*Baedeke*

W9-CRG-820

# Cape Town
## West Coast · Winelands ·
## Garden Route

www.baedeker.com

Verlag Karl Baedeker

# SIGHTSEEING HIGHLIGHTS ★★

Table Mountain, the Cape of Good Hope and two oceans, famous vineyards, Big Five safaris and endless dream beaches, Greenmarket Square, the Bo-Kaap quarter and the mega entertainment and shopping venue of the V&A Waterfront … hard choices face those who can't spend several weeks at the Cape. We have gathered together what you should not miss during your visit.

**Cape of Good Hope**
*Stand at the Cape of Good Hope just once!*

CAPE OF GOOD HOPE
THE SOUTH-WESTERNMOST POINT OF THE AFRICAN CONTINENT

**Stellenbosch**
*Colonial gem with picturesque house in Cape Dutch style*

**Cape Town carnival**
*Loud and colourful, with lots of music*

# BAEDEKER'S BEST TIPS

**Baedeker Tips provide insider information going beyond the major sights. Before you set off, here is a selection of the best tips for Cape Town and the Cape region: beautiful, useful and fascinating.**

### ■ »The Long Road to Freedom«
Nelson Mandela's memoirs are a testimony to human greatness ► **page 53**

### ■ Andulela
Football tours, jazz safaris, drum sessions and township jewellery workshops ► **page 121**

### ■ »Beyond all expectations«
Caramelized quail, delicate springbok fillet or fluffy raspberry soufflé – the Buitenverwachtung vineyard is one of South Africa's top ten ► **page 171**

### ■ Forest and valley
Try the shiraz with a faint chocolate aroma at the stunningly beautiful Boschendal vineyard. ► **page 182**

### ■ Botlierskop Game Reserve
Set off on the back of an elephant to spot black impala and the »Big Five«. ► **page 186**

**On safari**
*Elephant ride in the Botlierskop Wildlife Reserve*

### ■ Pan African Market
The largest selection of traditional craftwork from all over Africa ► **page 155**

**African craftwork**
*Sales at the Pan African Market support township families*

## 🔲 Top-class-putting
Non-members are welcome on the Fancourt Golf Resort's championship courses.

**San heritage**
*Tour of rock art by the original inhabitants*

## 🔲 Knysna Oysters
Fresh, cheap and excellent: eat the best oysters in Knysna.

## 🔲 African Dream
»Out of Africa« feeling in old-time luxury tents and candlelight dinners in the middle of Addo Elephant Park

## 🔲 Tea time at the »Nellie«
Take tea at the legendary Mount Nelson hotel.

## 🔲 Jazz wanted
Not only jazz fans like to come to Harvey's for Sunday brunch.

## 🔲 There she blows!
Southern Right Charter boats are permitted within 50m/150ft of the whales at Hermanus.

## 🔲 Summer Sunset Concerts
Classical concerts with open-air picnics in the Kirstenbosch National Botanical Garden

## 🔲 Cheetahland
See cheetahs, white lions and Bengal tigers at the Cango Wildlife Ranch near Oudtshoorn.

## 🔲 All gold
Visitors can design their own jewellery in the workshop of the Gold of Africa Museum.

## 🔲 Sundowner Cruises
Brick-red sails fill in the gentle evening breeze when the three-masted schooners set off for sunset cruises from the V&A Waterfront.

## 🔲 Bushmans Kloof Wilderness
Fascinating tours to ancient San cave paintings

**Golfer's paradise**
*There are wonderful golf courses all around Table Mountain and along the Garden Route*

THE GOLFER

A Knysna lourie: this rare
parrot only lives along the
Garden Route
▶ page 113

# BACKGROUND

*Smart souvenirs: varnished ostrich eggs*
▶ page 245

# PRACTICALITIES

# TOURS

*The call of the mountain: a superb view over Cape Town can be had from Table Mountain*
► **page 274**

*Franschhoek: a charming centre of wine-making with French atmosphere*
▶ **page 176**

# SIGHTS FROM A to Z

*Ashanti art in the Gold of Africa Museum*
► page 273

*Heartwarming: the friendliness of the people is magnetic*
► page 226

# Background

WHAT YOU SHOULD KNOW ABOUT CAPE TOWN: ITS BEGINNINGS, ITS COLONIAL AND APARTHEID HISTORY, ITS ECONOMY AND CULTURE, ITS PEOPLE – A BRIEF PORTRAIT OF SOUTH AFRICA'S FASCINATING »MOTHER CITY«.

# »THE FAIREST CAPE WE SAW...

**... in the whole circumference of the earth« wrote Sir Francis Drake enthusiastically in the log of his first rounding of the Cape of Good Hope in 1577. The amazing magnetism of the southern tip of Africa endures, and today its pulsating 3.5 million metropolis on Table Bay is one of the world's top destinations. No matter what time of year you choose, »South Africa's Mother City« is well worth the visit!**

Its unique location at the foot of Table Mountain between the Atlantic and the Indian Ocean gives Cape Town a special atmosphere. A cosmopolitan city, it is full of life, colour and light: a vibrant melting pot of all nations, cuisines and cultures, with inhabitants who no longer stay apart. Cape Town spoils visitors with top-class restaurants and hotels, with legendary clubs, laid-back cafés and a lot of room for relaxation.

## Oh, Mother City!

There is a new sense of ease at the old harbour, where the waterfront has been transformed into a massive entertainment and shopping venue, today South Africa's no. 1 tourist attraction. The beautiful and the rich meet under Table Mountain on the palm promenades of the stunning Clifton and Camps Bay beaches, which have long since become home to increasing numbers of Europeans. To this day, though, the heart of the »Mother City« is still around Jan van Riebeeck's Company's Garden, where Parliament, the South Africa

**Welcome!**
*The New Year is inaugurated with the colourful Minstrel Carnival*

Museum and the National Art Gallery are located. Desmond Tutu, winner of the Nobel Peace Prize, spent many years attacking apartheid in his sermons at St George's Cathedral here, and in the mid 1990s the Truth and Reconciliation Commission convened there. Greenmarket Square is the place to haggle for wood carvings, bead jewellery and colourful textiles from all over Africa, while in St George's Mall fashion, diamonds and modern art are sold. The trendiest place to meet in the city is Long Street: for example, at Kennedy's for cool jazz, or at Mama Africa for kudu, crocodile or os-

← *Cape Town's violet hour, and a Cape Agulhas figurehead*

trich steak to the sounds of kwaito music. For sundowners, Capetonians like to head up Table Mountain to get the best views of the sea of light below. The cable-car journey to the summit is a must, as is a stroll through the colourful Bo-Kaap district and a drive along the

**Local life**
*Bo-Kaap, a colourful village idyll
in the middle of the city*

**Natural world heritage**
*Exuberant beauty of the fynbos protea*

**Whale watching**
*Jumping humpback whale near Hermanus*

**Grape picking**
*A rich harvest around Stellenbosch*

**Western Cape**
*Raging surf at the Cape of Good Hope*

**Emblem**
*Take the cable car up Table Mountain*

serpentine panorama road around the Cape Peninsula, all the way to the continent's storm-battered southern tip.

## Cultural Heritage, Wine and Contradictions

The earth's most species-rich flora flourishes at the Cape: fynbos shrubland with its thousands of endemic plants is a Unesco Biosphere Reserve of exceptional beauty. South Africa's national flower, the king protea, also grows here, and it can be admired in all its splendour at Kirstenbosch, where the Botanical Garden is a flowering Noah's Ark. Nowhere else on earth can whales be so easily spotted from land as from Hermanus, on Walker Bay. Between Paarl, Stellenbosch and Franschoek ambitious vintners produce fine wines in historic vineyards, and visitors can dine on haute cuisine made from local produce in Cape Dutch mansions. The former prison island of Robben Island, where Nelson Mandela was incarcerated for 18 years before becoming »Father of the Rainbow Nation«, evokes mixed feelings. A decade and a half after Mandela initiated reconciliation, Cape Town exudes an irrepressible optimism. This innovative city obliterates all contradictions with its creativity, passion and openness to the world. It lives up to the challenge of the developed and undeveloped worlds coexisting side by side, of skyscrapers and corrugated iron huts. The colour of skin is no longer of primary importance, and working co-operation between blacks and whites is now a commonplace.

**Wine & Dine**
*Exclusive lodge with sea views*

## Eternally Breathtaking

The countryside of the Cape Province is also intoxicatingly beautiful. Three hours' drive north of the Mother City, the sandstone cliffs of the Cederberg Mountains, formed by wind and weather into bizarre shapes, seem almost unreal. The San, who have populated the Cape for thousands of years, have left mystical rock paintings up there. For many Cape Town visitors, the attractions of the Garden Route along the Indian Ocean are the crowning glories: crystal-clear water and endless white beaches, enchanted lagoons and dramatic coastal mountains, fascinating climbing tours and malaria-free Big Five safaris. For others the Garden Route is an urgent reason to return with a great deal more time, because the magic of Africa has cast its spell.

# Facts

**What does »fynbos« mean and what is the Cape Doctor responsible for? Who belongs to the Big Five, what is a dassie, and which woman rules South Africa's Mother City?**

# Mediterranean Cape

Fossil finds testify to the fact that the **Cape Rocks**, which run over 700km/450mi parallel to the coast, are up to 440 million years old. They once belonged to the huge mountain range of the prehistoric continent of **Gondwanaland**, which began to break up around 130 million years ago, and parts of which can now be found in South America, Antarctica and eastern Australia. The folding of the Cape Rock mountain chains (**Swartberg Mountains, Langberg Mountains and Tsitsikamma Mountains**) was the result of tectonic activity caused by the movements of continental plates. The South American continental plate pushed under the African plate at the end of the Cretaceous period, about 70–100 million years ago. The highest elevation, at 2326m/7632ft, is the Seweweeksport Mountain, but the most famous of them is Cape Town's emblem, the 1086m/3563ft **Table Mountain**, which falls steeply to the sea. The Cape Rocks consist predominantly of Table Mountain sandstone, quartz, slate and Cape granite, which is the result of earlier volcanic activity. Large sections of the Cape Rocks were covered in glaciers during the late Pleistocene, about 30,000–10,000 years ago. Erosion caused by wind and water has given the rocky coast its present form, with broad sandy beaches. At 129,370 sq km/49,950 sq mi, the Province of the Western Cape takes up almost 11% of the country's land area. The **most southerly point of the African continent** is not the famous **Cape of Good Hope** at the southern tip of the Cape Peninsula, but storm-battered Cape Agulhas at 20º east longitude.

**Formation of the Cape Rocks**

All around Cape Town, a **Mediterranean climate** of dry summers and damp winters spoils its residents with an average of 3000 hours of sunshine per year. The reasons for this climate are the site of the city below the sub-tropical belt of high pressure and two ocean currents: the warm **Agulhas Current** from the **Indian Ocean** meets the cold Antarctic **Benguela Current** from the **Atlantic** here. Good weather is brought by the southern Atlantic St Helena high-pressure front and another high-pressure front from the Indian Ocean. Asthe region is in the southern hemisphere, the sea around Cape Town is at its warmest between February and March. However, at a maximum of 17°C/63ºF, swimming in the Atlantic here is only something for the very keen, while the seas of False Bay and the Garden Route, warmed by the Agulhas Current, enjoy year-round water temperatures of around 22°C/72º.

**Dream beaches on two oceans**

The **Cape Doctor** is an unusual phenomenon. This is the name for a stiff **south-easterly breeze**, often lasting for weeks at a time during

**Table Mountain's tablecloth**

← *Dense white clouds hang like a white tablecloth over the majestic »Twelve Apostles« at Table Mountain* summer, which not only throws up a great deal of dust, but also ensures a necessary exchange of air in the basin below Table Mountain. A spectacular feature of this dry trade wind is the white »**table-cloth**«, a dense blanket of clouds on top of Table Mountain.

# Cape Flora and Fauna

**Unesco World Heritage**

The unique plant world of the south-western Cape (known as the Cape Floral Region) has been listed by Unesco as World Heritage since 2004, and comprises eight protected areas. The **smallest of the world's six floral regions** contains the greatest variety of species relative to its size. Many of the over 8500 plants can only be found here: on the Cape Peninsula alone, almost 2300 species grow, of which 90

are endemic. During the spring blossoming in August and September, broad swathes of countryside are transformed into a paradise of wild flowers. The Cape Flora, known as **fynbos** (Afrikaans: fijn = fine; bosch = bush) in South Africa, is perfectly adapted to the summer dryness. The shrub-like plant community here includes over 600 species of **erica**, but also the largest carnivorous plants found on earth. 400 different members of the Proteaceae family have been recorded, including 85 **proteas**, among them South Africa's national plant, the pink-flowering **king protea**. Carl Linnaeus (1707–78) named these plants after Proteus, an ocean god of Greek mythology who was capable of many incarnations. Asters, strawflowers, wild geraniums, 1400 different kinds of bulb flowers and rhizomes, 96 types of gladioli, irises, lilies, and freesias complete the sea of flowers. Among the **orchids**, the **red disa** is considered the finest. **Rooibosch**, honeybush and the aloe cactus are used in

*A feast for the eyes: the sunbird loves the sweet nectar of the king protea*

homeopathic medicine. In damp regions such as the Knysna Forest and the Tsitsikamma National Park there are **giant trees** over 40m/130ft high, such as mahogany, ironwood, stinkwood and yellow-wood. Clanwilliam cedars and snow proteas only grow in the Cederberg Mountains.

The big game that was once numerous at the Cape can now only be seen in **game parks**. Three-hour safari tours by jeep or on horseback are opportunities to encounter the »**Big Five**« – lions, leopards, buffaloes, rhinos and elephants – but alsogiraffes, cheetahs, zebras, warthogs, impalas, kudus, antelopes and springboks in open countryside. Many visitors combine the Garden Route with a visit to the Addo Elephant Park north of Port Elisabeth, where over 400 elephants live. The fact that the rabbit-sized **dassies** (►photo p.277) native to Table Mountain National Park are related to elephants can only be ascertained from two teeth in their upper jaws. Baboons, mountains zebras, gnus and springboks live at the Cape of Good Hope. The **bontebok**, which only lives here, has been given its own national park near Swellendam. A magnet for tourists at Simon's Town is the **penguin colony** at Boulders Beach. **Whales and sharks** can be sighted from July to December at False Bay, Hermanus and along the Garden Route. The **amazing underwater world** of the Atlantic and Indian Oceans is presented at the Two Oceans Aquarium at Cape Town's Waterfront. Really brave visitors can encounter white sharks by descending in a water cage. The Tsitsikamma National Park also has an underwater trail for snorkellers. The **ostrich**, the world's largest bird, is bred in giant farms in Oudtshoorn in the Little Karoo region. Sea eagles, pelicans, cormorants, gannets, albatross and South Africa's national bird, the **blue crane**, are all native to Cape Town's coasts. The World of Birds Wildlife Sanctuary at Hout Bay is entirely dedicated to birds. Among the 20 species of snake, the **puff adder** and the **Cape cobra** are poisonous.

*Malaria-free safari!*

*Wildlife in black and white: dozens of former farms at the Cape are private game reserves today*

## *Facts and Figures* Cape Twon

*Cape Town's flag since 1999*

### Government
▶ Capital of the Western Cape (West-Kaap) Province and seat of the South African parliament
▶ Ruling mayor: Helen Zille

### Economy
▶ Cape Town contributed 11.2% of the country's GDP in 2007. The most important economic sectors are: manufacturing, tourism, textile production, agriculture, IT, advertising, film industry, transport and trade.
▶ Tourism: 5.5 million visitors in 2007
▶ Unemployment: 22.1% in 2007

### Transport
▶ Cape Town International Airport is South Africa's second-largest airport.
▶ Cars and taxis are the most common form of transport. There are hop-on hop-off double-decker buses for sightseeing tours. Cape Metrorail operates trains to Muizenberg, Simon's Town, Paarl and Stellenbosch.

### Languages
▶ English, Afrikaans and Xhosa

### Telephone codes
▶ National: 021
International: +2721

### Time
▶ Two hours ahead of Greenwich Mean Time

### Cape Town
▶ Cape Town / Kaapstad / iKapa
As the first town founded during colonial times, it is also known as South Africa's »Mother City«

### Location
▶ Southern tip of Africa, 45km/28mi north of the Cape of Good Hope
▶ 33° 55 south latitude, 18° 29 east longitude

### Area
▶ 2499 sq km/965 sq mi

### Emblem and highest point
▶ Table Mountain (1086m/3563ft)

### Population
▶ 3.3 million (2007)
▶ Population density: 1321 per sq km/510 per sq mi

### In comparison
▶ London: 7.3 million inhabitants
▶ Rome: 3.7 million inhabitants
▶ New York: 8.1 million inhabitants

# Population · Politics · Economy

With 48.7 million people, South Africa is the most densely populated country in Africa. After Johannesburg and Durban, **Cape Town** (Afrikaans: **Kaapstad**, Xhosa: **iKapa**), is the third-largest city in the country. Cape Town is the **seat of the South African parliament** and the **capital of the Western Cape Province** (West-Kaap). As it was the first town founded during the colonial era, many South Africans also like to call it the **»Mother of all the country's cities«** (Moederstad, Mother City).

**Mother City**

Cape Town has undergone a fundamental change since the end of apartheid. The city centre has become safer and, thanks to generous regeneration programmes, many districts have been modernized. Tourism is booming in the host country of the 2010 World Cup Football Championship, there is much investment at the Cape and property prices are going through the roof. The Greater Cape Town area now encompasses a population of **3.3 million** (2007), and the Western Cape Province as a whole has 5.3 million residents (2007). Almost half of all Capetonians are under 20 years old, and only 5% are older than 65. The Mother City at Table Mountain has long since become the most popular place to live in the country, and one in ten South Africans now live in the Western Cape.

**Vibrant metropolis**

Even though the quality of life in Cape Town is significantly higher than in South Africa's other provinces, the city is burdened by substantial **infrastructure problems** due to the **massive increase in population** and persistent immigration from rural areas. Only a minority of Capetonians live in the City Bowl, as the city centre is known. The majority still live in the Cape Flats districts, where despite notable efforts by the government, living conditions are only being improved very slowly. In 2007 there was a housing shortfall of 400,000 units, according to the city administration, and almost a quarter of all households in the huge **townships** still lacked electricity, drinking water and toilets.

**Flipside of Cape Town**

Cape Town's extraordinary size of 2499 sq km/965 sq mi is the result of several communal area reforms. In December 2000, seven autonomous municipalities joined Cape Town's boroughs to become the so-called **Unicity of Cape Town**. Cape Town's **council** consists of 210 councillors who are chosen by 105 electoral districts. The mayor is elected by the council. The most recent communal elections in 2006 were won by the **present mayor, Helen Zille,** (►Famous People) from the Democratic Alliance Party. The party gained 91 seats and therefore took over from the ANC, which retained 81 seats but lost power after 13 years. In April 2009 elections Zille's DA gained the majority in the Western Cape province.

**City government**

**Rainbow Nation** Cape Town is the only city in South Africa where **coloureds** are the largest group (49%). They are the descendants of unions between white settlers and the Cape Khoi people, slaves and Cape Malaysians. **Blacks** make up 31% of the population, compared with 79% in South Africa as a whole. The **whites**, who until 1994 were politically, economically and culturally dominant, make up 18.5% of the population. Only 1.5% are **Indian or Asian**. Most Capetonians are bi-lingual, speaking Afrikaans and English or one of those languages with one of the other nine official languages. 42% of the population speak **Afrikaans** at home, 29% speak **Xhosa** (pronounced »cosa«), and 28% speak **English**. 1% speak Sesotho, Zulu, Setswana or one of the other languages of the **Rainbow Nation**. More than three quarters of Capetonians are **Christians**. A tenth describe themselves as non-religious, 9.7% are **Muslim**, 0.5% Jewish, and 0.2% Hindu. Despite a

**Education** continued shortage of **qualified labour**, considerable successes have been achieved in the sphere of literacy.. By 2007, the percentage of 20-year-olds without schooling was less than 5% (10% nationally). Almost 12% of Cape Town's schoolchildren gain places at the **University of Cape Town** (UCT), the **University of the Western Cape** (UWC), the **Cape Peninsula University of Technology** founded in 2005 (CPUT), or the highly regarded university in nearby Stellenbosch.

## Economy

**Boomtown** At 124 billion rand, Cape Town contributed around **11% of South Africa's gross national product** in 2007 and, together with the Province of the Western Cape, over 14%. Significant financial institutions, insurance houses and international oil businesses are based in the city, and South Africa's most important trading partners also have their seats here. Cape Town's business district spreads across the City Bowl and the harbour district around the Victoria & Alfred Waterfront. Almost half of all output is produced in the Central Business District (CBD), in Claremont, Century City, Durbanville and Tygerburg.

**Light and shade** According to the most recent predictions of the business magazine *The Economist*, South Africa has firmly established its leading role on the African continent: economic growth of between 3% and 6% over the past decade, a low balance of payments deficit and a stable currency are the reason. Yet the **huge wealth gap** between blacks and whites still divides society and is the main cause of the high crime rate and the resurgence of racism on both sides. On the other hand, an influential and wealthy **black elite** has emerged that is gradually gaining control of political and economic power. The **Black Economic Empowerment Law** (BEE, passed in 2004 and intended to ensure economic parity for blacks, states that all South African firms must employ a majority of black partners, managers and employees. It is

*Faces of the Rainbow Nation*

an attempt to reverse the results of apartheid, but it also causes new problems, since not productivity but membership of the black majority counts. In 2007, the average annual income for a white middle-class household stood at US$20,000, while an uneducated labourer at the World Cup Stadium in Green Point was only earning US$1.25 per hour. Officially, the **unemployment rate** in Cape Town stood at 26%, and at 22% for the Western Cape Province as a whole in 2007. The almost 40% of all households that live on or under the **poverty line** remain excluded from the economic miracle. Health statistics show that, although medical provision for **Aids** in the Cape region has improved in recent years, especially for women, the number of **tuberculosis cases** has almost doubled in the last ten years.

The sector with the strongest growth is **tourism**, which accounts for over 10% of GDP. In addition to the three million South Africans who visited the Cape in 2007, almost two million foreigners travelled there, a fifth of all visitors to South Africa. Record numbers are expected for **2010**, when the international football world will be arriving for the World Cup. Important employers are the textile and food industries, with emphasis on **wine production** and **fruit**, of which over 50% is grown for export. The advantageous exchange rates, Western infrastructure, superb locations and weather have also made Cape Town a top destination for the **film and fashion industries**, which come here to film everything from movies to adverts. Despite continuously rising prices, the real estate market is booming, and roads and hotels are being modernized and built everywhere for the 2010 Football World Cup. The Achilles heel remains energy supply. **Power cuts** are a regular occurrence. A new wind-power station is due to start up in 2010, and a new coal-fired power station in 2013.

A positive economic trend

# City History

When did the first inhabitants of the Cape arrive? Who was Jan van Riebeeck, and who was Cecil Rhodes? How did apartheid happen and what was the purpose of the Truth and Reconciliation Commission? Cape Town's history reflects that of the entire country, from the Khoisan to the young »Rainbow Nation«.

# Cradle of Mankind

| 3.5 million years ago | First hominids at the Cape |
|---|---|
| 77,000 BC | Earliest traces of human art in the Blombos Cave |
| 28,000 BC | Stone Age hunters and gatherers at the Cape |
| AD 700 | Khoikhoi cattle breeding |

**Hominids and Homo sapiens**

South Africa and the Cape region are considered cradles of mankind. The oldest human skeletal finds at Sterkfontein, a Unesco World Heritage site, prove that **hominids** already lived in South Africa around 3.5 million years ago. These were early kinds of humans (Australopithecus) considered to have been at a stage of development between humans and primates. The oldest finds of stone tools date from 1.5 million years ago. At the Cape, it is **Homo sapiens**, in particular, who has left traces. Fossilized footprints at the **Langebaan Lagoon** have been dated as 120,000 years old. Upper jaw bones and skeletal remains 100,000 years old have also been found in the Klasies River Mouth Caves on the south coast, between Cape Town and Port Elizabeth.

**The world's oldest art**

In December 2001, an excavation team led by the Capetonian archaeologist Chris Henshilwood discovered finds of global significance at the **Blombos Cave** at Cape Agulhas. The ochre stones with abstract engravings have been dated to **77,000 BC** and are now considered the oldest art by humankind. In 2004, Henshilwood also found 41 pea-sized snail shells with holes drilled by human hands, as well as ochre traces. This necklace was made around 75,000 BC and is the world's oldest piece of jewellery. Further bone and tool finds at Fish Hoek on Cape Town's foreshore, and on the Cape Peninsula, prove human presence and continuing development in about 30,000 BC.

**Hunters and gatherers**

Ancestors of the San and Khoikhoi tribes have lived in South Africa and at the Cape for 40,000 years. Collectively known as the **Khoisan**, as they are close relations, around 28,000 BC they created thousands of **rock paintings and engravings** that testify to their life as hunters, belief in magic and artistic creativity. Countless finds prove the continued existence of Khoisan at the Cape right up to the beginning of the 20th century. From AD 700, there is evidence of cattle breeding among the Khoikhoi. The language, history and culture of the San

← *Former president Frederik de Klerk took his oath in front of Cape Town's Truth and Reconciliation Commission prior to his hearing in 1997*

*Jan van Riebeeck lands at Table Bay on 6 April 1652*
*(painting by Charles Davidson Bell)*

was recorded at the end of the 19th century by **Dr Wilhelm H. Bleek** and Lucy Lloyd. Bleek's daughter Dorothea succeeded in making unique sound recordings in the early 20th century.

# Explorers at the Cape

| | |
|---|---|
| **1488** | Bartolomeu Diaz sails around the Cape of Good Hope |
| **1497–98** | Vasco da Gama discovers the sea route to India |
| **1503** | Antonio de Saldanha is the first European to set foot on Africa's most southerly point |
| **1601–08** | The Dutch christen the Cape »Table Bay« (Tafel Baai) |
| **1605** | British East India Company ships land at the Cape |

**Records from antiquity** Phoenicians in the service of the Egyptian pharaoh Nekho (609–594 BC) and, according to Herodotus, Carthaginians too already circumnavigated Africa before Christ was born. Reputedly, one of the Genoese brothers Vadino and Ugolino Vivaldi also achieved this in AD 1291.

## The First Europeans

**Portuguese seafarers** **Bartolomeu Diaz** circumnavigated the »**Cape of Storms**« in 1488 after first landing at Walvis Bay. He sighted cows and shepherds at Mossel Bay on 3 February that year. King João II of Portugal was so thrilled by Diaz' report that he optimistically renamed the Cape the Cabo de Boa Esperança. During his search for the sea route to India,

**Vasco da Gama** succeeded in circumnavigating the »**Cape of Good Hope**« on 22 November 1497. Four years later, a navigational error helped **Antonio de Saldanha** discover Table Bay. He was the first European to go ashore and climb Table Mountain, claiming the territory as **Saldania**. Like Saldanha before him, his fellow countryman **Francisco de Almeida** also clashed with the Khoikhoi on this spot, in 1510. After an attempt at cattle rustling and stealing children, less than half of his 150 men returned to the ship alive.

In 1601 and 1608, ships belonging to the **Dutch East India Company** (Vereenigte Oostindische Compagnie; **VOC**) anchored in Saldanha Bay and began to barter with the Khoikhoi. The new name of Table Bay (Tafel Baai) emerged at this time. Ownership claims by ships belonging to the **British East India Company** (BEIC) were made in 1605. Also under that company's orders, the Khoikhoi chief **Xhoré** was kidnapped and taken to England in 1613, but was allowed to return to the Cape six months later.

**Dutch and British**

# Cape Dutch Colony

| | |
|---|---|
| **1652** | Jan van Riebeeck founds a permanent settlement at the Cape on the orders of the Dutch East India Company |
| **1679** | Foundation of Stellenbosch |
| **1688** | Huguenots settle in Franschhoek and plant the first grapevines |
| **1779** | Start of the first Xhosa War at the Great Fish River |

In March 1647, the *Nieuw-Haerlem*, a ship owned by the VOC, ran aground in Table Bay. The stranded crew built a temporary fort, planted a vegetable garden and sought initial contact with the indigenous population. The subsequent report by the merchants Jansz and Mathys Proot on those events, on the strategic location of Table Bay and the emerging competition with England persuaded the Dutch East India Company to recruit **Jan van Riebeeck** to develop a permanent provisioning post in Ta-

**Foundation of Cape Town**

**? DID YOU KNOW ...?**

- ... that Cape Town was not originally planned as a city? De Kaap merely served as a provisioning post for food and water for VOC ships in the years from 1652. Jan van Riebeeck only gave permission for nine free company employees to build farms on the Liesbeck River in 1657. That same year, the first slaves arrived from Batavia and Madagascar. When Riebeeck left the Cape in 1662, 35 free burghers, 15 women, 22 children and 180 slaves lived in the tiny settlement.

ble Bay in 1651. Riebeeck's ships, the *Drommedaris*, *Reijger* and *Goede Hoope*, reached Table Bay on **6 April 1652** – the first three of five vessels. 82 men and eight women went ashore, among them van Riebeeck's wife Maria de la Quellerie, and this day is now considered the date on which **Cape Town was founded**.

## Early Settlers

*The young Cape colony*

Initially, despite several difficulties, the needs of the **Dutch East India Company** were regularly fully met. From 1657 onwards, this was first and foremost ensured by the use of **slaves** from the Dutch East Indian colonies, Mozambique and Madagascar. Cape Town's fort, the **Castle of Good Hope** begun in 1666, is today the oldest stone building in South Africa. In 1669 Stellenbosch was the second settlement founded at the Cape, by the later governor Simon van der Stel. Shortly afterwards it was joined by Swellendam. In 1676, the Dutch East India Company changed its immigration policy for the Cape, which was to feed itself from then on. Settlers arrived from Holland, Germany and France, becoming »**Boers**« (»boeren«, »free citizens«).

*The Huguenot Memorial in Franschhoek recalls its first settlers*

They also settled the surrounding area of the Cape. Among the French there were many **Huguenots**, who left their homeland due to religious persecution after the repeal of the **Edict of Nantes**. In 1688, the first 164 Huguenots arrived at the Cape on Dutch ships. They settled in **Franschhoek** (»French Corner«) and planted the first vines there. Battles with the **Khoikhoi and San** were reported in 1659 and 1671. As a result, the »Bosjesman« – as the »**Bushmen**« were derogatorily called, retreated further inland. A glaring shortage of women inspired the Dutch East India Company to fetch Dutch girls – mostly orphans – to the Cape. However, marriages also took place between settlers, slaves and native peoples, from which the ancestors of the »coloureds« were born. **Sheik Yusuf** was banished to the Cape after an insurrection on Java in 1693, and subsequently founded the first Muslim community of Cape Town, together with his supporters.

## Colonization

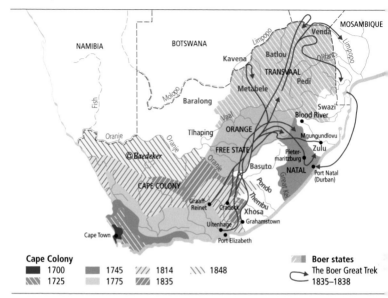

**Cape Colony**

| | | | |
|---|---|---|---|
| ■ 1700 | ■ 1745 | /// 1814 | \\\ 1848 |
| \\\ 1725 | ■ 1775 | /// 1835 | |

**Boer states**
The Boer Great Trek
1835–1838

## The Rise and Fall of the Dutch East India Company

By 1720 Table Bay, Paarl, Stellenbosch, Franschhoek, Drakenstein and Tulbagh were settled and the native San and Khoikoi had largely been driven out. Employees of the **Dutch East India Company** (Vereenigte Oostindische Compagnie; **VOC**), who were not permitted to own land themselves, successfully co-ordinated the development of the colony. Everything was under the company's control: from the price of food to the trade in ivory, furs, leather, ostrich eggs and slaves. Smallpox epidemics in 1713, 1755 and 1767 were serious setbacks. Nevertheless, there were already 1200 solid houses in Cape Town by around 1750, built in the **Cape Dutch style** with white-washed walls and curved gables. By 1743, 4000 Boers lived at or around the Cape, in addition to the free coloureds and slaves. By 1761, the Burgherwacht Huys, today's Old Town House at Greenmarket Square, had been built.

*Everything under control*

Due to the falling price of wine and cereals, more and more farmers began to keep cattle and sheep, which required less capital and work. In search of new pastures, the semi-nomadic »Trekboers« set off inland with their herds, heading up the east coast and onwards to uninhabited land. In 1779, they clashed with the Xhosa (Bantu) at the Great Fish River. It was the first of nine bloody **Xhosa Wars** which lasted until 1878.

*Heading inland*

**Collapse of the Dutch East India Company** In 1782, the Dutch East India company paid a dividend for the last time. The Anglo-Dutch wars between 1780 and 1783 signalled the collapse of the company. French allies were enthusiastically received at the Cape and a fashion trend was even inspired. However, dissatisfaction with corrupt and ineffective administrators, unpaid wages and ideas emanating from the French Revolution of 1789 ensured unrest. **Revolutionary national assemblies** founded by Boers in Swellendam and Graaff-Reinet in 1795 declared their territories free republics.

# British Colony

| 1795 | First British occupation |
|------|--------------------------|
| 1802 | The Cape Colony becomes Dutch once more |
| 1806 | Second British occupation, Cape Town becomes capital of the Cape Colony |
| 1834 | Abolition of slavery |
| 1835–41 | The great trek |
| 1899–1902 | Second Boer War |
| 1910 | Foundation of the South African Union |

**Republican intermezzo** **British troops** landed at Muizenberg in July 1795, and the Dutch East India Company capitulated within six weeks. Three years later, Cape Town was devastated by fire, and that year was also the end of the Dutch East India Company. In 1798, 6000 whites lived in Cape Town and Stellenbosch, and another 12,000 itinerant »Trekboers« were present in the hinterland. In addition, there were 15,000 Khoikhoi and around 22,000 slaves. After the **Peace of Amiens in 1802**, the Cape Colony had to be returned to Holland. Euphoric republican innovations including land reform, sponsorship of wine-growing, the introduction of Spanish merino sheep to improve wool quality, and the secularization of education only gained a brief hold in the »**Batavian Republic**«, however. In 1806, 4000 British troops landed at the Cape and were victorious at the **Battle of Blouberg**. Cape Town became the **capital** of the British Crown Colony founded in 1814. Certain freedoms were granted in 1809, including the »**Hottentot Law**«, which made the Khoikhoi British subjects and prohibited forced labour. Slavery, which had been forbidden on British ships since 1807, was officially banned at the Cape on 1 December 1834. The **end of slavery** set free 59,000 people.

! **Baedeker TIP**

**»The chains of silence are breaking«**
... is the name of the impressive exhibition at the Iziko Slave Lodge on Adderley Street, where the Dutch East India Company's slaves were kept for 132 years (► p.151).

*The Khoikhoi were also used as guides
(painting at the Castle of Good Hope, Military Museum)*

## Exodus and Gold Rush

The arrival of 6000 British citizens in around 1820, the establishment of English as the official language and British law for the legal system, drought and a shortage of land – especially, however, the abolition of slavery and liberal policies founded on ideas of equal rights – provoked the »Great Trek« among Boers. **10,000 Boers**, about 20% of the white population, left the Cape Colony heading east in several waves in the period up to 1841. They were known as the **Voortrekkers** (pioneers). While the Boers were fighting in the Xhosa border wars and against the Zulu at the Battle of Blood River and founding their **Boer Republics**, Cape Town gained limited self-governance in **1853**. Its constitution granted **suffrage to free coloureds and property-owning blacks**. The first electric light shone at Table Bay in 1882. The discovery of diamond and gold at Kimberly and Johannesburg also fascinated the Cape Colony, and set another wave of settlers on their way. Meanwhile, Cape Town expanded. In 1865, the **Crown Colony** had also taken possession of Ciskei and, by 1871, Basutoland (Lesotho).

The Great Trek (Groote Trek)

## The Road to Unity

By the end of the 19th century, the country was connected by **railway routes** from Cape Town to Kimberly and Johannesburg. Cape Town boomed, and from 1860 onwards prison labourers built sea defences and the **Alfred Docks** in the wind-protected Table Bay.

Second Boer War

Under prime minister **Cecil Rhodes** all the land between the Kei River and Natal was annexed to the Cape Colony in 1894. In 1885 the region south of the Molopo River came under British domination as the Crown Colony of Bechuanaland, and was incorporated into the Cape Colony in 1895. The gold rush, a permanent influx to the Boer republics, fear of anglicization and the failed British-planned Jameson Raid of December 1896 sparked the Second Boer War in 1899. After initial victories, the Boers were defeated and a drawn-out **guerrilla war** began, during which 34,000 Boers, 22,000 British subjects and 15,000 blacks lost their lives. The British pursued a »scorched earth policy«: the fighting Boers' farms were burnt down and women and children were interned in **concentration camps**, where over 26,000 of them died of malnutrition and unhygienic conditions.

**Separation of races ▶**

When **bubonic plague** broke out in Cape Town in 1901, the Cape government used the epidemic as an excuse for the physical **segregation of the black population** into special districts near the docks and Maitland.

**South African Union**

After the **Peace of Vereeniging** in 1902, the Boer republics were incorporated into the British colonies, and the reconstruction of war-ravaged lands allowed the Boers and the British to work more closely together. On 31 May 1910, the British-sponsored union of the colonies of Natal, Cape Colony, Transvaal and Oranje resulted in the South African Union, which was officially part of the British Empire. The union contained 1.2 million white and 4.6 million non-white inhabitants. Pretoria became the seat of government, Cape Town the seat of parliament,  and Bloemfontein the seat of the supreme court. The **new constitution** gave the vote exclusively to whites. The exception remained the Cape Colony, where more liberal law for wealthy blacks and coloureds that had been in force since 1853 were retained. However, the blacks lost their voting rights in 1936, the coloureds in 1956. The **first race laws** enacted were the 1911 mine workers' laws, the abolition of the right to strike and, in 1913, the **Native Land Act**, which prohibited blacks from purchasing land outside permitted areas (later known as the Homelands).

# Apartheid and Resistance

| 1923 | Division of Cape Town districts according to skin colour |
|---|---|
| **From 1948** | Tougher apartheid laws |
| 1961 | Foundation of the Republic of South Africa |
| 1966 | Violent clearance of District Six |
| 1986 | Pass Laws abolished |

*Anti-apartheid badge from the 1980s*

# AFRICAN NATIONAL CONGRESS

**Politically, the ANC is the dominant force in South Africa. The party has controlled every province in the country since the last election and – except in Cape Town – holds the post of mayor of all major cities. Originally founded to represent the interests of black South Africans, and later a spearhead in the fight against apartheid, the ANC today forms the bedrock of stability.**

In January 1912 black intellectuals in Bloemfontein founded the South African Native National Congress – renamed the **African National Congress** in 1923. Founder members included the ministers of religion John Dube and Walter Rubusana, the author Sol Plaatje, the chieftain Thomas Mapikela, the lawyer Pixley Seme and others. From the outset, the organization never saw itself as an exclusively African interest group, but rather welcomed all skin colours and accepted Christianity and the English language. In practice, however, it was a black opposition party that fought against racism and ethnic rivalries, as well as for the political empowerment of the black majority population. Blacks were not only denied suffrage. From 1913 they were only permitted to live in designated areas and were not allowed to purchase land outside them. Boycotts and strikes, the principal political tools of the early ANC, were mostly used to combat appalling working conditions, for example during the mineworkers' strikes of the early 1920s.

## Escalation

Inspired by the 1941 **Atlantic Charter** in which Roosevelt and Churchill announced a free world order as one of their war aims, the ANC demanded full citizens' rights for black South Africans in 1943. J.C. Smuts' government replied to this demand with a clear refusal, however. From then onwards, the ANC became radicalized. In 1944, the ANC Youth League, which demanded tougher measures, was founded by the freedom fighters Nelson Mandela, Walter Sisulu and Oliver Tambo. The goal was now no longer integration into the white political system, but liberation from that system. In answer to the ever more repressive apartheid laws after 1948, the ANC organized boycotts, strikes and – inspired by Gandhi's peaceful resistance – civil disobedience. In 1952, when white South Africa celebrated the 300th anniversary of Jan van Riebeeck's landing, tens of thousands of blacks participated in a mass counter-demonstration for the first time. On 26 June

*New man at the helm: South Africa's president Thabo Mbeki congratulates his successor as party leader, the newly elected chairman of the ANC Jacob Zuma (right)*

1955, 3000 representatives of all South African races – blacks, coloureds, Indians and also whites from the new Liberal Party – met in Soweto for a national congress against apartheid. It formulated the **Freedom Charter**, which included a demand for equal rights for all races, and was the foundation of the ANC's political programme right up until the 1990s. After the congress, the South African government arrested 156 leaders of the various movements and indicted them for treason. However, after a court case lasting five years, all the accused were released without charge. One of them, the ANC leader **Albert Luthuli**, was given the Nobel Peace Prize in 1960. But the congress alliance of 1955 quickly disintegrated, mostly because of disagreements on future strategy. There were also tensions within the ANC itself: the pluralists demanded equal rights, while the Africanists – in opposition to ANC policy so far – aspired to liberation from white rule in South Africa. The result was a split in 1959, when the Africanists broke away from the ANC to found the **Pan Africanist Congress** (PAC).

## The war ...

For 1960 the ANC and PAC planned major campaigns against the hated Pass Laws. The PAC announced a peaceful demonstration in front of **Sharpeville police station** for 21 March 1960. The police, who felt threatened, shot into the crowd, killing 69 demonstrators. The rest of the world responded with shock and outrage. Strikes and demonstrations occurred throughout the country, resulting in even more loss of life. The government reacted brutally. On 8 April 1960 it banned the ANC and PAC, who then continued their work underground and in exile. Both parties founded fighting organizations. The ANC founded **Umkhonto we Sizwe** (»Spear of the Nation«) with **Nelson Mandela** as its leader. Mandela had been elected president of the ANC and had risen to be leader of the black movement after the banning of Luthuli and the conviction of Sobukwe. The organization successfully mounted several spectacular attacks. Nevertheless, by 1963 it had been smashed. Mandela, who had been arrested and condemned to five years of prison in 1962, was given a life sentence in 1963, after material found at Umkhonto's central office was used to convict him of sabotage. For a time, it seemed the government had successfully destroyed black opposition. Activists were occasionally incarcerated without trial, and many died in police custody. Executions reached record levels. New organiza-

tions were founded in the 1970s, including those determined to create a »black consciousness«, after the example of the Black Panther movement in the USA. When the government wanted to establish Afrikaans – the »language of the white oppressors« – as the exclusive language of instruction in schools, 20,000 school children demonstrated in **Soweto** on 16 June 1976. The police shot indiscriminately into the crowd of unarmed children and teenagers. Two were killed (▶ photo p.37). Bloody unrest followed all over the country, and this time it took the government until the end of 1977 to regain control of the situation. It banned and persecuted all radical opposition organizations. **Steve Biko**, the leader of the Black Consciousness Movement, died as a result of torture in prison, in 1977.

## ... and its end

Abroad, sympathy for the ANC and Nelson Mandela grew. Foreign governments recognized the ANC as the foremost South African freedom fighting organization. In 1990, **state president Frederik de Klerk** – »Africa's Gorbachev« – legalized the ANC, PAC and the Communist Party, despite strong opposition from within his own ranks and from the white extreme right. He released Mandela from imprisonment and initiated dialogue with his former adversary. The ANC emerged as the strongest party, with 62% of the vote, during the first free parliamentary elections in South Africa in April 1994.

In 2004, the ANC gained almost 70% of the votes. In more recent times, reports of corruption and accusations against party leader **Jacob Zuma** have cast a shadow over the ANC. As Thabo Mbeki's acknowledged successor, Zuma was elected as the new leader of the ANC in December 2007. Although the ANC lost its 2/3 majority in the elections in April 2009 Zuma was elected state president.

The accusations against him were dropped before.

**Restriction of freedom**

After the end of the First World War, thousands in Cape Town died in the Spanish flu pandemic. Bloody suppression of strikes between competing white and black workers in the early 1920s was followed by the **Urban Areas Act** in 1923, which established the division of urban districts according to skin colour. In 1927, the **Immorality Act** came into force. It made sexual relations between people of different races punishable by prison sentences. Under prime minister Hertzog, **Afrikaans** became the second official language in 1925. After a seven-year construction period, Chapman's Peak Drive was opened in 1922 and, in 1929, the Table Mountain cable car and the Botanical Gardens at Kirstenbosch were inaugurated. In 1935, downtown Cape Town was expanded seawards by land reclamation. The South African Union under prime minister Jan C. Smuts joined the Allied side in the **Second World War** on 6 September 1939.

*District Six Museum recalls the legendary sixth municipal district, in which people from all continents, of all colours and from all regions once mixed*

## Toughening of Apartheid

After the 1948 **election victory of the National Party**, the government of Daniel F. Malan began to enshrine in law the complete separation of the races, a concept known as **apartheid**. The **Population Registration Act** of 1950 divided the population of the South African Union into whites, blacks, Indians and coloureds. The **Group Areas Act** of the same year dictated that people were only allowed to live and work in their allocated areas. In 1956, under **J. G. Strijdom**, blacks and coloureds lost their right to vote. Hundreds of additional laws ensured that apartheid became established in everyday life. The ANC, for its part, organized peaceful opposition, strikes and protest marches and, in 1960, proclaimed the **Freedom Charter** (▶ Baedeker Special, p.33). The **Sharpeville Massacre** during a peaceful anti-apartheid demonstration in March 1960 caused worldwide outrage. When, in the same year, over 30,000 inhabitants of the **Cape Town townships** protested against the new Pass Laws, which obliged all non-whites to carry a Book of Life complete with all records of border crossings and employers, the government proclaimed a state of emergency, and the ANC and PAC were banned.

*A picture that went around the world: the bloody Soweto Uprising by schoolchildren*

## Increased Resistance

In October 1960, prime minister **Hendrik Verwoerd** presided over a popular referendum on whether South Africa should become a republic: 52.3% opted for an **independent republic**, although only whites were allowed to vote. As a result of ever more vociferous criticisms of apartheid from London, South Africa withdrew from the British Commonwealth on 15 March 1961. Within a short time, the laws were further hardened and mass arrests took place. At the

**South African Republic**

same time, the **ANC** gained more influence. Its national secretary, **Albert Luthuli**, was awarded the Nobel Peace Prize in 1961. **Nelson Mandela** was arrested on 5 August 1962 and in 1963 sentenced to life imprisonment on Robben Island at the Rivonia Trial. The government decided to demolish Cape Town's **District Six** in 1966. In the same year, the head of state, Verwoerd, was assassinated. Christiaan Barnard successfully carried out the world's **first heart transplant** in the Groote-Schuur hospital in 1967. Millions of blacks were forcibly relocated to the Homelands during the 1970s. In 1976, the death of over 500 people during the **Soweto Uprising** of school children ensured renewed worldwide condemnation (photo p.37).

## Attempts at Reform, Boycotts and States of Emergency

Limited political rights were granted to coloured and Indians via a **change in the constitution** under the government of **Pieter Willem Botha** in 1984. However, the ANC campaign begun that same year was mercilessly repressed; over 2300 people died and tens of thousands were arrested. After years of massive international economic sanctions, Botha repealed the 1985 Prohibition of Mixed Marriages Act and, in 1986, the Pass Laws. Thousands of blacks came to seek their fortune at the Cape from that time. The **demand for Nelson Mandela's release** received worldwide support. After failed secret talks in 1986, Botha met Mandela for the first time on 5 July 1989. However, neither Botha nor the National Party were seriously prepared to share power and, after **bloody clashes** in the townships, Botha imposed the **state of emergency** that was to last until 1990.

# Mandela and the New Beginning

| | |
|---|---|
| **1994** | The ANC wins the first democratic elections and Nelson Mandela becomes state president. |
| **1996–98** | Truth and Reconciliation Commission |
| **1997** | The new South African constitution comes into force. |

**New era**    In 1989, the ANC, UDF and Cosatu joined in coalition. Thousands demonstrated against apartheid in Cape Town. Pressure from abroad also intensified. The heavy sanctions paralysed the economy, and banks and foreign capital withdrew. On 15 August 1989, **Frederik Willem de Klerk**, secretary of the National Party, became the new state president. During his historic speech in Cape Town for the opening of parliament on **2 February 1990**, he also inaugurated a new era at the Cape. He annulled the ban on the ANC and PAC, relaxed the state of emergency and announced negotiations on a new

*Truly a historic moment: South Africa's new president Nelson Mandela, flanked by his deputy and later successor Mbeki (left) and ex-president de Klerk on 9 May 1994*

constitution. **Nelson Mandela's** imprisonment on Robben Island ended after 27 years on 11 February 1990. A year later, the **laws governing the separation of the races were abolished**. Mandela and de Klerk were both awarded the **Nobel Peace Prize** in 1993 for their efforts at reconciliation and work towards a democratic South Africa.

More than 7 million blacks living in the Homelands were granted South African citizenship once more in 1994. The **first democratic elections** on 27 April 1994 returned the ANC as clear victor. Of the 23 million eligible voters almost 18 million were black, and **Nelson Mandela** became **South Africa's first black state president** on 10 May. After 342 years, white hegemony at the Cape was ended.

Democratic elections

*South Africa established a new state emblem in 2000. It has a shield embraced by ears of wheat, with two human figures inspired by the rock paintings at Linton. The shield is also framed by two tusks on either side. Above are a crossed spear and knobkerrie, a protea, and a secretary bird with wings outspread crowned by the rising sun. The tusks are joined by the state motto »Unity in diversity« written in Khoisan.*

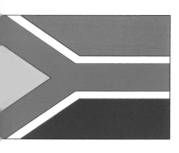

**South Africa's national flag**, introduced in 1994, shows six colours: black for the non-white population, gold for the mineral wealth and the constant sunshine of South Africa, green for the green land, red for the blood that was spilt during the battle for freedom, blue for the oceans and the sky, and white for the white population. The »Rainbow Flag« is an expression of the intention to pursue unity and reconciliation.

**Truth and Reconciliation Commission**

To help the country come to terms with its past, Mandela established the **Truth and Reconciliation Commission** with Desmond Tutu as its chairperson in the summer of 1996. Its purpose was to examine the human rights abuses that occurred during apartheid and, despite the fact that major figures responsible, such as P.W. Botha, remained untouched, the commission made an important contribution towards the **process of reconciliation** between the different peoples of South Africa.

**New constitution**

A new South African constitution was adopted after two years of negotiations, on 8 May 1996, and came into force on 4 February 1997. In December of that year, **Thabo Mbeki** took over the leadership of the ANC and the presidency from Nelson Mandela.

*Boundless enthusiasm on the streets: Capetonians celebrate in May 2004, when South Africa was chosen to host the Football World Cup for 2010*

# Cape Town Today

| 2004 | Electoral success for the ANC, South Africa chosen for the FIFA World Cup in 2010 |
|------|----------------------------------------------------------------------------------|
| 2006 | Helen Zille becomes mayor of Cape Town. |
| 2007 | Jacob Zuma becomes new party leader of the ANC. |

**Ambitious goals**

In 2002 the ANC and the NNP (New National Party, later dissolved in 2005) formed a coalition in order to retain control of government at the Cape. In 2003 Cape Town built the country's largest conference centre: the **Cape Town International Convention Centre** (CTICC). In the same year, millions of people all over the world watched the first **Aids Benefit Concert »46664«** – the number being Mandela's old prisoner's identification number – held in the Greenpoint Stadium. During the third elections held since democracy was established, the **ANC** won, gaining 69.7% of the vote on 14 April 2004. After failed attempts to bring the Olympic Games to Cape Town, South Africa was chosen on 15 May 2004 as host nation for the **2010 Football World Cup**. That year the city council also voted to realize the **N2 Gateway Project**, which envisages road and housing construction in the Langa Township between the airport and the city at a cost of 3 billion rand. The battle against wide social disparities, high unemployment, shortage of qualified workers and the continued spread of Aids remain priorities for the city.

**2006**

On 15 May, **Helen Zille** of the liberal Democratic Alliance (DA) was unexpectedly voted the new mayor of Cape Town, by 106 to 103 votes. She has resolutely been fighting corruption and nepotism ever since. Building commenced for the new **World Cup Arena at Greenpoint** at the end of October that year.

**2007**

The Democratic Alliance elected Helen Zille as its new chairperson with a clear two thirds majority. On 29 October, Cape Town celebrated the success of the »Springboks« with a huge parade after defeating the title-holders England 15:6 in the final of the **rugby world championship** in Paris. **Jacob Zuma** was voted the new party leader of the ANC and successor to Thabo Mbeki in December.

**2008**

At the end of January, over 900 tourists were trapped on Table Mountain for half the night due to **a power cut**, but passengers on the two cable cars were hoisted to safety by emergency services.

**2009**

In the elections of April 2009 the ANC lost its two-thirds majority, but once again its candidate, now Jacob Zuma, was elected as state president. It suffered a bitter defeat in Western Cape province, where Helen Zille and her Democratic Alliance won a majority.

# Arts and Culture

The San heritage, elegant Cape Dutch mansions and colourful township art are a testament to the diversity of cultures at the Cape. Lively African music, the internationally celebrated jazz greats, and the political cabaret of Pieter Dirk Uys are no less interesting.

## San Rock Art

Thousands of **rock paintings and engravings by the San** (once known as **Bushmen**), who have inhabited the continent for 40,000 years, have been found in South Africa. The oldest examples have been dated to 3000 BC. Images of horses and representations of white settlers prove that this art was still being practiced in the 19th century. The most common images are of hunters, gatherers and large mammals such as giraffes or antelopes. There are also fascinating trance pictures of the »dream dances« practised by healers and shamans. They show transformations into fabulous animals, ritual nose-bleeding during transitions to the Other World and mystical »ear snakes«. White settlers discovered a bag on a San belt containing ten colour pigments, including ones made of **metal and plant substances**, and a mixture made of burnt chalk and the blood of wild animals. Sadly, almost all rock art is threatened by weather erosion, but in the Western Cape it is possible to take an informative tour of 130 San cave paintings at the **Bushmans Kloof Wilderness Reserve** at the foot of the Cederberg Mountains. The new **South African emblem**, introduced in 2000, shows two San figures. The motto of the emblem is also inspired by the extinct Khoisan language Xam: »!ke e: /xarra //ke«, meaning »unity in diversity« (▶image p.39).

*Honoured on the national emblem*

## Cape Dutch and Victorian Architecture

The white settlers ignored native African traditions, instead looking to Europe for their models. Thus they created their own so-called **»Cape Dutch architecture«**, building elegant mansions all around the Cape. Beautiful examples can be seen at the Dorp Museum in Stellenbosch and on the many **vineyards** of the Constantia Valley, as well as around Paarl, Stellenbosch, Franschhoek, Groot Constantia, Boschendal, La Motte and Lanzerac. Several of these types of house can also be seen in Cape Town itself, complete with their plain symmetrical ground plans in either a T, H or U form, with curved gables, a raised veranda and thick whitewashed walls. Originally **thatched**, the houses were often re-roofed with flat roofs in the mid-18th century, as can be seen at Cape Town's Rust en Vreugd. Cape Town's oldest buildings are the **Slave Lodge** erected in 1660 on Adderley Street, and the **Castle of Good Hope**, which was begun in 1666. The Koopmans de Wet House dates from the late 18th century and was the work of the French architect **Louis Michel Thibault** (1750–1815), who also built the state residence, De Tuynhuis, on Parliament Avenue and numerous buildings in the back country for the Dutch East India Company (VOC). An important artistic influence came from the wood carver **Anton Anreith** (1754–1822), originally from Freiburg in Germany, who among other works carved the pulpit in the

*Snow-white gabled houses*

← *Jewel in the Cape Dutch style: Lanzerac Manor*

Groote Kerk. The colourful little houses of the Bo-Kaap district were built at the end of the 18th century.

**British influences**    After South Africa became a British colony, the classically influenced **Georgian style** of architecture took hold. A late example of this is **Bertram House**. The **Victorian era** impressively re-shaped the appearance of Cape Town. Attractive verandas and exuberant front gardens sprang up everywhere. Cast-iron balconies such as those on **Long Street** became fashionable in the mid-19th century. The gold and diamond rush financed monumental buildings such as the **neoclassical parliament**. The neo-Gothic style came to dominate church building at the end of the 19th century. Its main proponent was the renowned lighthouse builder **Carl Otto Hager** (1813–98), who built the Moederkerk in Stellenbosch. **Sir Herbert Baker** (1862–1946) built the Groote Schuur residence for Cecil Rhodes in a Cape Dutch revival style. **City Hall** on Grand Parade, the former town hall with Italian neo-Renaissance elements, marked the end of the Victorian era.

**Art Deco and modern architecture**    Many Art Deco buildings were built around Greenmarket and along Adderley Street in the 1930s. A highlight from this era is the **Old Mutual Building** with its impressive façade on Darling Street, restored in 2001. The depressing **townships** with their endless settlements of corrugated-iron **shacks** are a legacy of the **apartheid era** and are home to most inhabitants of the **Cape Flats** to this day. Since the end of apartheid, state building programmes for housing, such as the new N2 Gateway Project by the motorway between the airport and the city centre, have aimed to create urgently needed new living space. In the 1970s Jack Barnett designed a new building for the renowned **Baxter Theatre** in Rondebosch. At the turn of the new millennium, the giant shopping complex of **Century City** in Durbanville set the tone for the future. Meanwhile, the **V & A Waterfront** continues to be developed and has long been one of South Africa's most successful visitor attractions.

*Esther Mahlangu paints exuberant geometric patterns*

## Traditional Folk Art and Township Art

The women of the **Ndebele** tribe from the country's north-east create striking pictures with glowing colours and geometrical patterns. Their paintings and beadwork are sold in Cape Town's **craft markets** and in numerous shops, alongside art from all over Africa. Typical souvenirs are traditional animal figures of wood, masks, fetishes and magic potions, jewellery, pottery, baskets and woven textiles. A good selection –

*City Hall was built towards the end of the Victorian era*

in contrast to cheap mass-produced »airport art« – can be found at the V & A Waterfront, on Church Street, on **Greenmarket Square** and at the **Pan African Market** on Long Street. Ndebele artists of international renown are Dorah Sibanyoini, Mainah-Mbonani and **Esther Mahlangu**, who painted a BMW 520i with a typical Ndebele design for the 75th anniversary of the car manufacturer. The bead jewellery and cloth dolls decorated with beads made by **Zulus** are also wonderfully colourful. Zulu beadwork can be purchased at **Monkeybiz** on Rose Street, for example, and also at the Bead Centre of Africa at 223 Long Street, where courses and bead materials are also on offer (www.beadmerchantsofafrica.com). Leaves and feathers are favoured motifs on the colourful and high-quality wares at **Africa Ceramica**. Many white designers are inspired by African influences: for example the potter and founder of Monkeybiz **Barbara Jackson**, and **Carrol Boyes**, who makes exclusive cutlery and interesting lifestyle accessories out of English pewter (www.carrolboyes.com).

The former jazz pianist **Gerard Sekoto** (1913–93) is considered the father of **township art** , and was already creating memorable portraits of the hard life of South Africa's black ghettos in the 1940s. Today, many inhabitants of the townships supplement their income through their skills as craftsmen. They make practical items, original tin toys, Christmas tree decorations or humorous collages from **old tin cans, cork, wire and old plastic**. There is a wealth to choose from at Greenmarket Square, **Streetwires** and the **Pan African Market**.

**Recycling as art**

*Abdullah Ibrahim (once known as Dollar Brand) is one of the jazz greats*

# ALL THAT JAZZ

**Cape Town celebrates life with verve and soul. Night after night jazz is played in the leading clubs and bars below Table Mountain, and during the international Jazz Festival at the end of March, global stars such as Abdullah Ibrahim, »Mama Africa« Miriam Makeba and Grammy-winning Nestor Torres come to play.**

The figurehead of South African jazz is the composer, pianist and band leader **Abdullah Ibrahim** – formerly Dollar Brand – one of the most influential jazz musicians of our times. After decades of exile in Europe and the USA, he has lived in Cape Town once more since 1990. According to Ibrahim, »jazz is a universal language understood by everyone – a means of fighting oppression and violence, and also an expression of reconciliation«. The jazz legend Ibrahim grew up in Kensington, one of Cape Town's grimmest black ghettos. »Music saved my life« says Ibrahim, who composed the music of *Manenberg*, the unofficial anthem of the liberation movement, with **Basil Coetzee** in 1974.

The first bars of **South African jazz music** were heard in the Cape townships in the early 1930s. A mixture of marabi and American bebop, rhythm & blues, jump and jive dominated clubs and dance halls in Cape Town just as much as kwela and phata-phata dancing. Like many of his contemporaries, the young Adolphus Brand bought jazz records from American sailors at the port during the 1950s. As he always had a few dollars in his pocket for this purpose, he was soon known as **Dollar Brand**. Under this artist's name he accompanied vocal groups and joined South Africa's most famous jazz band, the **Jazz Epistles**, in 1959, alongside the talented trumpeter **Hugh Masakela**. Their music became known as the »Sound of Freedom«, an answer to the ever increasing pressure of apartheid. However, after the bloody Sharpeville Massacre, Brand (now known as Abdullah Ibrahim following his conversion to Islam) left the country in 1962. He returned to the Cape only after the end of **apartheid**.

## The roots of Cape jazz

Cape jazz enjoyed its heyday during the 1950s, when it became a political expression of freedom and self-confidence in the face of a racist police state. This was not without risk: saxophonist **Winston Mankunku** only

played his legendary *Hakhal Inkomo* (roaring bull) behind a curtain. A diversity of roots quickly turned Cape jazz into an authentic sound: ancient Khoisan and Xhosa rhythms with their ghoema drums and trance singers mixed with kettledrums, trumpets and the marches of the colonial rulers, as well as with the musical heritage of slaves: the banjos and brass instruments of the »minstrels«. Eventually, the exodus caused by apartheid took **Cape jazz** all over the world. Pianists such as Tete Mbambisa, Hotep Galeta and Mark Fransman, saxophonists like Basil Coetzee, Morris Goldberg and Buddy Wells, and guitarists like Jonathon Butler and Alvin and Errol Dyers enjoyed international success. But the »godfather of Cape jazz« was always Abdullah Ibrahim, who now performs in his home town with his 16-strong **Cape Town Jazz Orchestra**. Among other established Capetonian jazz interpreters are the guitarist and composer **Mac McKenzie** and his Ghoema Captains of Cape Town, **Hilton Schilder** and his cult band The Genuines, and the alto saxophone player Robert **Edward Jansen**. The top events for jazz lovers are the **Cape Town International Jazz Festival** at the end of March (www.capetownjazz fest.com) and the **Cape Jazzathon** on the Waterfront in January (www.jazz athon.co.za). The International Jazz Festival offers jazz workshops, master classes, events for kids as well as a free open air concert, all in two days.

## Jam sessions live

Life is celebrated with mainstream jazz at the Waterfront in the **Manenberg Jazz Café** in the Clock Tower Centre (tel. 021/421 5639). Outstanding musicians such as Jimmy Dludlu, Sylvia Mdunyelwa or Gavin Minter regularly play on the stage of the **Green Dolphin** in the Victoria and Albert Hotel (tel. 021/421 74710); in **Kennedy's Cigar Bar** at 251 Long Street (tel. 021/ 424 1212) and at **Marco's African Place** at 15 Rose Lane in Bo-Kaap (tel. 021/ 423 5412). On Sundays, people meet for a jazz brunch at the **Winchester Mansions** hotel at Sea Point. **Dizzy's Jazz Café** stages hot jazz sessions on Fridays and Saturdays (41 The Drive, tel. 021/ 438 2686). **Coffee Beans Routes**, 285 Long Street (tel. 021/ 424 3572) produces ghoema, Cape jazz and classic jazz concerts on Church Square and at the Spier Estate near Stellenbosch (www.coffee beans.co.za). Andulela's **Cape Town Jazz Safaris** last five hours. The start is at Distrix Café on Hanover in Zonnebloem, 106 Darling Street, at 7pm. Stops include the jazz school »M 7« founded by Abdullah Ibrahim in 1998, a township jazz club and a visit to local jazz greats (tel. 021/ 790 2592).

## Contemporary and Modern Artists

Booming art scene
The Capetonian painter **Marlene Dumas** (born 1953), who moved to Holland in 1976, is just one of many representatives of the booming art scene originating from the Cape. The variety of contemporary South African art reflects its new, confident identity. New studios and galleries are opening every month, and information on the changing art community can be found at www.arthrob.co.za. Work by South African contemporary painters, such as Jane Alexander, Willie Bester and William Kentridge, but also examples of young **township art** and naïve Cape art, are exhibited at the **South African National Gallery**. The work of **Irma Stern**, who was deeply influenced by Expressionism, can be seen at the Irma Stern Museum in Rondebosch. Idiosyncratic touches in the cityscape are added by Brett Murray's statue of *Africa* at St George's Mall, and Gavin Young's *Still Life with Ice-Cream Cone and Blue Cheese* – a homage to Cézanne made of Californian redwood near the Clock Tower at the Waterfront.

**Baedeker TIP**

### Art map
The annually revised arts & crafts map published by Cape Town Tourism provides information on opening times, locations and a short description of the most important galleries, curio shops and art and craft markets on the Cape Peninsula.

## Cool Jazz and Hot Rhythms

Cape jazz, marabi and kwaito
Cape Town celebrates life with music that has its very own feeling. The top clubs play every kind of music and style, from jazz to kwaito, from hip-hop to house. As Cape Town is one of the world's great **jazz centres**, visitors should treat themselves to at least one jam session at the Green Dolphin, Kennedy's or the Table Bay Hotel. Alternatively buy tickets to see the old maestro Abdullah Ibrahim and his Cape Town Jazz Orchestra. Under the name ghoema jazz the folk songs of the coloureds have also found their place within Cape jazz at the **Cape Town Carnival** (▶Baedeker Special, p.153). **Marabi** music evolved from African and Western musical influences in the 1920s to become the unmistakable style of the black working class. This music is enjoying a comeback, just as much as the traditional African drumming that can be experienced at the Drum Café in District Six, but the music that expresses the lifestyle and self-confidence of South Africa's black youth like no other is **kwaito**. Originally popularized in the multi-cultural district of Hillbrow in Johannesburg, this explosive mixture of hip-hop, rhythm & blues, ragamuffin, reggae and drum & bass music has become the music of the post-apartheid era. Since the late 1990s, thanks to the private radio station YFM, this protest music has also successfully infiltrated the listening habits of white middle-class youth. The lyrics are sung in a combination of

African languages, English and Scamtho, the slang of the townships. The most popular voice of kwaito in the early 1990s was **Brenda Fassie**, the »Madonna of the Townships« (►Famous People). Today, the first letters from the names of three high school kids stand for the most successful kwaito band: **TKZee** stands for Tokollo Tshabalala, Kabelo Mabalane and Zwai Bala. Other bands with an international following are **Bongo Maffin**, whose front man is called Appleseed; Zola; and the **Prophets of da City**.

## Curtain Up!

The University of Cape Town teaches **ballet**. Here the choreographer **John Cranko** (1927–73) received his early training before emigrating at the age of 19. World-class performances are presented at the **Cape Town City Ballet**, the Cape Dance Company and the Jazz Art Dance Theatre in the **Art Scape Theatre Complex**, which is also renowned for its brilliant operas, theatre performances and musicals. William Kentridge enjoyed a resounding success there with Mozart's *Magic Flute* in 2007. Modern pieces, dance and concerts are performed on the three stages of the **Baxter Theatre**. Up-and-coming artists introduce their talents at the Little Theatre or in the Observatory quarter. Shakespeare fans meet at the Open Air Theatre in Maynardville. Wit and style are the hallmarks of Evita Se Perròn, the cult character created by cabaret artist **Pieter-Dirk Uys** in Darling. Ever since the successful world tours of *District Six*, there has a boom in musicals at the Cape. During the first African opera festival in Cape Town, in 1995, Roelof Temmingh's *Enoch, Prophet of God* was the first performance of an »African opera« that combined traditional African sounds with contemporary music. Mark Dornford-May won the Golden Bear at the 2005 Berlin Film Festival for his film of Bizet's opera *Carmen* in Xhosa, entitled ***U-Carmen e-Khayelitsha***.

*Theatre, dance and cabaret*

*»Good vibrations!«* – Cape Town has its own rhythm

# Famous People

**Who was considered Public Enemy No.1 for over a quarter of a century? Why did Nelson Mandela and Desmond Tutu receive the Nobel Peace Prize? How does Evita Bezuidenhout get away with acts of provocation at the Cape?**

## Christiaan Barnard (1922–2001)

During the night of 3 December 1967, »Chris« Neethling Barnard **Heart surgeon** successfully completed the world's first **heart transplant** (► photo p.228). During a nine-hour operation, Barnard transplanted the heart of a 25-year-old woman who had died in an accident into the 55-year-old grocer Louis Washkansky and, although Washkansky died of pneumonia just 18 days later, subsequent heart transplants were more successful. Since then, about 80,000 hearts have been transplanted worldwide. Barnard and his team at the **Groote Schuur Hospital** completed 420 heart such operations, including spectacular **»heterotopic transplants«**, in which the donor heart was connected to the recipient's heart. Barnard, the son of a Protestant missionary from the desert town of Beaufort West in the Great Karoo, became a pioneer in heart surgery as well as an international jet-setting play-boy. He adorned the covers of glamour magazines alongside Sophia Loren and Gina Lollobrigida, but his three marriages ended in di-vorce. Severe arthritis forced Barnard to retire in 1983. From then on, the »Master of Hearts« dedicated himself to the Christiaan Bar-nard Foundation, set up to help children with heart disease all over the world, and also published popular health books. As a committed opponent of apartheid, he took Greek nationality in 1993 and died of an acute asthma attack on Cyprus on 2 September 2001.

## Wilhelm Heinrich Immanuel Bleek (1827–75)

Bleek, the son of a Berlin theologian, studied African languages in **Linguist** Bonn and Berlin. In 1854 he participated in an expedition to the Ni-ger and Chad, and a year later researched a Zulu dictionary and grammar reference book after receiving an invitation from the Angli-can bishop Colenso in Natal. After gaining a doctorate, Bleek moved to the Cape in 1856, becoming the first **curator of the South African Library** as well as the official translator for Governor Grey. He dedi-cated himself to researching the **Bantu and Khoisan languages** and also collected African stories and fables. His ***Comparative Grammar of South African Languages*** is considered a milestone of African lin-guistic research. In 1862 he married Jemima Lloyd and settled in the Cape Town suburb of Mowbray. To better study the language, cul-ture and religion of the Khoisan, Bleek took prisoners from Robben Island and Breakwater Prison back to his home, and up to 28 »Bush-men« lived with him. After his premature death in 1875, his sister-in-law **Lucy Lloyd** and his daughter Dorotea continued his research, and in 1911 published his 13,000-page work on the Khoisan. Unesco added this work to the list of World Heritage in 1997. Since 2006 it

*← Schalk Burger and Helen Zille delight in holding the Webb Ellis Trophy: all Cape Town celebrated in 2007, when South Africa won the rugby world championships*

*Winner of the Nobel Prize for Literature: John Maxwell Coetzee*

has also been available in digital format at the South African Museum and on the internet at www.lloydbleekcollection.uct.ac.za.

## John Maxwell Coetzee (born 1940)

The Capetonian Coetzee spent much of his youth in Worcester, which is the setting for his novel *Boyhood*. After studying English and mathematics at the University of Cape Town, he spent three years working as a computer programmer for IBM in England. He completed his studies at the University of Texas in Austin in 1969, and then taught at New York State University before returning to the Cape in 1972. He taught at the University of Cape Town until 2000, latterly as **Professor of Literature**. Coetzee became internationally famous in 1977 with the publication of **In the Heart of the Country** – a depressing portrayal of a father-daughter relationship on a lonely desert farm that was filmed with Jane Birkin in 1984. The film, entitled *Dust*, won the Silver Lion at the Venice Biennale. A parable on power and powerlessness, his novel *Waiting for the Barbarians*, published in 1980, won South Africa's highest literature prize, the CAN Literary Award. In 1984, he received the **Booker Prize** for *The Life and Times of Michael K.* Two years later, Coetzee worked on a new edition of the Robinson Crusoe tale in *Mr Cruso, Mrs Barton and Mr Foe*. He was the first author to win the Booker Prize twice, the second time in 1999 for his grim novel *Disgrace*. He was honoured with the **Nobel Prize for Literature** in 2003. In the citation, Coetzee was praised for his analytical brilliance and for being a conscientious doubter, merciless in his critique of the Western world's flimsy morals. In 2002 Coetzee and his partner Dorothy Driver moved to Australia, where he now teaches at the University of Adelaide. After his novel *Slow Man*, his most recent publication was *Diary of a Bad Year*, in 2007.

## Brenda Fassie (1964–2004)

**Madonna of the Townships**  Both Nelson Mandela and Thabo Mbeki came to the bedside of the 39-year-old **pop star** Brenda Fassie at Johannesburg's Sunninghill Hospital before she died after 13 days in a coma, on 9 May 2004.

The press was told an asthma attack had caused a heart attack and the subsequent coma. An autopsy published later, however, mentioned a cocaine overdose. The **Queen of Kwaito** – South African township music – was the youngest of nine children in Cape Town's oldest township of Langa. Brenda's mother, a pianist, christened her in honour of the American Country singer Brenda Lee. Brenda's father died when she was two years old, and she was already earning her first money at the age of five, singing for tourists. At sixteen, she moved to Soweto and appeared with the band Joy before becoming lead singer for the **township band Brenda and the Big Dudes**. One of the band's musicians became the father of her son **Bongani »Bongz« Fassie** in 1985. Following in his mother's footsteps, he contributed to the soundtrack of the Oscar-winning movie *Tsotsi*. Bongani's track *I'm so sorry* was dedicated to Brenda. In her kwaito songs she used the township pidgin of the movie, known as *Tsotsitaal*: a mixture of English, Afrikaans, Zulu, Sotho and Tswana. Her marriage in 1989 to the former convict Nhlanhla Mbambo lasted only two years. Wild times followed, but neither her drug problems and 30 hospitalizations, nor her excessive lifestyle, cancelled gigs and her bi-sexuality damaged her **incredible popularity**. The lowest point of her life came in 1995, when she was found in a hotel room next to her lover Poppie Sihlahla, who had died of a cocaine overdose. Brenda survived her and went on to produce annual new solo albums. Her greatest comeback success was *Memeza*, which became South Africa's best-selling album in 1998. Three years later, *Time* magazine anointed her »Madonna of the Townships«.

## Nelson Mandela (born 1918)

Nelson Mandela spent more than a quarter of a century behind bars, considered Public Enemy No 1. Then, although he had never been allowed to vote before, Mandela became the first black person to take the office of **state president** after the first democratic elections in 1994. Rohlihlahla Dalibhunga Mandela – thus his full name at birth, meaning »troublemaker« or, colloquially, »pulling on the branch of a tree« – was born in the tiny village of Mvezo near Umtata, the capital of Transkei, on 18 July 1918. His father was a chieftain and advisor to Jongintaba, King of the Thembu, a member of the Xhosa tribes. He received a »civilized« name from his school teacher on his first day at school and became known as Nelson. A further »1000 insults induced a rage in me

! *Baedeker* TIP

**»Long Walk to Freedom«**
Nelson Mandela began writing his autobiography in 1975 in his eleventh year in prison. It matches Mandela's stately grace with wise reflection on his life and the freedom struggle that defined it (Publisher's Weekly, 1994). Under the title "Touch of Mandela" the clock tower Gallery on the Waterfront exhibits Mandela's lithographs, which also reflect his time on Robben Island.

*Bearers of hope for reconciliation: Nelson Mandela and his wife Graça Machel*

and a rebellious attitude that drove me to fight the system that enslaved my people«; and so he qualified as a lawyer and, in 1944, joined the **African National Congress** and founded the youth league of the ANC together with Walter Sisulu, Oliver Tambo and others. In 1952, Mandela and Tambo opened **South Africa's first black law practice**, and Mandela quickly became the symbolic figurehead of the black majority. After his call for the peaceful breaking of the Race Laws in 1952, the government banned him from all political work. Nevertheless, he remained active for the ANC. He married the black social worker **Winnie Nomzamo Madikizela** on 14 June 1958. After the Sharpeville Massacre of 1961, the ANC was banned and Mandela went underground. He organized a general strike, which was brutally crushed; this meant the end of the phase of non-violent resistance – for Mandela, too. He ended up in **»Umkhonto we Sizwe«**, the militant wing of the ANC known as the »Spear of the Nation«, carrying out sabotage operations alongside Joe Slovo. Mandela was arrested in 1962 and condemned to five years imprisonment at the Rivonia Trial. This sentence was extended to life imprisonment in 1964, and his

**prison number 46664** (marking him as the 466th convict of 1964) became synonymous with the battle against apartheid. He was released by **President Frederik de Klerk** on 11 February 1990, after **28 years in jail**, most of it spent on Robben Island, and following numerous secret negotiations and increasing pressure internally and from abroad. Together, de Klerk and Mandela then committed themselves to the **abolition of apartheid** and a policy of reconciliation. For this effort they jointly received the Nobel Peace Prize in December 1993. Nelson Mandela began his term in office as **South African state president** on 10 May 1994. Bridging the gaps in his divided society and the reconciliation of all South Africans was the heart of his political work. Mandela divorced his wife Winnie in 1996, after she was indicted for criminal activities and forced to resign all political posts. With Mbeki's election in 1999, the »grand old man of Africa« – affectionately known as **»Madiba«** – and one of the most impressive politicians of the 20th century, stood down from office. He married Graça Machel, the widow of the former president of Mozambique, on his 80th birthday. Since 2003, Mandela's prisoner number has also become a symbol in the **fight against Aids**. Every year on 1 December a benefit concert for Aids is held, the first occasion being the **46664 World Aids Day Concert** in Cape Town in 2003. Mandela's second son, the lawyer Makgatho Mandela, died of Aids aged 54 in 2005. For Mandela's 90th birthday, London's Hyde Park was the venue for the 2008 Aids Day Concert.

## Jan van Riebeeck (1619–77)

Johan Anthoniszoon van Riebeeck, the son of a surgeon in Culemborg in the Netherlands, was born on 21 April 1619. He served the **Dutch East India Company** (VOC) as a scribe and assistant surgeon in Djakarta from 1639, also visiting Japan and overseeing the trading post at Tonkin in Vietnam. He was withdrawn from that post when it emerged that he had done business on his own behalf as well. In 1649, Riebeeck married the 20-year-old **Maria de la Quellerie**, who bore him eight sons during her short life. She died in Malacca in 1664. In 1651 he was given the chance to rehabilitate himself. Van Riebeeck was put in charge of establishing a **support base at Table Bay** responsible for provisioning ships on their long journey between Europe and Asia with fresh groceries, especially with meat and vegetables. The first three of five ships set anchor in the bay with 82 men and eight women on board on **6 April 1652**. (► ill. p.26). The first winter was hard, and 20 people died in damp huts. Van Riebeeck built a fort for protection and mounted a signal mast for passing ships on it. Fruit and vegetables were cultivated and meat was obtained by bartering with the Khoikhoi. The harbour was made safe against storms with the construction of a quay, and workshops and a hospital soon followed. Riebeeck's suggestion to settle free farmers found support and, in 1657, the first slaves  arrived. When Riebeeck

**Founder of Cape Town**

left the Cape in 1662 to take up the post of commander in the Moluccas, Cape Town had four streets with simple houses, 200 white inhabitants and 180 slaves. Van Riebeeck died in Jakarta in 1677.

## Joe Slovo (1926–95)

**Left-winger**

For decades, Yossel Mashel Slovo was one of the most influential whites in South Africa's **anti-apartheid movement**. Slovo was born in the Jewish ghetto Obeliai in Lithuania on 23 May 1926, and came to South Africa with his parents at the age of nine. In the 1940s he worked as a lawyer. He became a member of the South African Communist Party (SACP) in 1942. He fought as a volunteer in the Springbok Legion in North Africa for the Allied side during the Second World War. In 1949, Slovo married the journalist and anti-apartheid activist Ruth First, with whom he had three daughters. As representative of the Congress of Democrats allied to the ANC, he participated in the drafting of the Freedom Charter in 1955. He was arrested in December 1956. Active in the militant wing of the ANC and also a leading theoretician, Slovo went into exile in 1963, with periods in England, Zambia and Mozambique. His wife Ruth fell victim to a letter bomb in 1982, addressed to him. **General Secretary of the SACP** from 1986 onwards, he resigned his office due to ill health. (His successor was Chris Hani, who was assassinated in 1993). In 1990, Slovo was notable for his reasoned contribution to the negotiations with President de Klerk, and it was his consensus-building suggestion that a transitional Government of National Unity should be formed. Nevertheless, he never forgot his communist convictions and always wore red socks during negotiations. He became minister for housing in Mandela's government in 1994, but died of bone-marrow cancer a year later. Slovo made an appearance in the 2006 movie *Catch a Fire*, whose script was written by his daughter Shawn.

## Desmond Mpilo Tutu (born 1931)

**Confrontational bishop**

Desmond Tutu was born a **Xhosa** in the Transvaal mining town of Klerksdorp. The family moved to Johannesburg, where his father was a teacher, when he was twelve. He originally wished to study medicine, but the family was unable to pay for this, and Tutu became a teacher. Later he studied theology and was ordained as an Anglican priest in 1960. Bishop of Lesotho from 1976 onwards, he received the **Nobel Prize for Peace** in 1984 for his work as general secretary to the South African Church Council. That same year he also became the **first black bishop** of Johannesburg. Two years later, he became

*Desmond Tutu during the first free elections in Cape Town's Guguletu township, in 1994*

archbishop of Cape Town and thus also the head of the Anglican Church in South Africa. He had been president of the Pan-African Church Conference since 1987, and made Cape Town's **St George's Cathedral** a stronghold of **peaceful resistance**. As negotiator between the ANC and Inkatha during the 1990s, he was able to advance the cause of the democratization process. From 1996 to 1998, Tutu was chairman of the **Truth and Reconciliation Commission**, entrusted with working through the crimes committed during apartheid. His warm-hearted and humorous message for the world is encompassed in his book about those years: *No Future Without Forgiveness*.

## Pieter-Dirk Uys (born 1945)

The **provocative cabaret artist** Pieter-Dirk Uys was always a thorn in the side of the apartheid regime, but it never dared to attack him openly. His popularity was his protection. The son of a Calvinist father from an old Boer family and a Jewish mother who arrived in South Africa after fleeing the Nazis, Uys began his acting career in

*A formidable lady:*
*Uys alias Evita Bezuidenhout*

1969. He appeared in over 30 one-man shows during the 1970s, also penning over 20 dramas and appearing on South African television. *Paradise is Closing Down*, *God's Forgotten* and *Foreign Aids* achieved international success. »PDU«, as he is known, became famous as the shrill drag queen **Evita Bezuidenhout**, who lives in the old train station of Darling, north of Cape Town. The »Evita of the Cape« has voiced even the most terrible truths with **black humour** and has maintained her critical stance despite the dawning of the new South Africa. Evita Se Perrón (platform in Afrikaans) has exposed the pseudo-liberals in the new South Africa in *Truth Omissions* and *You ANC Nothing Yet*. Today, as a committed **Aids activist**, he also visits townships and schools at the Cape with his HIV educational programme entitled *For Facts Sake!* Meanwhile Evita involved herself in elections in 2003, with her show *Elections and Erections* and, in 2007, she cheekily announced her own candidature in *Evita for President*. More details of his life and the complete texts of his plays can be found at www.pdu.co.za. Dates for contemporary performances in Darling can be found at www.evita.co.za.

## Helen Zille (born 1951)

**Cape Town's mayor** Cape Town's courageous mayor Helen Zille (►photo p.50) has a vision: »This city can and must become one of most prominent cities of the world«. Born on 9 March 1951 in Johannesburg, she is the great grandniece of a famous Berlin caricaturist, **Heinrich Zille**, and is proud of her ancestor: »his commitment to the common people is typical of my whole family«. Her Jewish parental home stood firm against apartheid. Her father fled to South Africa from German racial hatred in 1934, her mother in 1936. Helen Zille gained great respect as a young **journalist** on the Rand Daily Mail. She bravely exposed the truth about the death in 1977 of the popular civil rights campaigner **Steve Biko**, who had died in custody not due to a hunger strike but from beatings by the security police. Four years later, Zille resigned her post because her chief editor was forced to leave for his critical stand against apartheid. Subsequently, she was active in a variety of **civil rights movements** and also became press officer for the University of Cape Town. From 1994 onwards, Zille (also fluent in Afrikaans and Xhosa) became involved in the **Democratic Alliance Party** (DA), becoming minister for education in the Western Cape in 2000, and also deputy party chairperson. On **15 March 2006**, Zille unexpectedly won the Cape Town communal elections, ousting the ANC mayor Nomainda Mfeketo, who had been in office for the past 13 years, with a three-vote majority. Cape Town is therefore the only city in South Africa in which the ANC has lost control. Zille's first test of strength came with the sacking of the council leader Wallace Mgoqi, which she finally enforced by court order. The **battle against corruption** was more complicated: up to four highly-paid directors in the town hall, all ANC members, were holding the same post when she took office. When attacks against her by the ANC did not stop, Helen Zille went on the offensive and took the unilateral decision to cut the provincial government's electricity and water for their refusal to pay bills that amounted to millions. She has been considered a **force to be reckoned with** ever since. Helen Zille lives in Cape Town's multi-cultural quarter of Observatory with her husband, sociology professor Johann Marre, and their two grown-up sons. On 6 May 2007 she succeeded Tony Leon as **chairperson for the Democratic Alliance Party** and is already being touted as a possible presidential candidate. When she was arrested for breaking the law governing public gatherings during a demonstration against drugs in the township of Mitchell's Plain in September 2007, she used her court case to accuse the minister for police of unjustified arrests. Four weeks later, Zille and all her co-defendants were found not guilty. As part of the run-up to the 2010 FIFA World Cup, she lent her support to a Cape Town project set up by the aid organization **Power Child**, which is planning to build a new campus with sports facilities that will offer township children safe leisure amenities and protection against sexual abuse.

# Practicalities

WHAT ARE BILTONG, BRAAI AND BRODIE? WHERE IS THE BEST SEAFOOD TO BE FOUND? WHERE ARE THE BEST PLACES FOR SHOPPING? WHEN IS THE ENTIRE CITY OUT DANCING? FIND OUT HERE – IDEALLY BEFORE ARRIVING FOR YOUR HOLIDAY AT THE CAPE.

# Accommodation

Accommodation grading

The **Tourism Grading Council of South Africa** (TGCSA) carries out annual inspections of hotels, pensions, B&Bs and camp sites and grades them according to a system ranging from one to five stars (www.tourismgrading.co.za). The tourist boom of recent years at the Cape means there are **wonderful places to stay in all price categories** in Cape Town: from luxury 5-star hotels with sea view and spa to stylish Victorian guest houses and cosy B&Bs, as well as good backpacker hostels. **Timely reservations** are essential during high season from November to April, and also during the Football World Cup in 2010.

## Price categories

- Luxury: over 2000 rand
- Mid-range: 1000–2000 rand
- Budget: under 1000 rand. Prices are for one night's accommodation for two people in a double room including breakfast.

## ▶ RECOMMENDED CAPE TOWN HOTELS Map p.64–65

### LUXURY

▶ ① **Cape Grace Hotel**
West Quay Road,
V & A Waterfront
Cape Town 8002
Tel. 021 / 410 7100
Fax 021 / 419 7622
www.capegrace.com
Surrounded by water on three sides, this 5-star hotel refurbished in 2008 is a member of the Fair Trade Hotels and the Leading Small Hotels of the World. All 122 rooms have views of either Table Mountain or the Waterfront. Also has an award-winning restaurant, onewaterfront (▶p.94), and the Bascule Bar with over 460 whiskies from all over the world. Spa with suitably African décor.

▶ ② **Ellerman House**
180 Kloof Road, Bantry Bay
Cape Town 8060
Tel. 021 / 430 3200
Fax 021 / 430 3215
www.ellerman.co.za
The former residence of the English shipping magnate Ellermann is decorated with South African art by Maggie Loubser, George Pemba, Irma Stern and John Meyer. The classical style of the house is enhanced by the new Ellerman Villa & Spa with 21st-century architecture; there are 16 elegant rooms and suits. The restaurant specializes in seafood and the wine cellar has over 12,000 bottles of top-class South African wines.

▶ ③ **Mandela Rhodes Place**
Corner of Burg / Wale Street
Central
Tel. 021 / 481 4000
Fax 021 / 481 4001
www.threecities.co.za
www.mandelarhodesplace.co.za
Opened in 2007, this ultra-modern city hotel has luxury apartments. A recommended dish in the restaurant is Synergy on 7:

Dominique Guebert's rack of lamb with butternut, capers and mint.

► ④ **Mount Nelson Hotel**
76 Orange Street, Oranjezicht
Cape Town 8001
Tel. 021 / 483 1000
Fax 021 / 483 1001
www.mountnelson.co.za
The pink palace once owned by the shipping magnate Sir Donald Currie has received guests in its inimitable luxurious style since Victorian times. The »Nellie« has hosted royals and VIPs from all over the world. Winnie Mandela once booked a total of ten rooms at the same time. The Librisa Spa opened in 2008 promises relaxation, while head chef Ian Mancais spoils guests with culinary delights in the Cape Colony restaurant. For Mediterranean cuisine, head for the Oasis restaurant. At least drop by for a drink! ►Baedeker Tip p.202

► ⑤ **The Bay Hotel**
69 Victoria Road, Camps Bay
Cape Town 8040
Tel. 021 / 438 4444
Fax 021 / 438 4433
www.thebay.co.za
Wonderful view of Table Mountain and the beach promenade with luxurious pool area set back from the hurly-burly of Camps Bay. Gourmet cuisine in Tides restaurant, sundowners on the wooden deck of the Sandy B bar or in the Traders bar.

► ⑥ **The Table Bay Hotel**
Quay 6, V & A Waterfront
Cape Town 8001
Tel. 021 / 406 5000
Fax 021 / 406 5656
www.suninternational.com/Destinations/Hotels/TableBay

All 329 rooms of this maritime luxury hotel on the Victorian Breakwater pier have wonderful views of either Table Mountain or the harbour. A member of the Leading Hotels of the World, it contains five stylish restaurants and bars. Jazz lunches on Sundays. The Health Spa offers relaxation with aromatherapies and »hot stone massage«. VIPs have left their mark at the seal monument at the main entrance.

*Baedeker recommendation*

► ⑦ **Twelve Apostles Hotel and Spa**
Victoria Road, Camps Bay, Cape Town
Tel. 021 / 437 9000
www.12apostleshotel.com
Just the location, at the foot of the Twelve Apostles right by the Atlantic, is spectacular. This exclusive 5-star hotel has 55 rooms and 15 suites and, in addition to two wonderful pool gardens above the ocean, the Azure gourmet restaurant (►p.95). A grotto with spa and a private cinema are also available, plus 72 different Martini cocktails to choose from in the Leopard Bar!

► ⑧ **Villa Belmonte**
33 Belmonte Avenue, Oranjezicht
Cape Town 8001
Tel. 021 / 462 1576
Fax 021 / 462 1579
www.villabelmontehotel.co.za
Tabea and Cliff Jacobs' enchanting Victorian villa has 15 rooms and a large pool. The Cajun chicken with game paté is a great treat.

► ⑨ **Winchester Mansions**
221 Beach Road, Sea Point
Cape Town
Tel. 021 / 434 2351

## *Cape Town* Hotels and guest houses

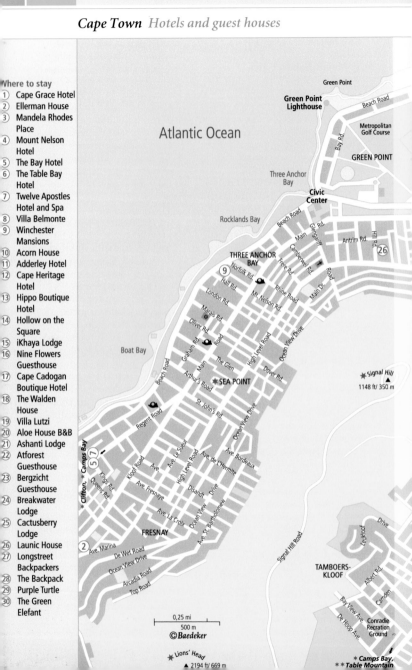

**Where to stay**

1. Cape Grace Hotel
2. Ellerman House
3. Mandela Rhodes Place
4. Mount Nelson Hotel
5. The Bay Hotel
6. The Table Bay Hotel
7. Twelve Apostles Hotel and Spa
8. Villa Belmonte
9. Winchester Mansions
10. Acorn House
11. Adderley Hotel
12. Cape Heritage Hotel
13. Hippo Boutique Hotel
14. Hollow on the Square
15. iKhaya Lodge
16. Nine Flowers Guesthouse
17. Cape Cadogan Boutique Hotel
18. The Walden House
19. Villa Lutzi
20. Aloe House B&B
21. Ashanti Lodge
22. Atforest Guesthouse
23. Bergzicht Guesthouse
24. Breakwater Lodge
25. Cactusberry Lodge
26. Launic House
27. Longstreet Backpackers
28. The Backpack
29. Purple Turtle
30. The Green Elefant

Atlantic Ocean

Green Point

Green Point Lighthouse

Beach Road

Metropolitan Golf Course

GREEN POINT

Three Anchor Bay

Civic Center

Rocklands Bay

Beach Road

Antrim Rd.

26

THREE ANCHOR BAY

9

Norfolk Rd.
Hall Rd.
London Rd.
Marais Rd.
Oliver Rd.

Mt. Nelson Rd.

High Level Road

Dover Rd.

Ocean View Drive

Boat Bay

Beach Road

The Glen

Arthur's Road

★ SEA POINT

★ Signal Hill
1148 ft/ 350 m

St. John's Rd.

Regent Road

Ocean View Drive

King's Rd.
Queens Rd.

Kloof Road

Ave. Le Sueur
Ave.
Ave. Fresnaye

High Level Road

Ave. de l'Hermite

Ave. Bordeaux

Disandt

Ocean View Drive

2
Ave. La Croix

FRESNAY

Ave. Marina

De Wet Road

Ocean View Drive

Arcadia Road

Top Road

Ocean View Drive

Ave. St. Bartholomew

Signal Hill Road

TAMBOERS-KLOOF

Kloof

Drive

Albert Rd.

Camden

Bay View Ave

De Hoop Ave

Conradie Recreation Ground

0,25 mi
500 m
©Baedeker

★ Lions' Head
▲ 2194 ft/ 669 m

★ Camps Bay,
★★ Table Mountain

★ Clifton, ★ Camps Bay

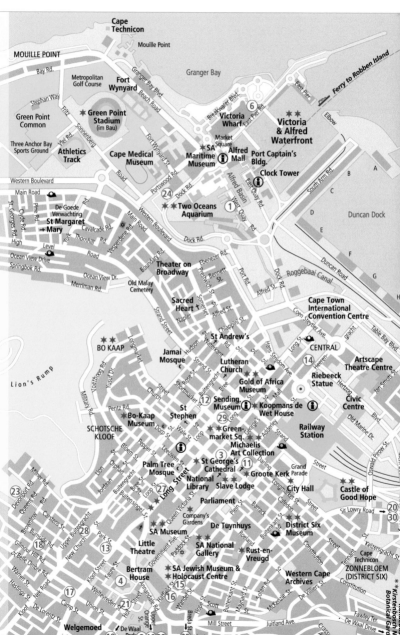

*Superb accommodation at the Twelve Apostles Hotel with a sea view*

Fax 021 / 434 0215
www.winchester.co.za
Elegant boutique hotel in colonial style with Atlantic views under the renowned management of South Africa's 2001 Hotel Manager of the Year, Nils Heckscher. Jazz fans meet at Harvey's here, for brunch on Sundays. (►Baedeker Tip, p.208).

### MID-RANGE

► ⑩ **Acorn House**
1 Montrose Avenue
Oranjezicht, Cape Town 8001
Tel. 021 / 461 1782
Fax 021 / 461 1768
www.acornhouse.co.za
This protected monument, a masterpiece by Sir Herbert Baker built in 1904, was designed with generous verandas, pillared walkways in warm wood tones and a great deal of white stucco. All eight double rooms exhibit great attention to detail. There is also a pool, garden and well-stocked wine cellar.

► ⑪ **Adderley Hotel**
31 Adderley Street, Central
Cape Town 8000
Tel. 021 / 423 1426
Fax 021 / 423 1439
www.relaishotels.com/adderley. Three Victorian houses and an 11-storey tower on one of Cape Town's main boulevards form the central hotel complex. 28 large suites, a cocktail bar and roof top pool with sundeck are just some of the features. Try the homemade butternut ravioli or Thai chicken in the Bowl Restaurant.

► ⑫ **Cape Heritage Hotel**
90 Bree Street, Central, Cape Town 8000
Tel. 021 / 424 4646
Fax 086 / 616 7281
www.capeheritage.co.za
This elegant boutique hotel housed in an 18th-century building with a pretty courtyard has 15

*Romantic dinner at the Cape Colony restaurant at the Mount Nelson Hotel*

individually styled rooms. A selection of six good restaurants can be found all around Heritage Square.

▶ ⑬ **Hippo Boutique Hotel**
5–9 Park Road, Gardens, Cape Town 8001
Tel. 021 / 423 2500
Fax 021 / 423 2515
www.hippotique.co.za
Design hotel with a successful blend of classical and modern: king-size beds, cotton bedding, cherrywood parquet floor, leather chairs and internet access in all 20 rooms. Children must be a minimum of 12 years old.

▶ ⑭ **Hollow on the Square**
9 Ryk Tulbagh Square, Hans Strijdom Ave, Central, Cape Town 8001
Tel. 021 / 421 5140
Fax 021 / 421 4648
www.hollowonthesquare.co.za
Modern city hotel two minutes from the Congress Centre. 115 rooms, delicious cuisine in the Amici restaurant, also a cocktail lounge and spa.

▶ ⑮ **iKhaya Lodge**
Mill Street
Dunkley Square Gardens
Cape Town 8010
Tel. 021 / 461 8880
Fax 086 / 631 3292
www.ikhayalodge.co.za
IKhaya, meaning »home« in Xhosa, is a boutique hotel in African style. The restaurant with its breakfast and lunch buffet is also African influenced. In addition there are self-catering apartments and safe parking.

▶ ⑯ **Nine Flowers Guesthouse**
133–135 Hatfield Street, Gardens, Cape Town 8001
Tel. 021 / 462 1430
www.nineflowers.com. In a historic Victorian building, where each room's colour scheme is inspired by a different Cape flower.

▶ ⑰ **Cape Cadogan Boutique Hotel**
5 Upper Union Street
Tamboerskloof, Cape Town 8001
Tel. 021 / 480 8080
Fax 021 / 480 8090
www.capecadogan.com. This hotel
with excellent personal service, a
farmhouse in the 19th century,
was declared a national monument in 1984. 12 beautiful rooms,
a pool, an open fireplace and a
well-stocked library. The President
Suite is in its own villa.

▶ ⑱ **The Walden House**
5 Burnside Road,
Tamboerskloof, Cape Town
Tel. 021 / 424 4256
Fax 086 / 689 4802
www.walden-house.com. Colonial
villa dating from 1900, with seven
elegant rooms. Finest bedlinen
under mosquito nets and a wonderful garden.

▶ ⑲ **Villa Lutzi**
6 Rosmead Avenue
Oranjezicht, Cape Town 8001
Tel. 021 / 423 4614
Fax 021 / 426 1472
www.villalutzi.com. Villa with excellent personal service run by
Dagmar and Eric Lothaller. All 15
rooms are spacious and the interior design is full of personal
touches. Large pool and a beautiful garden with views towards
the Lion's Head. Safe parking.

## BUDGET

▶ ⑳ **Aloe House B & B**
12 Howe Street, Observatory
Cape Town 7925

*Colonial style: Hotel Cape Cadogan*

Tel. 021 / 448 5337
www.aloehouse.co.za
Frank Gaude rents out a Victorian
cottage with two pretty rooms
complete with lounge and open
fire (non-smokers only). Gaude
also runs city sightseeing tours and
organizes picnics with the pelicans
at the nature reserve of Rondevlei.

▶ ㉑ **Ashanti Lodge**
11 Hof Street, Gardens
Cape Town 8001
Tel. 021 / 423 8721
Fax 021 / 423 8790
www.ashanti.co.za
Comfortable single, double and 6-
to 8-bed dorm rooms with private
bath. Also has a pool, the Kumasi
Café and the Travel Centre.

▶ ㉒ **Atforest Guesthouse**
14 Forest Road, Oranjezicht
Cape Town 8001
Tel. / fax 021 / 461 5484
www.safarinow.com/go/atforest.
Well-kept villa with six double
rooms including private bath and
air conditioning; also a pool and
grill area.

▶ ㉓ **Bergzicht Guesthouse**
5 Devonport Road
Tamboerskloof, Cape Town 8001
Tel. 021 / 423 8513
Fax 021 / 424 5244
www.bergzichtguesthouse.co.za
19th-century villa with wonderful
views towards Table Mountain
from the pool. Double rooms with
TV and a family room with small
kitchen.

▶ ㉔ **Breakwater Lodge**
Portswood Road,
V & A Waterfront, Cape Town
Tel. 021 / 406 1911
Fax 021 / 406 1070

www.breakwaterlodge.co.za
How about staying in the former
port prison? The historic north
wing still preserves graffiti by
British prisoners dating from
1903. Comfortable rooms, self-
service restaurant and a café.

*Baedeker recommendation*

▶ ㉕ **Cactusberry Lodge**
30 Breda Street, Oranjezicht
Cape Town 8001
Tel. / fax 021 / 461 97 87
www.cactusberry.net.ms
Stylish rooms at affordable prices. Nice
lounge, pool and sunbathing area on the
terrace, and also a quiet courtyard.
Wonderful breakfasts, and in the evenings there is wine under the eucalyptus
tree.

▶ ㉖ **Launic House**
10 Romney Road, Green Point
Cape Town 8005
Tel. 021 / 434 4851
Fax 021 / 434 0913
www.launichouse.co.za
Smart B&B in the heart of Green
Point. 17 non-smoker rooms.

## BACKPACKER HOSTELS

▶ ㉗ **Longstreet Backpackers**
209 Long Street, Central
Cape Town
Tel. 021 / 423 0615
Fax 021 / 423 1842
www.longstreetbackpackers.co.za
One of South Africa's best youth
hostels. Single, double and 4-bed
rooms. Clean showers, large
kitchen and grill area. On Sundays
free vegetable potjie.

▶ ㉘ **The Backpack**
74 New Church Street
Central, Cape Town

*Budget: the Purple Turtle hostel*

Tel. 021 / 423 4530
Fax 021 / 423 0065
www.backpackers.co.za
Award-winning youth hostel with
single, double, 4- to 8-bed rooms.
Gets five stars from the TGCSA.
Also a pool, cocktail bar, infor-
mation exchange and tours.

▶ ㉙ **Purple Turtle**
31 Shortmarket Street, Cape Town
Tel. 021 / 424 7811
www.capetownbackpacker.co.za
Recently renovated youth hostel

around the corner from Greenmarket Square. There are double
rooms and a dormitory, a bar,
restaurant and lockers.

▶ ㉚ **The Green Elefant**
57 Milton Road, Observatory
Tel. 021 / 448 6359
Fax 021 / 448 0510
www.hostels.co.za
Three guest houses with personal
service in the heart of the student
district with large double rooms.
Book the Dolphin or Lion Room!

# Arrival · Before the Journey

## Arrival

By air   There is no shortage of airlines that fly direct to Cape Town daily or
several times weekly: South African Airlines (SAA), British Airways,
KLM, Air Namibia, Lufthansa and Virgin Atlantic are all worth con-
sidering, and it may be cheap or convenient to fly via Amsterdam,

! *Baedeker* TIP

**Camera film, batteries and storage media**

Analogue or digital, photographic equipment is more expensive in Cape Town than in Europe or North America, so it is highly advisable to bring sufficient film, rechargeable batteries and memory sticks from home, and not forget the adapter! The best light conditions for photos are in the morning before 9am and in the afternoon from 4pm onwards, because the sun is very bright during the day. Occasionally, it is also a good idea to leave the camera behind and just focus on the experience of South Africa: let the country work its magic on you.

Frankfurt or Johannesburg instead of direct from London. Most flights from European airports take 12–13hrs; as the time zone is the same as in central Europe, jet lag is not an issue! Night flights with a morning arrival are ideal. Kulala and 1time are budget airlines connecting Cape Town with other South African cities. During high season (Dec–March), reservations should be made three months in advance; good-value flights can be had during the South African autumn (April–June). Scheduled flights must normally be **re-confirmed** with the relevant airline company three days prior to the return flight. Always check travel conditions printed on the flight ticket or attached documents.

Planes arrive at **Cape Town International Airport (CTIA)**, which is just under 24km/15mi east of the city centre and  reached in 30mins by car via the N2 motorway. Shuttle buses operate between the airport and city centre and the larger hotels have their own shuttle services. Alternatively, take a taxi, the only authorized ones being Touch Down Taxis (► p.132). The major international car rental firms (► p.132)are represented at the airport; it is best to make bookings prior to arrival. *Hotel transfers*

Numerous European and South African **tour operators** sell package holidays via travel agents or the internet: from tailor-made tours for self-drive holidays to all-inclusive holidays of several weeks. Local tour operators and travel agents can be found, among other places, on Cape Town Tourism's website www.tourismcapetown.co.za *Package tours*

Visitors from the UK, North America, Australia and New Zealand require a **passport** with an expiry date no less than six months beyond the date for the return journey. Children must travel on their own passports with photographic ID. There must also be at least two *Travel documents*

## ARRIVAL INFORMATION

### CAPE TOWN AIRPORT

► **Cape Town International Airport (CTIA)**
Tel. 021 / 937 1275
Fax 021 / 936 2937
Flight information:
Tel. 086 / 727 7888
www.acsa.co.za
www.airports.co.za.

### AIRLINE COMPANIES

► **South African Airways (SAA)**
Tel. at the airport CTIA:
021 / 936 2230
www.flysaa.com

► **Air Namibia**
Tel. at the airport CTIA:
021 / 936 2755
www.airnamibia.co.na

► **British Airways**
Tel. 021 / 936 9000
www.ba.com

► **KLM**
Tel. at the airport CTIA:
021 / 935 8500, www.klm.com

► **Lufthansa**
Tel. in Cape Town:
021 / 415 3735
www.lufthansa.com

► **Virgin Atlantic**
Tel. at the airport CTIA:
011 / 340 3400
www.virgin-atlantic.com

► **1 Time**
Tel. 021 / 036 3040 1190
www.1time.aero
value for money internal flights

► **Kulula**
Tel. 086 / 158 5852
www.kulula.com
Value for money internal flights

► **Nationwide**
Tel. 021 / 936 2050
www.flynationwide.co.za

blank pages available in the passport for entry and exit stamps. Visits of more than three months require a visa. Proof of a return flight and sufficient funds can be required, though a credit card is often sufficient. Additional information can be found through the relevant South African embassy or consulate (►p.100). Photocopies of travel documents should always be stored separately.

*Driving licence* Visitors need an **international driving licence**, though car rental firms also accept the new EU licence. Minimum age for car hire is 21 years.

*Health* The Western Cape Province, including Cape Town, the Winelands and the Garden Route, is a **malaria-free zone**. No particular vaccinations are required, though you should be up-to-date on polio, tetanus, diphtheria and hepatitis A and B. The quality of Cape Town's **drinking water** is outstanding. South Africa enjoys good medical provision, and Cape Town has several excellent private clinics. When **medical services** are needed, payment is either by cash or credit card. Visitors' national state health insurances will not cover the cost of medical care in South Africa. It is therefore essential to take out sufficient **medical insurance** including repatriation cover before the journey.

! *Baedeker* TIP

**Good day, sunshine!**

The sun shines with much greater intensity at the Cape than in Europe. Sunglasses, sun hat and sun cream with high UV protection factors should therefore always be part of your luggage.

South Africa accepts goods free of duty to the following limits: 1 litre of spirits, 2 litres of wine, 400 cigarettes, 50 cigars, 250g of tobacco, 250ml of eau de toilette and 50ml of perfume. Furthermore, gifts to a value of 500 rand. More detailed information is available from the Department of Customs and Excise, Pretoria/Tshwane, tel. 012 / 428 7000. Plant and animal products, such as trophies, can only be exported by special permission. Trade in endangered plants and animals is strictly prohibited.

*South African customs regulations*

Visitors over the age of 17 returning to the EU from non-EU countries are permitted to import for private consumption: 1 litre of spirits, 2 litres of wine or beer, 200 cigarettes or 250g of tobacco, as well as gifts to the value of € 175 (no gold alloys).

*Return journeys to the European Union*

*Fine lodgings at the Botlierskop Game Reserve*

# Beaches

Wind and waves
Capetonians love the water and beach life, and go sailing in all weathers. With 150km/95mi of coast all around the Cape they have plenty of opportunities, whether for sunbathing, swimming with all the family, snorkelling or surfing. On the west coast, water temperatures rarely rise above 20ºC/68ºF, even during summer. The beaches along the **rough Atlantic side** are relatively protected from the summer winds, but the sea is a good five degrees cooler than along the beaches of **False Bay**. The most pleasant water temperatures, however, are along the Garden Route on the Indian Ocean.

Dream beaches on the Indian Ocean
The Indian Ocean awaits with turquoise waters, long white sandy beaches and some of the best water sports facilities in the world. **Strand Beach**, at the gates of Somerset West, is a hot spot for Hobie Cat sailors and surfers, while Melkbaai Beach with its two tidal pools is recommended for sun worshippers and for long beach walks. Smart yachts dot the harbour of **Gordon's Bay** and its wide Bikini Beach is popular with volleyball players. One of the most popular bathing beaches is at **Muizenberg**, where the water is warm and the long beach has very fine-grained sand. Colourful beach cabins and wood fencing provide protection from the common breezes. The best-known surfing spots around here are Sunrise Circle and Surfer's Corner. Beach marshals ensure safety at False Bay during the summer months. Families favour the gently sloping beaches at **Fishhoek** and **Kalk Bay**. The beautiful beach set among large blocks of granite at **Boulders** is also loved by 3000 small jackass penguins. Divers, surfers and kayakers gather all around the Cape. The best beaches at the

## ℹ The loveliest beaches

- Camps Bay: fashionable and with palm promenade
- Clifton No. 4: family-friendly Blue Flag beach near the city
- Blouberg Beach: best Table Mountain panorama
- Dolphin Beach: hot spot for kite surfers
- Muizenberg: colourful beach huts, with protection from wind and warm water
- Bikini Beach: meeting place for volleyball players and sailors
- Sandy Bay Beach: topless sunbathing is OK here
- Buffels Bay: quiet beach with views across False Bay

Cape of Good Hope Nature Reserve are **Platboom Beach, Buffels Bay** and **Diaz Beach**, though they are all unsupervised by life guards. Watch out for the strong currents.

Experienced **kite surfers** can enjoy high waves on the Atlantic Coast, especially at Sunset Reef, Crayfish Factory, 365s and Outer Kom. The ultimate wave at **Dunes Beach** near Noordhoek is strictly for professionals (www.wavescape.co.za). Meanwhile, the 8km/5mi Long Beach at **Noordhoek** is ideal for beach horse-riding. Two safe beaches for families on the otherwise rough Atlantic can be found at **Hout Bay**, which is also the beginning of Chapman's Peak Drive. To the north lies **Sandy Bay Beach**, Cape Town's nudist beach. **Llundudno** is a popular meeting place for surfers, but no place for beginners. For sunbathing, surfing and beach volley ball, the broad beaches near the city at **Camps Bay** are ideal. They are usually full at weekends, but very trendy, always good for a beach party, and the service along the palm promenade is first class. Huge granite blocks divide the beach at **Clifton** into four sections: the first one is known for posing, while the fourth is a family beach, protected from the wind and endorsed by a blue water quality flag. Hot spots for kite surfers are to the north of Cape Town, at **Dolphin Beach** and along **Blouberg beach**, which also has the most spectacular view of Table Mountain. Wind surfers from all over the world congregate at **Sunset Beach**.

*Surf spots and wind-protected bays along the Atlantic*

# Children in South Africa

South Africa is very **child-friendly** and many attractions all around the Cape are suitable for children. Several can be visited free with the **Cape Town Pass** (www.thecapetown pass.com, ►p.100). The best places to eat with kids can be found at **www.eatingoutwithkids.co.za.**

*Never boring!*

Shark diving at the **Two Oceans Aquarium** is exciting for the entire family, as is the whale and dinosaur exhibition at the **South African Museum**. The Planetarium also organizes special children's programmes. On Table Mountain, meanwhile, your children will surely be charmed by the **rock dassies** and amazed to discover that these cuddly little animals are supposedly related to elephants! The obligatory drive around the Cape Peninsula must include a stop to see the **penguins at Boulders Beach**, and **Tygerberg Zoo** has a touch-and-feel enclosure, as well as lions, antelopes and chimpanzees. The attractions at Hout Bay are the exotic **World of Birds** and a fascinating boat trip to **Duiker Seal Island**. The shows by the young artists of the **Zip Zap Circus** School at Founders Garden (Jan Smuts Street, tel. 021/421 8623; www.zip-zap.co.za) are definitely worth seeing. Children from age ten can learn drumming every Thursday at 6.30pm at the **Drum**

*Cool for kids*

**Café**. Be sure to get the latest information on tides and currents for the **beaches**. **Tidal pools** are usually a safer bet. There are water slides and **surfing courses** at the beach at Muizenberg. Sunscene (www.suns-cene.co.za ), Downhill Adventures (▶ p.127) and Gary's School in Muizenberg organize **mountain bike tours** and **sand boarding** in the dunes around Cape Town. If you have a Cape Town Pass one sand boarding session is free at Scarborough with Gary's School. At **Century City** kids can explore crocodile swamps and Ratanga Junction Adventureland, as well as try go-carting, ride double-decker carousels or the Cobra rollercoaster. A unique experience is **whale watching** in Hermanus, where the gentle giants swim very close to the mainland coast. At the end of Route 62, a visit to an **ostrich farm** is a must, but neighbouring **Cheetahland** with its cheetahs and white tigers, and the giant **Cango Caves** are also unforgettable. Wonderful sandy beaches and magical lagoons await along the **Garden Route**. The »Big Five« **can be seen without risk of malaria** at the new private wildlife reserves on former farms such as the **Aquila Game Reserve** two hours' drive from Cape Town in the southern Karoo; alternatively visit the **Botlierskop Game Reserve** near Mossel Bay. Last but not least: the whole family can swing through the rainforest like Tarzan at the Treetop Canopy Tour in the **Tsitsikamma National Park**. Great fun!

## Cinema

The standard Hollywood films all play in Cape Town. Tuesdays is cinema day with reduced entrance tickets. The cinema programme can be found at **www.moviesite.co.za**, and tickets can be purchased via **Computicket** (▶p.128). Interesting contributions with an African context can be seen at the SA World Film Festival in Nov/Dec, during the documentary film festival Encounters in July, and at the Three Continents Film Festival in September.

## ▶ CINEMAS AT THE CAPE

▶ **Labia on Orange**
68 Orange Street, Gardens
Tel. 021 /424 5927
www.labia.co.za
Best cinema with four screens.
Thu and Fri from 4pm, meals at
the cinema. The subsidized series
entitled The African Screen promotes South African films.

▶ **Cavendish Nouveau**
Lower Level, Cavendish Square
Dreyer Street, Claremont
Tel. 021 / 683 4063
Film classics on 8 screens.

▶ **Azure Cine 12**
Twelve Apostles Hotel
Victoria Road, Camps Bay
Tel. 021 / 437 9000
www.12apostleshotel.com
The small cinema at this luxury
hotel has just 16 seats, where non-
residents can also see new films
daily at 10am, 3pm, 6pm, 8pm
and 10pm. »Dinner & Movie« is a
special cinema menu offered by
the Azure restaurant.

▶ **Cinema Starz!**
Grand West Casino
1 Vanguard Drive
Goodwood
Tel. 021 / 534 0250
Cinema for the whole family on
six screens daily from 10am.

# Electricity

The power supply in South Africa is 220/230V and sockets are for
rounded three-pronged plugs. European (though not UK) plugs fit,
but it is better to bring an adapter. Sockets for electrical shavers and
hair driers are usually adapted for the continental European plug.

# Emergency Services

## IN CAPE TOWN

▶ **Emergency phone number**
Tel. 107; tel. 112 (from mobiles)

▶ **Police**
Tel. 10111; tel. 021 / 421 5115
(tourist assistance)

▶ **Ambulance**
Tel. 10177

▶ **Fire brigade**
Tel. 021 / 590 1900

▶ **Mountain rescue**
Tel. 021 / 480 7700
(Table Mountain and Table
Mountain National Park)
Tel. 021 / 948 9900
(Western Cape)

▶ **Groote Schuur Hospital**
Main Road, Observatory
Tel. 021 / 404 9111

▶ **Poison centre**
Tel. 0800 / 333 444

▶ **Sea rescue**
Tel. 021 / 449 3500

▶ **Air ambulance**
Tel. 021 / 937 1211

▶ **Automobile Club
South Africa AA**
Tel. 021 / 419 6914

Tel. 0800 / 010101
(breakdown assistance)

Tel. 0800 / 033 007
(accident assistance)
www.aasa.co.za

# Entertainment

*Cape Town nights are long!* Cape Town offers something for every taste: fashionable rendezvous, relaxed jazz bars and hot nightclubs with cool DJs. The scene changes fast. Venues disappear or are added almost every week and there is always a special party happening somewhere in Cape Town. Jazz, kwaito, hip hop, funk, retro or house – every nightclub has its own unmistakable style. Hot spots for the city's night life are the **V & A Waterfront**, **Long Street** and the streets around **Greenmarket Square**, as well as the beach promenades of **Clifton** and **Camps Bay**, the **Observatory** student quarter, and the »Waterkant« at **Greenpoint**.

 GOING OUT map p. 80–81

### WHEN AND WHERE?

▶ **Parties, DJs, club nights and festivals**
www.tourismcapetown.co.za
www.capetownmagazine.com
www.tonight.co.za
www.thunda.com
www.capeetc.com/calendar
The *Cape Argus* publishes a nightclub column every Tuesday and an overview of the most important weekend events every Thursday. The *Cape Times* and the *Mail & Guardian* both have inserts on Fridays that include an events schedule for the following week.

### AFRICAN RHYTHMS

▶ ① **Drum Café**
32 Glynn Street
District Six
Tel. 021 / 462 1064, 461 1305
www.drumcafe.net
Mon, Wed, Fri 7pm–2.30am
Pretty noisy, but great fun, this is the Cape's most alternative drum club. Workshops are held on Mondays and there is a djembé drum circle from 9pm on Wednesdays, including drum rental. On Thursdays from 6.30pm to 8pm there is also drumming for children from age 10. On Fridays there is live music.

*Kwaito band at »Mama Africa«*

► ② **Mama Africa**
178 Long Street, Central
Tel. 021 / 426 1017;
Mon–Fri from 4.30pm, Sat from
6pm
First choice on Cape Town's
nightlife strip of Long Street, with
daily live music, including mar-
imba, swing, jazz and kwaito.
Delicious African cuisine from all
over the continent.

BARS AND TAVERNS

► ③ **Alba Lounge**
First floor, above the Hildebrand
restaurant, Waterfront
Tel. 021 / 425 3385
www.alblounge.co.za
Cocktail lounge daily from 5pm;
restaurant daily 8am–7pm
Linda and Aldo Girolo have

turned the old offices of
Hildebrand & Sons into the top
Italian restaurant at the port. For
evening cocktails try AlbaTiser,
Chequita or the Buffalo Soldier.
Delicious canapés and finger food
are also served. During the Cape
winter, the »Movies at Alba« enjoy
cult status.

► ④ **Buena Vista Social Café**
1st Floor, Exhibition Building
81 Main Road, Green Point
Tel. 021 / 433 0611
www.buenavista.co.za
Mon–Sun noon–2am
Cuba at the Cape! Hand-made
cigars, excellent rum cocktails and
the best tapas in the city. Saturday
is salsa night.

# Cape Town *Restaurants, bars and taverns*

**Where to eat**
1. Aubergine
2. Azure
3. Baia
4. Beluga
5. Five Flies
6. onewaterfront
7. Savoy Cabbage
8. Tank
9. Africa Café
10. Anatoli
11. Bukhara
12. Khaya Nyama
13. Madame Zingara
    Theatre of Dreams
14. Manna Epicure
15. Manolo
16. Pigalle
17. Biesmiellah
18. Cape Town Fish Market
19. Marco's African Place
20. Posticino
21. Royale Eatery
22. Café Gainsbourg
23. Infocafé
24. Melissa's
25. Mount Nelson Hotel,
    Teatime
26. Obz Café
27. Café Mozart

**Where to go out**
1. Drum Café
2. Mama Africa
3. Alba Lounge
4. Buena Vista Social Café
5. Café Caprice
6. Green Dolphin
7. Ignite Bar
8. Kennedy's Cigar Lounge
9. La Med
10. Marvel
11. M-Bar Lounge
12. Planet Champagne Bar
13. Relish Rest. & Bar
14. Grand West Casino &
    Entertainment World
15. Club Deluxe
16. Hemisphere
17. Jo'burg
18. Opium Club
19. Orchard Bank
20. Rhodes House

Cape Technicon

Mouille Point

MOUILLE POINT

Bay Rd.

Granger Bay Blvd.

Granger Bay

Metropolitan Golf Course

Fort Wynyard

Stephan Way

Green Point Common

Fritz Sonnenberg Rd.

★ Green Point Stadium (im Bau)

Three Anchor Bay Sports Ground

Vlei Rd.

Athletics Track

Cape Medical Museum

Breakwater Blvd.

East Pier

Ferry to Robben Island

Elbow

③ Victoria Wharf

Victoria & Alfred Waterfront

East Pier Rd.

⑱ Market Square

★ SA Maritime Museum

Alfred Mall

Port Captain's Bldg.

③ Clock Tower ⓘ

South Arm Rd.

B

A

De Goede Verwachting

St. Margaret + Mary

Cavalade Rd.

Western Boulevard

Main Road

④

Clyde Rd.

Pine Rd.

York Rd.

Thornhill

High

Level

Ocean View Drive

Springbok Rd.

Ocean View Dr.

Merriman Rd.

Portswood Rd.

Dock Rd.

ⓘ Alfred Basin

⑥

⑥ ★★ Two Oceans Aquarium

West Quay Rd.

Duncan Dock

C

D

E

Dock Rd.

Duncan Rd.

Roggebaai Canal

F

G

★★ Theater on Broadway

Ebenezer Rd.

Prestwich St.

Bennett St.

Port Rd.

Alfred St.

Boundary Rd.

⑯

Old Malay Cemetery

Strand Street

Somerset Rd.

Napier

Alfred St.

⑩

★★ Sacred Heart

⑱

Chiappini St.

Cape Town International Convention Centre

Coen Steytler Ave.

H

J

BO KAAP

Lion's Rump

Longmarket

Yusuf Dr.

Voetboog Rd.

Pentz Rd.

Millart Rd.

⑰ Bo-Kaap Museum

SCHOTSCHE KLOOF

Hudson

Rose St.

Loop St.

Buitengracht

Church St.

Bree

⑦

⑨

St. Stephen

★★ St. Andrew's

⑧

⑲ ★★ Lutheran Church

Gold of Africa Museum

Sending Museum

ⓘ Koopmans de Wet House

⑪

⑯

CENTRAL

Long St.

Hans Strijdom Ave.

Heerengracht

Adderley

★ Riebeeck Statue

Artscape Theatre Centre

Civic Centre

Old Marine Dr.

Hertzog Blvd.

Jan Smuts St.

Table Bay Blvd.

⑳

⑳

Deroni

⑬

SA Museum

Company's Gardens

De Tuynhuys

District Six Museum

Palm Tree Mosque

② ⑤

★ St. George's Cathedral

⑯ ★ Groote Kerk

★ Slave Lodge

National Library

Parliament

⑮

Greenmarket Sq.

⑳ ★ Michaelis Art Collection

Railway Station

Grand Parade

City Hall

★★ Castle of Good Hope

Sir Lowry Road

⑳

Queen Victoria St.

Little Theatre

Bertram House

SA National Gallery

SA Jewish Museum & ★★ Holocaust Centre

★ Rust-en-Vreugd

Western Cape Archives

ZONNEBLOEM (DISTRICT SIX)

Kirstenbosch Nat. Botanical Garden

De Waal Drive

⑫

Welgemoed

De Waal Park

Mill Street

Myrtle Rd.

Juitland Ave.

▶ ⑤ **Café Caprice**
37 Victoria Road
Camps Bay
Tel. 021 / 438 8315
Kitchen open daily 9am–10pm;
bar daily 9am–2.30am
Cool place for enjoying sunsets
right at the beach of Camps Bay.
During the summer season open
daily, otherwise DJ music at
weekends. The most popular
cocktail is the Cranberry Long
Island. The restaurant serves
breakfast complete with eggs
Benedict, as well as tapas, salads,
burgers and grilled dishes.

▶ ⑥ **Green Dolphin**
Victoria & Alfred Arcade Pier
head, V & A Waterfront
Tel. 021/421 7471;
www.greendolphin.co.za
Traditional African jazz with out-
standing musicians, such as Sylvia
Mdunyelwa, Dave Ledbetter and
Gavin Minter, as well as good
evening meals.

▶ ⑦ **Ignite Bar**
2nd floor, The Promenade
Victoria Road, Camps Bay
Tel. 021 / 438 7717
www.ignitebar.co.za
Wed–Sat 6pm–2.30am
Gigs last into the mornings too.
One of the Cape's hottest night-
clubs. Hip hop with DJ Leighton
Moody, and the »endless summer
night party« happens every
Thursday. Beach bar with gor-
geous views.

▶ ⑧ **Kennedy's Cigar Lounge**
251 Long Street, Central
Tel. 021 / 424-1212
www.kennedys.co.za
Mon–Sat noon–3am
Heavy leather chairs, excellent
whiskies, relaxing piano music and
first-class jazz. The restaurant

*First-class jazz is played at the Green Dolphin and Kennedy's*

serves Californian cuisine with an African twist. Smokers can choose between hand-rolled Davidoffs, Montecristos and Cohibas.

► ⑨ **La Med**
Glen Country Club
Victoria Road, Clifton
Tel. 021/438 5600
www.lamed.co.za
Mon–Fri from 11am, Sat–Sun from 9am
Popular destination for sundowners on balmy summer evenings, with views of Lion's Head. From 9pm onwards it's party time with DJ music. During the Cape winter, rugby fans meet here.

► ⑩ **Marvel**
236 Long Street, Central
Tel. 021 / 426 5880
Daily 8pm–4am
Cool bar with hip hop and electronic sounds. Two pool tables and a tiny dance floor that is always jumping.

► ⑪ **M-Bar Lounge**
Metropole Hotel
38 Long Street, Central
Tel. 021 / 424 72 47
www.metropolehotel.co.za
Daily 11am–2am
Designer bar in deep reds. Hot meals on the veranda. Fridays from 9pm No Pop Music; Sat live music from 9pm.

► ⑫ **Planet Champagne Bar**
Hotel Mount Nelson
76 Orange Street, Gardens
Tel. 021 / 483 1000
www.mountnelson.co.za/planet
Sat–Thu from 5pm, Fri from 3pm
This exclusive bar in an elegant colonial style is just the place for drinking champagne and exotic cocktails.

*To La Med for sundowners*

▸ ⑬ **Relish Restaurant & Bar**
770 New Church Street
Tamboerskloof
Tel. 021/422 3584
www.relish.co.za
Mon–Fri from noon, Sat from 5pm
Stunning views onto Table
Mountain. Set on three floors, this
is an ideal place for sundowners
and refined eating. Try the frozen
daiquiri.

## CASINO

▸ ⑭ **Grand West Casino**
1 Vanguard Drive, Goodwood
Tel. 21 / 505 7777
www.grandwest.co.za
The casino was built in the style of
1900 with buildings inspired by
District Six and opened on the eve
of the new millennium. Apart
from the games tables, there is also
a giant ice skating arena, a bowling
ally, cinemas and jazz at the
»Hanover Street«.

## CLUBS & NIGHTCLUBS

▸ ⑮ **Club Deluxe**
Unity House
159 / 161 Longmarket Street
Central
Tel. 021 / 422 4832
Wed–Sat 10pm–4am
The place for techno and house
music.

▸ ⑯ **Hemisphere**
31st Floor, ABSA Centre
Riebeeck Street, Central
Tel. 021 / 421 0581
www.hemisphere.org.za
The venue has a »no jeans, no T-
shirts« policy and is a stylish place
for sundowners from 4.30pm onwards. From 9pm onwards, this
elegant club offers dancing complete with stunning views of Table
Mountain.

▸ ⑰ **Jo'burg**
218 Long Street, Central
Tel. 021 / 422 0142
Mon–Fri 5pm–4am, Sat 2pm–4am
Dance to hip hop, funk, soul and
house into the early hours of the
morning. On Sunday live jazz.

▸ ⑱ **Opium Club**
6 Dixon Street, Waterkant
Tel. 021 / 461 8701
www.opium.co.za
Nightclub with stylish designer
interior. Fri–Sun from 9pm live
music; Thu DJs play funk.

▸ ⑲ **Orchard Bank**
229b Long Street, Central
Tel. 021 / 423 8954
Daily 9pm–4am
Fashionable bar with leather chairs
and a dance floor alive to dub, hip
hop and mainstream pop.

*Baedeker recommendation*

▸ ⑳ **Rhodes House**
60 Queen Victoria Street, Gardens
Tel. 021 / 424 8844
www.rhodeshouse.com
Thu–Sat 10pm–4am
Cape Town's smartest club with intimate
bars on two floors and a stylish interior
where the beautiful and rich dance to
house music.

# Etiquette and Customs

It is common practice to wait at the entrance of **restaurants** before being seated, rather than to find your own table. Although VAT is included in bills, **tips** are not. A 10% tip is standard and since many waiting staff earn their wages almost entirely from tips, it is fair to give 15% for good service. On safaris, a minimum 50 rand tip per person and day is standard for the tipping box.

»Please wait to be seated!«

Capetonians like to be sporty and prefer **casual clothing**. During the summer especially, men can leave their suit jackets in the wardrobe, and casual elegance is also fine for dinner. There are a few exceptions – top hotels, restaurants and nightclubs that insist on a certain dress code, such as »no sports clothing«.

Clothing

You should always ask permission before photographing people. This is particularly important in rural areas, but also in Muslim communities and in the townships. Military installations are taboo!

Photography

South Africans have become highly sensitized to word choice ever since the sea changes of the 1990s. This is not only evident in the many re-namings of settlements and streets. Many words still carry the odour of apartheid and are disappearing from common usage, little by little. For example, the word »kaffer« in all its variations has long been replaced by more appropriate descriptions, even in the naming of flora and fauna.

Language

# Festivals, Holidays and Events

Capetonians are as mad on sport as they are on entertainment. In January they celebrate carnival African style, while during summer at the Cape, jazz, cricket and spectacular cycle races are all on the calendar. A variety of festivals celebrate the blooming of wild flowers during spring, the grape harvest, the return of the whales or the beginning of the oyster season in Knysna. For a detailed overview, see **www.capeetc.com/calendar** and **www.tourismcapetown.co.za**.

Festivals all year round

▶ EVENTS CALENDAR

**HOLIDAYS**

**1 January**: New Year's Day
**21 March**: Human Rights' Day, (Sharpeville Day 1960)

**March / April**: Good Friday; Easter Monday (Family Day)
**27 April**: Freedom Day (recalls the first democratic elections in 1994)

**1 May**: Workers' Day
**31 May**: Day of the Republic
**16 June**: Youth Day (commemorates the schoolchildren's uprising in Soweto in 1976)
**9 August**: National Women's Day
**24 September**: Heritage Day (originally Shaka Day celebrating Zulu culture)
**16 December**: Day of Reconciliation. Originally Day of the Vow recalling events prior to the Battle of Blood River between Voortrekkers and Zulus in 1838. It is also the anniversary of the founding of ANC's militant wing Umkhonto we Sizwe in 1961.
**25 December**: Christmas Day
**26 December**: Day of Goodwill. If it falls on a Sunday, the following Monday is a holiday.

## TICKET SERVICES

▶ **Computicket**
  ▶p.128

## FESTIVALS AND EVENTS IN JANUARY

▶ **Minstrel Carnival (»Coon Carnival«)**
New Year carnival held on 2 January with lots of tradition and costumed musical groups (▶ Baedeker Special, p.153, photo p.86).

▶ **Jazzathon**
Jazz festival in mid-January at the Waterfront (www.jazzathon.co.za)

▶ **J & B Met**
Not just a sporting event but a social occasion to see and be seen at Kenilworth Racecourse at the

*Colourful, different, rhythmical and exuberant: Cape Town's Minstrel Carnival*

end of January. Marvel at the most extravagant hats and the latest high fashion (www.jbmet.co.za).

FEBRUARY TO APRIL

▶ **Cape Town Festival**
Multicultural urban festival with music, theatre and dance (www.capetownfestival.co.za)

▶ **Cape Argus Cycle Tour**
140km/88mi-long cycle race around the Cape Peninsula in mid-March, when over 32,000 participants fight for their personal best (www.cycletour.co.za).

▶ **Cape Town International Jazz Festival**
Africa's biggest jazz festival lasts two days on the last weekend in March and is held at the International Convention Centre (www.capetownjazzfest.com).

**APRIL**

▶ **Two Oceans Marathon**
One of the most beautiful marathon routes in the world covers 56km/35mi around the Cape Peninsula ending at Constantia's Nek cemetery (beginning of April; www.twooceansmarathon.org.za).

▶ **Klein Karoo National Arts Festival**
Predominantly Afrikaaner art and cultural festival in Oudtshoorn (www.kknk.co.za)

**MAY**

▶ **Cape Gourmet Festival**
Ethnic food, typical Cape cuisine and choice wines in South Africa's capital for gourmets (www.gourmetsa.co.za)

▶ **V & A Waterfront Wine Festival**
Over 75 of the most important vineyards and wine-makers from the Cape exhibit here with stalls and wine-tasting (www.waterfront.co.za).

**JUNE TO NOVEMBER**

▶ **Whale watching**
Whales can be observed between False Bay near Cape Town and Plettenberg Bay on the Garden Route, who migrate to the Cape from Antarctica for calving (▶ Baedeker Special, p.214).

**JULY**

▶ **Oyster Festival**
The Knysna Oyster Festival lasts ten days (www.oyster festival.co.za).

▶ **Red Bull BWA (Big Wave Africa)**
July and August is the time to wait for that perfect wave at the mega surf festival. Venues at Dungeons, The Sentinel and Hout Bay (www.redbullbwa.com).

**AUGUST/SEPTEMBER**

▶ **Wildflower festivals**
Within a few days, millions of wild flowers bloom in a magnificent display of colour north of Cape Town – spectacular natural wonder that only lasts a few weeks and is celebrated in many places.

▶ **Whale Festival**
The return of the southern right whales is celebrated in Hermanus during the last week in September, complete with street markets, theatre and music (www.whalefestival.co.za).

▶ **Nederburg Wine Auction**
Wine experts from all over the world come to the auction at Paarl to buy top wines from the Cape (www.neder burg.co.za).

**NOVEMBER**

▶ **Sithengi**
South African film and television festival combined into the annual Cape Town World Cinema Festival (www.sithengi.co.za).

**NOVEMBER TO APRIL**

▶ **Summer Sunset Concerts at Kirstenbosch**
▶ Baedeker Special, p.223

**DECEMBER**

▶ **Mother City Queen Project**
Major gay parties from mid December until New Year with galas and masked balls (www.mcqp.co.za).

▶ **Christmas**
During the advent weeks before Christmas, Santa comes to the air-conditioned shopping malls and St George's pedestrian mall to delight children of all skin colours, complete with red coat, bobble hat and white beard. During the last few days before Christmas there are also tempting stalls on Adderley Street Night Market.

# Food and Drink

*Cosmopolitan cuisine at the Cape*

Cape Town is **South Africa's culinary capital** and has a varied restaurant scene – from low-cost takeaways to refined 3-star restaurants. African influences mix with the aromas of Oriental spices and European recipes, and **creative chefs** serve fascinating dishes accompanied by the region's **fine wines**. Gourmets get their money's worth at the Cape, for even the top-class restaurants with famous chefs and outstanding service are good value. A huge choice of fresh seafood awaits fish lovers, but visitors should also try game dishes, such as grilled kudu, crocodile or ostrich, not to mention a Cape Malay curry. South African **breakfasts** are as varied as British ones, with fresh juices, eggs, ham, bacon and grilled tomatoes all on the menu. Just a **light lunch** is usually eaten between 11am and 3pm. The main meal is **dinner**, which is eaten from 6pm onwards and can include several courses. In good restaurants advance reservations are needed, even during the week. Where eating venues do not have an alcohol licence, patrons can bring their own drinks and pay a small fee for corkage. Endorsed by Desmond Tutu, the aid organization Street Smart South Africa was founded in 2005 and **helps Cape Town's street children**. Member restaurants ask for an additional 5

**Price categories**

- Expensive: over 300 rand
- Moderate: 150 to 300 rand
- Inexpensive: under 150 rand
Prices are for a meal with starter, main dish and dessert without drinks.

*Street Smart South Africa ▶*

rand or more on the bill, 100% of which is spent on education and family reunification programmes. Look out for the logo: a 5 rand coin with a knife and fork (www.streetsmartsa.org.za).

## Cape Town Specialties

South Africans love meat. A typically macho meal is braai (BBQ): communal **outdoor grilling** of meat goes back to the Boers. People get comfortable around an open fire with a beer in hand while game, beef, lamb or pork sizzles over the embers. **Karoo lamb** is especially delicious, as sheep in the semi-desert feed on aromatic herbs. Of course **boerewors** is an essential ingredient: a sausage made of beef and mutton spiced with coriander. It is also sold as a hot dog with fried onions at many street stalls. Accompaniments to a braai include **mealie pap**, a firm corn porridge, as well as salads, pickles, spicy chutneys and **chakalaka**, a hot sauce made with tomatoes, onions and paprika. Many hotels and restaurants also put on braais. If you like your steak pink, be sure to ask for »medium rare« or even »rare«, as South Africans tend to eat their meat well-cooked. Capetonians also like to grill fish such as snoek or yellowtail at the beach.

Braai

◄ How do you like your steak?

*Cape Town delicacy from the sea: grilled crayfish*

*Vines all around Stellenbosch →*

# FINE VINTAGES FROM THE CAPE

South African wines now enjoy global success. A new generation of wine-makers is producing multi-faceted top-class wines using the latest technology on the fertile soils of Stellenbosch, Paarl, Franschhoek and Constantia.

The first grapevines arrived by boat from France on the orders of the Dutch East India Company and, on 2 February 1659, Jan van Riebeeck noted that »thanks be to God, the first wine was pressed from Cape grapes today«. Governor Simon van de Stel developed a vineyard on his Groot Constantia estate from 1680, and also promoted wine-making by founding Stellenbosch, today the capital of the winelands. Huguenot refugees from Bordeaux, Burgundy and Provence planted the first vines in Franschhoek in 1688 and established wine-making on a broad front. Quality remained poor in the 18th century, with the exception of Vin de Constance, which enjoyed great popularity at European royal courts and was an outstanding muscatel wine from Klein Constantia. England was only interested in Cape sherry at that time, while South Africans enjoyed brandy. That changed with the Continental blockade in 1806. Soon South African wine was replacing French vintages in London. Even Napoleon, in exile on St Helena, enjoyed the legendary muscatel of Constantia.

## Terra Terra Vinum

Cape Town's National Library discovered its special connection with the history of wine-making in 2006: the oldest public library in South Africa owes its foundation to a wine tax established in 1818 that funded the construction of the institution until 1822. Schools and hospitals were also funded by the wine tax. Peace with France and overproduction at the Cape caused profits to collapse until 1850, though a short-term upswing was ensured by phylloxera vastatrix, a sap-sucking insect imported from America that destroyed 75% of European vineyards. But then the pest also reached the Cape, and only a resistant American strain made recovery possible. By 1904 78 million vines, the number grown before the arrival of phylloxera, were established once again. The first wine syndicate was founded in 1889, and in 1906 the first wine-growing co-operative was founded in Tulbagh, but neither Baron van Babo, »Onze Jan« Hofmeyr nor Cecil Rhodes were able to establish new markets. Only the foundation of the Kooperatiewe Wijnbouwers Vereni-

ging van Zuid-Afrika (KWV) in 1918 in Paarl put an end to catastrophic overproduction. Today, South Africa is the world's tenth-largest wine producer, with 112,000 hectares (275,000 acres) of vines. Exports have increased more than sixfold since the end of apartheid.

A new generation of vintners has learnt to market what is special about their grapes. In 2002 they joined to form the Wine Makers of South Africa (WOSA). In addition to standard wines (from simple table wines to Trockenbeerenauslese), sparkling wines traditionally fermented in the bottle, port wines and distilled wines such as brandy are produced. There are around 350 private vineyards and 69 co-operatives, and the wine industry employs more than 350,000 workers.

## DOP STOP!

Several Khoisan were already being paid in ship's wine in 1688. Payment in kind with tobacco, wine and bread was continued by the Dutch East India Company. Until 1834, workers on the vineyards worked as slaves.

Later, hundreds of thousands received no pay, instead being given a weekly allowance of cheap wine, the amount depending on the whim of individual farmers. This practice was enshrined in law by the Liquor Act in 1928 and only abolished in 1960. This act prescribed exactly the daily ration per day and per worker. Rural farming families were not permitted to move away. The result over generations was widespread alcoholism, which various charitable projects have been working to alleviate since 1990. Cape Town has been supplying mobile medical assistance for alcoholics with its DOP STOP Programme since 1997, and in 2002 the South African wine industry paid 71 million rand towards a ten-year project working with the legacy of alcohol-related illnesses.

## Wine-makers with vision

The bankrupt vineyard north of Paarl bought by the Capetonian lawyer Alan Nelson in 1987 also paid its workers in wine. Nelson abolished the practice and turned 12ha/30 acres of his land

*Matthewes Thabo, one of the first black vintners, in the cellar of the »New Beginnings« estate*

over to the 16 black workers, on condition they continued to cultivate wine. It was the first vineyard run by blacks. They christened it New Beginnings. »Grown, ripened and filled in the new South Africa« stood on the pinotage bottles of the first vintage. Today these black wine-makers produce 30,000 litres (8000 US gallons) of red wine per annum. Nelson's example took off. Young wine-makers stop by, and the government supports their projects within the context of their Black Economic Empowerment policy designed to encourage self-reliance among blacks.

## Wine-making with seals of quality

The ideal conditions at the Cape are ensured by the mild Mediterranean-type climate, fertile earth in the hilly interior and the prevailing west winds that supply regular rainfall. The new key word »terroir« emphasizes micro-climate, soil type and the art of wine-making. The growing season is characterized by eight frost-free months. The main production area is within the magical triangle marked by Stellenbosch, Franschhoek and Paarl. This is the base of the Stellenbosch Farmer's Winery, which has been responsible for qualitative improvements since 1935. Outstanding white wines grow in the hills of Tulbagh, along with light steens and riesling, as well as strong wines used for making sherry. Tulbagh and Paarl have established the appellation Boberg for their »port« and »sherry«. Worcester, Robertson, Swellendam and Klein Karoo specialize in dessert wines and distilled wines. Since 1973, there has also been a seal of quality known as »Wines of Origin«, comparable with DOCG in Italy. Every indication of origin, variety, year, location and quality is confirmed by a state seal on bottlenecks, popularly known as the »bus ticket«. Ever since 1975, Cape vintners have also been producing »blends«, similar to cuvée.

## White and red

The most common grape is the high-yield white chenin blanc, a fine variety that has been grown in the Loire valley since the 9th century and presumably arrived in the country with Jan van Riebeeck. In South Africa it is known as steen. Johann Gaue perfected the variety at his estate at Nederburg from 1936. Twenty years later, this semi-sweet chenin

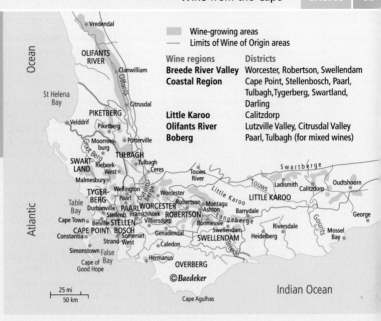

Wine-growing areas
— Limits of Wine of Origin areas

| Wine regions | Districts |
|---|---|
| **Breede River Valley** | Worcester, Robertson, Swellendam |
| **Coastal Region** | Cape Point, Stellenbosch, Paarl, Tulbagh, Tygerberg, Swartland, Darling |
| **Little Karoo** | Calitzdorp |
| **Olifants River** | Lutzville Valley, Citrusdal Valley |
| **Boberg** | Paarl, Tulbagh (for mixed wines) |

©Baedeker

blanc was one of the top-selling wines in the world. Nevertheless, its production has been in steep decline since 1990. Chardonnay and sauvignon blanc wines, on the other hand, are very popular. Among dessert wines, Hanepoot holds its own. Sultana grapes are used as table grapes and for making brandy.

The production of red wine is extremely successful. Georg Canitz already bottled his first pinot noir at the Muratie estate in 1927. The first South African zinfandel was created by Gilbeys in 1975. The genuinely South African grape pinotage, which produces a velvety fruity wine, has become famous and was created in 1925 by crossing a late Burgundy pinot noir with cinsaut (formerly known as hermitage in South Africa). Next to the late-ripening Bordeaux cabernet sauvignon grape, today's star is a very old one: namely the 3000-year-old Persian variety shiraz. It seduces all

taste buds, both on its own and in blends. Merlot is also up and coming, while cinsaut is used for young table wine.

## Vintners, wines and cellar tours

The continent's most important wine fair is the annual Cape Wine held at the Cape Town International Conference Centre (CICC) in September, and all major producers attend. Many vineyards at the Cape offer excellent restaurants, spa facilities and stylish accommodation in their Cape Dutch mansions alongside cellar tours and tasting sessions.

Wine tours can be booked via tourist offices in the Winelands or online at www.wine.co.za.

John Platter's renowned *South African Wine Guide* supplies annual reviews of South Africa's vineyards, wine-makers and almost 6000 wines (www.platter online.com).

| | |
|---|---|
| Biltong and game | The earliest settlers already ate biltong, an **air-dried meat** usually made of kudu, beef or springbok, South Africa's national animal. Biltong also tastes very good with beer and wine. In general, native **game** such as ostrich, antelope and even crocodile is excellent. |
| Bredie | In inclement weather, South Africans like to meet for a bredie, a heavy **lamb casserole**. This **national dish** is stewed in a cast-iron pot with a variety of vegetables, such as tomatoes, water lilies or cabbage and is also known as a **potjiekos** (meaning hot pot). The **water lily bredie** is made by slowly simmering mutton or lamb with the buds of Cape water lilies. |
| Cape Malay cuisine | The Cape Malay specialties are not to be missed! Popular dishes include fried **samosas** filled with vegetables or minced beef or chicken. **Sosaties** are meat kebabs made from marinated lamb or pork. **Bobotie** is a curry made from minced lamb. |
| Seafood | Of course local menus reflect the fact that Cape Town is by the sea. Cape delicacies include **crayfish** and **rock lobster**, grilled **kingklip** – a type of cod with firm meat – and **Cape salmon**, ideally served with lemon butter, garlic sauce and foil potatoes. The daily catch, referred to as **line fish**, frequently includes **Atlantic cod**, **yellowtail** (bream), **butterfish**, **snoek** (barracuda, ocean pike) and **perlemoen** (abalone), a hand-sized sea snail from the Atlantic. The best **oysters** come from Saldanha Bay on the West Coast and Knysna on the Garden Route. |

## ! *Baedeker* TIP

### Taste of Cape Town

The »Taste of Cape Town« gourmet festival, established in 2008, is a veritable attack on the taste buds held on the grounds of Camps Bay High School at the beginning of April. Visitors can twice daily watch and learn with star chefs from the best restaurants in Cape Town. Tasting sessions are accompanied by live music (www.tasteof capetown.com).

| | |
|---|---|
| Desserts and sweets | **Aromatic South African fruit** enriches the menu, and not just for dessert. Table grapes, apples, pears, citrus fruit, mangos and gooseberries grow at the Cape. To round things off, South Africans often order a **malva pudding**, a sweet cake made from milk, sugar, cream and apricot jam with custard. **Melktert** is a type of cheesecake with a puff pastry base that is served with strawberries or other fruit. Locals adore the extremely sweet, greasy and sticky **koeksisters**, small pastries soaked in syrup. |

## What to Drink

| | |
|---|---|
| Wine and beer | Following colonial British traditions, people like to enjoy a **sundowner**, which is usually gin and tonic or whisky. The vintners at the Cape are famous for their **world-class wines** (▶ Baedeker Special, |

p.90). Wine can be purchased at vineyards or in the supermarket, but beer and spirits can only be bought at a **liquor store**. An increasing number of local breweries are producing tasty alternatives to the South African market leaders in beer, dominated by Castle and Lions. Windhoek lager from Namibia is popular. There is good Bavarian beer with roast pork shank, sausages and an annual Oktoberfest at the **Paulaner Brauhaus** on the Waterfront in Cape Town. The Cape also produces an excellent **brandy**. **Mampoer** is a cherry liquor, **Witblits** a high-proof marc. **Amarula**, on the other hand, is a mild creamy-sweet liquor with just 17% alcohol made from the fruit of the marula tree. **Tap water** in Cape Town is completely safe to drink and the water quality among the best in the world. **Mineral water**, freshly squeezed **fruit juices** and the usual international **soft drinks** are available everywhere. An excellent thirst quencher without tannins and rich in vitamin C is the local **rooibos tea**.

Non-alcoholic drinks

 RECOMMENDED RESTAURANTS Map p.80–81

### RESTAURANTS ONLINE

► **www.eating-out.co.za**
**www.restaurants.co.za**
Cape Town restaurants, menus and prices

### EXPENSIVE

► ① **Aubergine**
39 Barnet Street, Gardens
Tel. 021 / 465 4909 (closed Sun)
www.aubergine.co.za
First-class restaurant in a 19th-century house that belonged to Judge John Wylde, among Cape Town's top ten. Harald Bresselschmidt and his team spoil patrons with clever French-Cape Malay cuisine and world-class wines. The soufflé makes for a divine finale.

► ② **Azure**
The Twelve Apostles Hotel, Victoria Road, Camps Bay
Tel. 021 / 437 9000
www.12apostleshotel.com/dining
Pure romance: candlelight dinners are served on the terrace with views of the Atlantic and Lion's

Head. Exquisite South African dishes are created under the leadership of Roberto de Carvalho, who also introduced »fynbos cooking« at the Cape. How about ostrich carpaccio, smoked snoek or springbok in morogo leaves? Meanwhile, the Leopard Room Bar offers a choice of 72 different vodkas and 46 port wines.

► ③ **Baia**
Shop 6262, upper level, Victoria Wharf, Portswood Road
V & A Waterfront
Tel. 021 / 421 09 35
On a sunny day there is no better place for lunch than the large terrace at Baia with views of the Waterfront. Voted best newcomer of 2006, the grilled kingklip is recommended.

► ④ **Beluga**
The Foundry, Preswick Street
Green Point
Tel. 021 / 418 2948
www.beluga.co.za
The beautiful people of Cape

Town have been meeting here ever since Oscar Kotzé opened his world-class restaurant in 2006, complete with café, sushi and cocktail bars. Patrons have included Bill Clinton, Kevin Spacey and Tiger Woods. Try Victor Claude's Pacific menu followed by the chocolate truffle tart!

▶ ⑤ **Five Flies**
14–16 Keerom Street, Central
Tel. 021 / 424 4442
www.fiveflies.co.za
Historic atmosphere in a Cape Dutch building combined with exciting combinations of the best ingredients from all over the world. The west coast grilled crayfish followed by iced orange soufflé is divine.

▶ ⑥ **onewaterfront**
West Quay Road, Cape Grace Hotel, V & A Waterfront
Tel. 021 / 410 7100
www.onewaterfront.co.za
Prize-winning gourmet address with spectacular views of Table Mountain. Star chef Phil Alcock has been creating sensational fish dishes here since 2007, along with his unmatched crème brûlée. Come for lunch after a stroll around the Waterfront.

▶ ⑦ **Savoy Cabbage**
101 Hout Street, Central
Tel. 021 / 424 2626
www.savoycabbage.co.za
Closed Sun
Only the finest ingredients from the region are turned into perfect meals in this elegant brick loft with champagne bar. Try the braised warthog.

▶ ⑧ **Tank**
72 Waterkant Street
Cape Quarter, Waterkant
Tel. 021 / 419 0007
www.the-tank.co.za
A 20,000-litre aquarium divides the bar from the trendy seafood restaurant with a large sushi selection. Try a tank cocktail to go with your food, made of Malibu, vodka, lemon grass and lychee juice.

**MODERATE**

*Baedeker recommendation*

▶ ⑨ **Africa Café**
108 Shortmarket Street, Central
Tel. 021 / 422 0221
www.africacafe.co.za
Take a culinary journey through Africa, from Morocco to Malawi, in the company of Cindy, Hector and friends to the sounds of drumming and dance performances. Patrons can buy relevant cook books and even the colourful plates. Supervised car park; reservations essential.

▶ ⑩ **Anatoli**
24 Napier Street, Waterkant
Green Point
Tel. 021 / 419 2501
www.anatoli.co.za (closed Sun).

*Africa Café: a culinary journey through the continent*

Excellent Turkish cuisine with 20 starters ranging from aubergines to chick pea puree and hot oven-baked bread.

▶ ⑪ **Bukhara**
33 Church Street, Central
Tel. 021 / 424 0000;
www.bukhara.com
A glass wall allows patrons to watch as northern Indian tandoori lamb and aromatic curries are made. Sabi Sabharwal also runs branches of this restaurant in the Grand West Casino and Stellenbosch.

▶ ⑫ **Khaya Nyama**
267 Long Street, Central
Tel. 021 / 424 2917
This »house of meat« guarantees a safari ambience to go with your crocodile, kudu, warthog or springbok steak, served with butternut. Guitar and djembé drum sounds accompany meals.

▶ ⑬ **Madame Zingara Theatre of Dreams**
Sable, corner of Ratanga Road
Century City
Tel. 021 / 426 2458
www.madamezingara.com
A large fire resulted in this popular show moving near to Century City in 2006. Artists from Chile, Argentina, Canada and South Africa offer dance, acrobatics, magic tricks and comedy. Chef Grethel cooks Italian food, but also Madame's famous chocolate chilli fillet using Belgian chocolate, of course!

▶ ⑭ **Manna Epicure**
151 Kloof Street, Tamboerskloof
Tel. 021 / 426 2413
Closed Sun and Mon
Designer venue with good wine list, fresh salads, excellent tapas and the best bread around. Pretty veranda for people watching on trendy Kloof Street.

► ⑮ **Manolo**
30 Kloof Street, Central
Tel. 021 / 422 4747
www.manoloeat.co.za
Closed Mon
Whether you eat in the Reed
Room, Gold Room or orange
Light Room, the food in this
fashionable restaurant is top class.
Reserve a table in the garden for
romantic evenings.

► ⑯ **Pigalle**
57 Somerset Road, Green Point
Tel. 021 / 421 4848
Closed Sun
Stylish Art Nouveau candelabras
light this glamorous restaurant
serving freshly caught seafood and
a select wine list. There is also a
dance floor and live band.

### INEXPENSIVE

► ⑰ **Biesmiellah**
2 Upper Wale Street, Bo-Kaap
Tel. 021 / 423 0850
Closed Sun
Plain interior, but delicious Indian
and Cape Malay delicacies and a
fantastic view of Signal Hill. No
alcohol licence.

► ⑱ **Cape Town Fish Market**
Shop 159, Kings Warehouse,
Portswood Close, Waterfront
Tel. 021 / 418 5977
www.ctfm.com
Ever since Douw Krugmann
bought his first fish shop on Cape
Town's Waterfront, his concept
has spread throughout South
Africa: restaurant, fish market,
teppanyaki grill and sushi bar.
Whether light meals or something
special from the wok, business is
always booming. Other branches
at Canal Walk, at Bloubergstrand
and Camps Bay.

*Baedeker recommendation*

► ⑲ **Marco's African Place**
15 Rose Lane, Bo-Kaap
Tel. 021 / 423 5412
www.marcosafricanplace.co.za (closed
Mon). Choose from juicy T-bone steaks,
oxtail curry or grilled springbok, kudu
or ostrich. Live music and jazz events
with popular musicians such as Jimmy
Dludlu, Hugh Masekela and Sylvia
Mdunyelwa.

► ⑳ **Posticino**
323 Main Road, Sea Point
Tel. 021 / 439 4014;
www.posticino.co.za
Enrico and Gioacchino's magic
crisp stone-baked pizza at the
»Postman«, and also pasta with
delicate sauces. Another branch at
Greenmarket Square.

► ㉑ **Royale Eatery**
279, Long Street, Central
Tel. 021 / 422 4536, (closed Sun).
Friendly waitresses serve the best
hamburgers at the Cape on two
floors. Also delicious milk shakes
and fresh salads.

### CAFÉS

► ㉒ **Café Gainsbourg**
64 Kloof Street, Gardens
Tel. 021 / 422 1780. Charming
bistro for cappuccino, good
wines, pasta and panini. If it is too
full, try the nearby Café Paradiso
at 110 Kloof Street
Tel. 021 / 423 8653.

► ㉓ **Infocafé**
Pinnacle Building, corner of Burg
& Castle Street
Tel. 021 / 426 4424
www.infocafe.co.za
Internet café serving small snacks,

latte macchiato and giant muffins. Anneke, Marie and Conwell are also happy to help at the computer.

► ㉔ **Melissa's**
94 Kloof Street, Gardens
Tel. 021 / 424 5540
www.melissas.co.za
Delicious pastries and Mediterranean lunch buffet and a relaxing place to read the newspaper. Foodies will find wonderful gifts without chemical additives. Branches in Green Point, Constantia and Stellenbosch.

► ㉕ **Mount Nelson Hotel**
► Baedeker Tip, p.202.

► ㉖ **Obz Café**
115 Lower Main Road,
Observatory
Tel. 021 / 448 5555
www.obzcafe.co.za
In-café in the Observatory student district with good breakfast, pasta, tapas and delicious salads. Host Tyrone is extremely well-informed on all events happening locally. Wed to Sat theatre performances, Tue and Sun live music.

*Baedeker recommendation*

► ㉗ **Café Mozart**
37 Church Street, Central
Tel. 021 / 424 3774
Closed Sun
This charming café next to the AVA Gallery exudes 19th-century charm and is a popular meeting place for Cape Town's artists. Classical music and sunny tables in front of the door.

# Information

 TOURIST INFORMATION

**SOUTH AFRICAN TOURISM**

► **Australia**
Suite 301, Level 3
117 York Street
Sydney NSW 2000
Tel. 02-92 61 50 00
Fax 02-92 61 20 00
Email: info.au@southafrica.net

► **UK**
6 Alt Grove, London SW19 4DZ
Tel 08 70-155 00 44
Fax 020-89 44 67 05
E-mail: info.uk@southafrica.net

► **USA**
500 5th Avenue
20th Floor, Suite 2040

New York, NY 10110
Tel. 1-800-593 13 18
Fax 212-764 19 80
E-mail:
info.us@southafrica.net

▶ **Cape Town Tourism**
The Pinnacle Building
Corner of Burg & Castle Street
P.O. Box 1403, Cape Town 8001
Tel. 021 / 487 6800
Fax 021 / 487 6859
www.tourismcapetown.co.za.
Reservations made for hotels, hire cars and tours; internet café and souvenir shop provided, along with information on the regions of the Western Cape Province. Additional information offices are located in the Clock Tower Centre at the Waterfront, at the base station of the Table Mountain cable car, and at Kirstenbosch Botanical Gardens.

▶ **Save with the Cape Town Pass**
The Cape Town Pass gives free entrance to more than 50 attractions in Cape Town and Cape Province, as well as providing 20 special offer reductions. It is valid for one, two, three or six days from the first time it is used. Minors between 4 and 17 years old can use the Children Cape Town Pass. Both are available in advance at travel agents and from the offices of Cape Town Tourism, as well as online at www.thecape-townpass.co.za.

**REPUBLIC OF
SOUTH AFRICA: EMBASSIES**

▶ **In Australia**
Rhodes Place, Yarralumla
Canberra, ACT 2600
Tel. 02-5273 2424
www.sahc.org.au

▶ **In Canada**
15 Sussex Drive, Ottawa
Ontario, K1M 1M8
Tel. 613-744 0330
www.southafrica-canada.com

▶ **In Ireland**
2nd Floor, Alexandra House
Earlsfort Centre, Earlsfort Terrace
Dublin 2
Tel. 01-661 5553
E-mail: info@saedublin.com

▶ **New Zealand**
Refer to embassy in Australia

▶ **In UK**
South Africa House
Trafalgar Square
London WC2N 5DP
Tel. 020-7451 7299
www. southafricahouse.com

▶ **In USA**
3051 Massachusetts Ave NW
Washington DC 20008
Tel. 202-232 4400
www.saembassy.org
Consulates in New York, Chicago and Los Angeles

**REPRESENTATION IN
SOUTH AFRICA**

▶ **Australia**
Embassy in Pretoria
292 Orient Street, Arcadia
Tel. 012-342 3740

▶ **Canada**
Consulate in Cape Town
19th Floor, Reserve Bank Building
60 St George's Mall, City Bowl
Tel. 021-423 5240

▶ **Ireland**
Consulate in Cape Town
54 Keerom Street, City Bowl
Tel. 021-423 0431

▶ **New Zealand**
Embassy in Pretoria
Block C, Hatfield Gardens
Arcadia
Tel. 012-342 8656

▶ **UK**
Consulate in Cape Town
Southern Life Centre
8 Riebeeck Street, City Bowl
Tel. 021-425 3670

▶ **USA**
Consulate in Cape Town
4th Floor, Broadway Industries
Centre, Foreshore
Tel. 021 421 4280

## INTERNET ADDRESSES

▶ **www.gov.za**
Website of the South African
government, a lot of information.

▶ **www.anc.org.za**
Website of the ruling party, press
statements, facts and figures, links

▶ **www.aarvark.co.za**
Good search engine.

▶ **www.ananzi.co.za**
Search engine for everything from
culture and entertainment to en-
vironment, industry, politics and
government, science, society and
people to tourism.

▶ **www.iafrica.com**
A large portal with good travel
information.

▶ **www.saeverything.co.za**
Everything to do with South
Africa, including events.

▶ **www.safrica.info**
South Africa's »official portal«.

▶ **www.southafrica.co.za**
South Africa online, good portal.

▶ **www.capetown-online.com**
Politics, business, travel, lifestyle,
property and more

▶ **www.aatravel.co.za**
Travel information and online
reservations from the South African Automobile Association

# Language

# LANGUAGE GUIDE FOR AFRIKAANS

## Pronunciation

Afrikaans is normally pronounced as it is written, but there are
sounds that don't exist in English which makes it a difficult language
for anglophones to pronounce correctly. Vowel pairs are not pronounced as a single diphthong, but as two separate sounds. A, e, i,
and o are often nasalized if they come before ng, n or m, but especially if they are followed by the letters f, g, h, l, r, s, v, w, or z. For
example: kans (kās), »chance«.

| | |
|---|---|
| aa, ae | long a, as in »awesome« |
| au, ou | o + u, as in »goat« |
| ee | long e, as in »erie« |
| ei | e + i, as in »play« |
| eu | as in »few« |
| ie | long i, as in »see« |
| oe | as in »loot« |
| oo | long o, as in »pool« |
| u | similar to »brew« |
| ui | as in »play« |
| y | as in »time« |
| g, ch | as in the Scottish »loch« |
| gh | as in »golf« |
| ng | ng as in »singing« |
| r | as in »very« |
| s | s as in »sun« |
| sj | sh as in »shin« |
| tj | ch, as in »Czech« |

## Useful phrases

| | |
|---|---|
| Good morning | Goeie more |
| Good day | Goeie middag / Goeie dag |
| Good evening | Goeie naand, naand |
| Good night | Goeie nag |
| Good-bye | Tot siens |
| Yes/no/maybe | ja / nee / ja-nee |
| Please | asseblief |
| Thank you | dankie |
| Excuse me | Ekskuus (tog) |
| Sorry | Verskoon my |
| That's fine | Plesier |
| Sir, Madam | Meneer, Mevrou |
| When does (do) … open? | Wanneer is … oop? |
| When does (do) … close? | Wanneer word … gesluit? |
| What time is it? | Hoe laat is dit? |
| How do I get to …? | Hoe kom ek na (by die) …? |
| How long will it take? | Hoe lank sal dit neem? |
| How far is it to …? | Hoe ver is dit na (tot by die) …? |
| Where can I get …? | Waar kan ek … kry? |
| Where is …? | Waar is …? |
| Please give me … | Gee my asseblief … |
| Do you have …? | Is daar …? |
| I need … | Ek het … nodig. |
| I want to have … | Ek wil graag … |
| Do you have …? | Het u …? |

| | |
|---|---|
| How much does it cost? | Wat kos dit? |
| I like that | Ek hou daarvan |
| I don't like that | Ek hou nie daarvan nie |
| That's too expensive | Dit is te duur |
| Don't you have anything cheaper (better)? | Het u nie iets goedkopers (beters) nie? |
| Can you change money? | Kan u geld wissel? |
| How do you say that in English (Afrikaans)? | Wat noem 'n mens dit in Engels (Afrikaans)? |
| Do you speak English? | Praat u Engels? |
| I don't speak … | Ek praat geen … nie. |
| I don't understand you. | Ek verstaan u nie. |
| Please speak a little slower. | Sal u asseblief 'n bietjie stadiger praat. |
| Please write that down. | Skryf dit asseblief neer. |
| Monday | Maandag |

»Amkela!«, »Welkom!«, »Welcome!«

| | |
|---|---|
| Tuesday | Dinsdag |
| Wednesday | Woensdag |
| Thursday | Donderdag |
| Friday | Vrydag |
| Saturday | Saterdag |
| Sunday | Sondag |

## Numbers

| | | | |
|---|---|---|---|
| 0 | nul | 19 | negentien |
| 1 | een | 20 | twintig |
| 2 | twee | 21 | een en twintig |
| 3 | drie | 22 | twee en twintig |
| 4 | vier | 30 | dertig |
| 5 | vyf | 40 | veertig |
| 6 | ses | 50 | vyftig |
| 7 | sewe | 60 | sestig |
| 8 | ag, agt | 70 | sewentig |
| 9 | nege | 80 | tag(gen)tig |
| 10 | tien | 90 | negentig |
| 11 | elf | 100 | (een) honderd |
| 12 | twaalf | 101 | honderd en een |
| 13 | dertien | 200 | twee honderd |
| 14 | veertien | 330 | drie honderd en derti; |
| 15 | vyftien | 1000 | duisend |
| 16 | sestien | 100,000 | honderd duisend |
| 17 | sewentien | 1 Million | een miljoen |
| 18 | agtien, agttien | 1 Billion | een miljard |

# Literature

Novels and stories
**Breyten Breytenbach**: *Dog Heart: A Memoir* (Harcourt, 1999). Dreams, comedy and horror accompany the renowned South African author's return to South Africa from exile. (▶ p.94). Insights into a divided nation that gets under your skin.

**André (Philippus) Brink**: *On the Contrary* (Vintage Paperback, 1994). The »rebel, soldier, traveller, master builder, lover and liar« Estienne Barbier looks back on life while awaiting his execution. Brink is literature professor at the University of Cape Town, writes in Afrikaans and has been nominated for the Nobel Prize in Literature several times. He came to fame outside South Africa after his novel *A Dry*

*White Season* (1988) was filmed with Donald Sutherland and Marlon Brando.

**J.M. Coetzee**: *Disgrace* (Vintage, 2008). A disturbing story that won the Booker Prize. A Cape Town professor of English begins an affair with a student, which sets in train a chain of painful events.

**❗ *Baedeker* TIP**

**»My Traitor's Heart« ...**

(Vintage paperback, 1990) is brilliant and compulsive reading. The author Rian Malan is an Afrikaner and descendant of one of the most reviled architects of apartheid. He went into exile in 1977 and returned eight years later to confront his heritage in a soul-searching classic.

**Athol Fugard**: *Tsotsi* (Penguin paperback, 1983). A township gang melodrama that South Africa's most famous playwright wrote as long ago as 1960. It remains a timeless parable of the good and evil in mankind. The 2006 film of this story won the »best foreign language film« Oscar.

**Nadine Gordimer**: *Loot and Other Stories* (Penguin, 2004). Surprising twists and ten human destinies in modern South Africa by the country's first author to win the Nobel Prize for Literature.

**Etienne van Heerden**: *The Long Silence of Mario Salviati* (Regan Books paperback, 2004). Art curator Ingi Friedlander leaves Cape Town in search of a famous sculpture and crosses the line between reality and magic.

**Nelson Mandela**: *Favourite African Folktales* (Norton & Co. paperback, 2004). A treasure trove of stories imaginatively illustrated. Chosen by the grand old man of South Africa himself, these stories give an authentic sense of Africa.. Reluctant readers can choose the audio CDs.

**James A. Michener**: *The Covenant* (Mandarin Paperback, 1980) A fictionalized, but immaculately researched, novel on the founding of South Africa. A long but fascinating panoramic view of South Africa's history.

**Alan Paton**: *Cry, the Beloved Country* (Scribner, 2003). A classic of South African literature, this novel tells the story of Zulu pastor Stephen Kumalo and his son Absalom during the grim era of the 1940s. A universal tale of human dignity in the face of adversity.

**Richard Rive**: *Buckingham Palace*, District Six. 2006.
A collection of stories about the inhabitants of District Six.

**Vivian Bickford-Smith, Elizabeth van Heyningen, and Nigel Worden**: *Cape Town in the 20th Century: An Illustrated Social History* (Human

Rights Watch, 2000). *Making of a City*, by the same authors, covers the earlier period of Cape Town's history.

Non-fiction **Breyten Breytenbach**: *The Memory of Birds in Times of Revolution* (Faber & Faber paperback, 1996). Key essays and two letters addressed to Nelson Mandela on the question of how South Africa's new freedoms can be preserved and how a genuine unity can be achieved. Breytenbach was jailed for being an anti-apartheid activist from 1975 to 1982. His marriage to a Vietnamese woman had earlier been prohibited under the apartheid race laws. Today, this son of an old Boer family from Bonnievale commutes as a professor between the universities of Cape Town, New York and Senegal.

**Craig Fraser**: *Shack Chic: Art and Innovation in South African Shacklands* (Quivertree, 2003). The creative and colourful architecture of the townships.

**Nelson Mandela**: *The Long Road to Freedom* ►Baedeker Tip, p.53

**David Mason**: *A Traveller's History of South Africa* (Interlink, 2003). A practically organized and easy-to-read introduction.

**Myrna Robins**: *Cape Flavour* (Struik, 2003). A culinary journey through twelve regions of the Western Cape, with recipes, details of wines and restaurants, and lovely photography.

**Allister Sparks**: *Beyond the Miracle: Inside the New South Africa* (Profile Books, 2003). A review of recent years and an assessment of the future by a distinguished anti-apartheid campaigner and one of the most respected commentators on South Africa.

**Jonny Steinberg**: *The Number* (Jonathan Ball, 2004). An account of the world of Cape Town's gangs from inside.

## Films in Cape Town

Cape Town's film industry is booming and the new **Cape Town Film Studios** have recently been built in Belleville. Many companies from all over the world have taken advantage of the great scenery and light, as well as lower costs. For example, in 2009, Cape Town was used as the setting for the historical drama ***Heaven & Earth*** about the life of Miranda Barry (Natasha McElhone). England's first female doctor, she was forced to disguise herself as a man in order to practice her profession in the 19th century, although she did have an affair with Cape Town's governor Lord Charles Somerset (James Purefoy), in the end. Advertising companies also take advantage of Cape Town's unique ambience, and serpentine Chapman's Peak is much used by international car firms looking for great location shots.

# Media

Among the country's serious national newspapers are the weekly ***Mail & Guardian*** (www.mg.co.za), the *Sunday Times*, and the *Sunday Independent*. The highly regarded **Sowetan** (www.sowetan.co.za), founded as an anti-apartheid paper in 1981, today has a readership of over 1.6 million – and not just among the black population. Two major English language newspapers are published daily in Cape Town: the ***Cape Argus*** (www.capeargus.co.za) and the ***Cape Times*** (www.capetimes.co.za), which has many useful events pages. The most important Afrikaans newspaper is *Die Burger* (www.die burger.com). **SA Citylife** is a monthly cultural listings magazine, while the restaurant guide ***Eat Out*** is published every two months.

*Newspapers and magazines*

The state-run **South African Broadcasting Corporation** (SABC) broadcasts eleven radio programmes on fm and medium wave. Fascinating discussions on the private station SAFM can be heard all over the country, as can radio stations 5FM, Metro FM and Radio 2000. Some of the most popular private radio stations are Bush Radio, Cape Talk, Good Hope FM, The Voice of the Cape and the youth music station YFM. SABC also broadcasts three TV programmes, of which the most interesting is the predominantly English-language third channel. Pure entertainment TV is shown on the private channel e.tv, and over 55 international programmes can be received via DStv. Many hotels have satellite TV and internet. There are also plenty of internet cafés in Cape Town.

*Radio, television and internet*

# Money

The national currency is the **South African Rand** (ZAR). 1 rand is divided into 100 cents. The front of bank notes are printed in English, while the other side always has two of the Rainbow Nation's eleven national languages on it. Bank notes come in denominations of 10, 20, 50, 100 and 200 rand. There are coins for 5, 10, 20 and 50 cents, as well as 1, 2 and 5 rand. 5000 rand per person can be brought in or out of the country and there are no regulations regarding other currencies. Exchange rates are better in South Africa than abroad.

*Currency*

**Travellers' cheques** can be cashed at all major banks, as well as in many hotels. ATM cash machines are available 24hrs a day for cash withdrawals with a **debit or credit card** in combination with your PIN number. Only use ATM machines with video surveillance at the larger banks to protect against cash machine robbers.. The usual credit cards are accepted by most hotels, restaurants, car hire firms and many shops. Opening hours for most banks are: Wed–Fri 9am–3.30pm, Sat 8.30am–11.30am.

*Travellers' cheques, ATM cash machines and credit cards*

## EXCHANGE RATES

1 GB £ = 13.63 rand
1 rand = 0.073 GB £

1 US$ = 9.53 rand
1 rand = 0.105 US$

1 euro = 12.63 rand
1 rand = 0.079 euros

## CONTACT DETAILS FOR CREDIT CARDS

Bank debit and credit cards and SIM cards that are lost or stolen should be reported and blocked immediately. In the event of lost bank or credit cards, can contact the following numbers in UK and USA (phone numbers when dialling from South Africa):

▸ **Eurocard/MasterCard**
Tel. 001 / 636 7227 111

▸ **Visa**
Tel. 001 / 410 581 336

▸ **American Express UK**
Tel. 0044 / 1273 696 933

▸ **American Express USA**
Tel. 001 / 800 528 4800

▸ **Diners Club UK**
Tel. 0044 / 1252 513 500

▸ **Diners Club USA**
Tel. 001 / 303 799 9000

Have the bank sort code, account number and card number as well as the expiry date ready.
The following numbers of UK banks (dialling from South Africa) can be used to report and cancel lost or stolen bank and credit cards issued by those banks:

▸ **HSBC**
Tel. 0044 / 1442 422 929

▸ **Barclaycard**
Tel. 0044 / 1604 230 230

▸ **NatWest**
Tel. 0044 / 142 370 0545

▸ **Lloyds TSB**
Tel. 0044 / 1702 278 270

# Museums and Exhibitions

Discounts   The **Cape Town Pass** (▸p.100) gives free access to 18 of the most significant museums in and around Cape Town. Many museums offer discounts to children, students and pensioners. A precise overview can be found at www.tourismcapetown.co.za.

Iziko Museums   14 of the most important museums are now under the umbrella organization of the **Iziko Museums of Cape Town**. »Iziko« – »hearth« or »fireplace« in Xhosa – is meant to indicate the central function of people coming together. The official members of this association now all have the word Iziko in their name: as in Iziko Slave Lodge (www.iziko.org.za).

# ▶ CAPE TOWN MUSEUMS

## ART AND ARCHAEOLOGY

▶ **Fish Hoek Valley Museum**
59 Central Circle, Fish Hoek.
Opening times: Tue–Sat
9.30am–12.30pm. The museum
shows prehistoric finds associated
with the 12,000-year-old »Fish
Hoek Man«, and also arranges
tours of the skeleton site in Peers
Cave.

▶ **Gold of Africa Museum**
▶Strand Street

*Golden Akan
crown in the
European style
(around 1900)*

▶ **Hugo Naudé &
Jean Welz Gallery**
115 Russel Street, Worcester.
Opening times: daily 9am–4.30pm
Modern art collection.

▶ **Irma Stern Museum**
▶Rondebosch

▶ **Iziko Michaelis Collection**
▶Greenmarket Square, Old Town
House

▶ **Iziko Rust en Vreugd**
▶Rust en Vreugd

▶ **Iziko South African Museum**
▶South African Museum

▶ **Iziko South African National
Gallery**
▶South African National Gallery

▶ **Marvol Museum**
▶Stellenbosch

▶ **Montagu Museum Complex**
▶Route 62, Montagu

▶ **Old Mutual Building**
▶Grand Parade

▶ **Rupert Museum**
▶Stellenbosch

## HISTORY / CULTURE

▶ **Afrikaans Language Museum**
▶Paarl

▶ **Bartolomeu
Dias Museum**
▶Garden Route, Mossel Bay

▶ **Beck Huis Museum**
▶Worcester

▶ **Boschendal Manor House**
▶ Baedeker Tip, p.182

▶ **Castle of Good Hope**
▶ p.162

▶ **Calitzdorp Museum**
▶Route 62, Calitzdorp

▶ **Clanwilliam Museum**
▶West Coast, Cederberg
Mountains

▶ **C. P. Nel Museum**
▶Route 62, Oudtshoorn

*Cape regimental uniforms in the Military Museum at the Castle of Good Hope*

► **Iziko Koopmans-de-Wet House**
►Strand Street, Koopmans-de-Wet House

► **Iziko Slave Lodge**
►Adderley Street, Slave Lodge

► **Kleinplasie Open Air Museum**
►Worcester

► **Knysna Museum**
►Garden Route, Knysna

► **Mayibuye Centre**
►Robben Island

► **Moravian Mission Museum**
►Overberg, Genadendal

► **Old Gaol Museum**
►West Coast, Cederberg Mountains, Clanwilliam

► **Oude Kerk Volksmuseum**
►West Coast, Cederberge Mountains, Tulbagh

► **Paarl Museum**
►Paarl

► **Robben Island Museum (RIM)**
►Robben Island,
►V & A Waterfront

► **Robertson Museum**
►Worcester

► **Simon's Town Museum (RIM)**
►Simon's Town, Fish Hoek

► **South African Jewish Museum**
►p.257

► **South African Missionary Meeting House Museum**
► Bo-Kaap, Sendinggestig Museum

► **The Heritage Museum**
►Simon's Town

► **Wupperthal Museum**
►West Coast, Cederberg Mountains, Wupperthal

## NATURE AND TECHNOLOGY

► **Air Force Museum**
►South African Air Force Museum

► **Cape Agulhas Lighthouse Museum**
►Bredasdorp, Cape Agulhas

► **Cape Medical Museum**
►Green Point

► **Castle Military Museum**
►Castle of Good Hope

► **Durbanville Clay Museum**
►Durbanville

► **Heart of Cape Town Museum**
►Observatory, Woodstock

► **Iziko Planetarium**
►South African Museum

► **Iziko South African Maritime Museum**
►V & A Waterfront

► **Josephine Mill**
►Newlands

► **Joubert House**
►Route 62, Montagu

► **Old Harbour Museum**
►Hermanus

► **Outeniqua Transport Museum**
►Garden Route, George

▶ **Shipwreck Museum**
▶Bredasdorp

▶ **South African Fisheries Museum**
▶Hout Bay

▶ **South African Naval Museum**
▶Simon's Town

▶ **Strandveld Museum**
Kusweg, Franskraal, Gansbaai.
Opening times: daily 10am–3pm.
Private museum in an old fisherman's house with the largest collection of wreck finds taken from *H.M.T. Birkenhead* (▶Hermanus), which sank off Danger Point.

▶ **The Carriage Museum**
Stellenbosch, Stellenbosch Wine Route, Blaauwklippen

▶ **Vasco da Gama Nautical Museum**
Van Riebeeck Street
Oorlogsvlei, Saldanha
Tel. 022 / 714 2088
The museum at Shelley Point is dedicated to the earliest navigators and seafarers who explored this coast.

▶ **Whale Museum**
▶Hermanus

**OTHERS**

▶ **Apple Museum**
▶Overberg, Grabouw

▶ **South African Rugby Museum**
▶Kirstenbosch National Botanical Garden, Around

# National Parks · Nature Reserves

Off to see the **Big Seven** – because around here the whale and the great white shark can be added to the lion, buffalo, leopard, rhino and elephant! Protection of the Cape's species-rich flora and fauna is not only under the jurisdiction of the state organizations **South African National Parks (SAN Parks)** and **Cape Nature Conservation**, but also the responsibility of numerous private initiatives and **private game reserves** on former farmland.

## National Parks

Addo Elephant National Park
**Location**: 75km/47mi north of Port Elizabeth. Tel. 042 / 233 8600, www.sanparks.org/parks/addo. **Special features**: over 400 elephants, the »Big Five« and, from 2010 onwards, also whales and sharks
▶p.199.

Agulhas National Park
**Location**: 230km/145mi east of Cape Town. Tel. 028 / 435 6222, www.san parks.org/parks/agulhas. **Special features**: Africa's most southerly point with fynbos vegetation such as the Cape plane tree, as well as whale watching and the wreck museum in Bredasdorp.
▶p.157.

## ▶ South African National (SAN) Parks

Central Booking Office
P.O. Box 787, Pretoria 01
Tel. 012 / 428 9111
Fax 012 / 426 5500
www.sanparks.co.za
SAN administers the country's 21 large national parks. Around Cape Town that includes: Addo Elephant Park (Eastern Cape), Agul-

has National Park, Bontebok National Park, Knysna National Lake Area, Table Mountain National Park, Tsitsikamma National Park, West Coast National Park and Wilderness National Park.

## ▶ Cape Nature Conservation

Cape Nature House
Belmont Park, Cape Town
Tel. 021 / 426 0723
Bookings: tel. 021 / 659 3500
www.capenature.co.za.
Responsible for 42 nature reserves at the Cape.

*Baedeker recommendation*

## ▶ Wild Card

Nature lovers can enjoy one year of free access to all of South Africa's national parks and nature reserves with the Wild Card, while the regional Cape Cluster card is valid for the Western Cape Province. Reservations at www.sanparks.co.za and www.capenature.co.za.

*Only native to Knysna Forest: the colourful Knysna lourie*

**Location**: 210km/130mi east of Cape Town. Tel. 028 / 514 2735, www.sanparks. org/parks/bontebok. **Special feature**: South Africa's smallest national park with rare bontebok antelopes ▶p.231.    Bontebok National Park

**Location**: 500km/300mi east of Cape Town along the Garden Route. Tel. 044 / 382 2095, www.san parks.org/parks/knysna. **Special features**: seahorses in the wonderful Knysna Lagoon. Only in Knysna Forest will you find the light-green Knysna lourie from the parrot family ▶p.193.    Knysna National Lake Area

**Location**: from Signal Hill to the Cape of Good Hope. Tel. 021 / 701 8692, www.sanparks.org/parks/table_mountain/, www.tmnp.co.za. **Special features**: a paradise for hiking, unique Cape flora, penguins and whale watching ▶p.275.    Table Mountain National Park

**Tsitsikamma National Park** **Location**: 700km/450mi east of Cape Town along the Garden Route. Tel. 042 / 281 1607, www.sanparks.org/parks/tsitsikamma, www.tsitsikamma.info. **Special features**: one of the country's last remaining rainforests with three of South Africa's most beautiful hiking routes ▶p.198.

**West Coast National Park** **Location**: 120km/75mi north of Cape Town. Tel. 022 / 772 2144, www.san parksorg/parks/west_coast. **Special features**: superb wild flowers blooming in Aug–Sept; penguins and breeding sites for migrant birds. ▶p.292.

**Wilderness National Park** **Location**: 650km/400mi east of Cape Town along the ▶Garden Route. Tel. 044 / 877 1197, www.sanparks.org/parks/wilderness. **Special features**: thousands of water birds and untouched sandy beaches ▶p.191.

## Personal Safety

Central Cape Town, in particular, has become much safer ever since the installation of CCTV and the use of numerous security firms. Nevertheless, it is generally advisable to **take care!** South Africa's new democracy has not progressed to such a degree that everyone can move freely in all places.

The crime rate is much lower than in Johannesburg, but many districts and houses are still highly secured. Township tours should only be taken with professional guides. Get the latest information on the local situation from your hotel. Only carry the most essential money, papers and credit cards etc with you. Cameras should remain in discreet bags and not be carried openly. Exchange money only in supervised banking outlets or at ATMs with video surveillance. Travelling on foot after dark should be limited to safe neighbourhoods. Use a taxi for evening trips to restaurants, theatre or cinema. Valuable items should stay in the hotel safe or, during car journeys, in the boot.

## Post and Communications

Post **Post offices** are open Mon, Tue, Thu and Fri 8.30am–4.30pm; Wed 9am–4.30pm, Sat 8am–noon. The main post office is on Parliament Street. **Letter boxes** are red. **Postage** for airmail postcards to Europe is around 4 rand, for a letter almost 5 rand. The first regular post ship travelled between Cape Town and England in 1857 and took around 42 days for the trip, depending on the weather. Today post takes less than one week to arrive.

## ▶ NATIONAL CODES

▶ **From outside South Africa**
to South Africa: tel. 00 27
to **Cape Town**: tel. 00 27 21

▶ **From South Africa**
to Australia: tel. 00 01
to Ireland: tel. 00 353

to UK: tel. 00 44
to USA and Canada: tel. 001

▶ **Directory enquiries**
For Cape Town: tel. 1023
nationally: tel. 1025;
international directory enquiries:
Tel. 0903

**Public telephone boxes** contain blue telephones for phone cards, which can be purchased in many shops, post offices and hotels, to the value of 15, 20, 50, 100 and 200 rand (www.telkom.co.za). **Mobile phones** can be rented at Cape Town airport using a credit card. Pre-paid SIM cards for national networks, such as MTN, Cell C, Virgin or Vodacom can be bought in supermarkets or at petrol stations and used in personal mobile phones.

*Telephones*

# Prices and Discounts

Prices at the Cape are generally **low**, though tourists notice fluctuations in the exchange rate. Not only petrol is significantly cheaper than in Europe, but also shopping and eating out. Inflated hotel prices can be expected for the 2010 Football World Cup, however. The best **opportunities for savings** are early bookings, flying out of season and the **Cape Town Pass** and **Wild Card**. The VAT refund for tourists also provides a saving of 14% on purchases (keep receipts).

*Value for money*

## ▶ WHAT DOES IT COST?

**Basic double room**
from 800 rand

**Simple meal**
from 40 rand

**Three-course menu**
from 100 rand

**Litre of petrol**
from 10 rand

**Cup of coffee**
from 8 rand

**Litre of mineral water**
from 20 rand

# Shopping

**Shopping paradise** Thanks to its **low prices**, Cape Town is a veritable shopper's paradise. Youthful fashions can be found in **Hout Street, Long Street** and **Kloof Street**. Book shops, Cape wines and good antique shops are on Church Street and Shortmarket Street, while the pedestrian zone of **St George's Mall** has department stores, diamonds and colourful street stalls. Bright printed cloths, bead jewellery, wood carving, soapstone items, masks and original artworks made of tin and metal from the townships can be found at **Greenmarket Square**. Art from all over Africa is sold at the **Pan African Market**, 76 Long Street. Many talented goldsmiths have also settled at the Cape. Leather goods and sports and outdoor clothing are good value for money. The ultimate for shopaholics is the **V & A Waterfront** and the retail temple of **Century City**, along the N1 highway by Milnerton. Opening hours for shops are normally Mon–Fri 9am–5pm, Sat 9am–1pm; shopping malls open daily till 9pm.

**Opening hours ▶**

## SHOPS

### ANTIQUES

▶ **Antique Arcade**
127 Long Street, Central. A dozen small antique shops with furniture, fine porcelain and silverware.

▶ **Church Street Antique Market**
Antiques, kitsch and junk can be found on the daily street market between Long Street and Burg Street during summer; during winter it operates between Thu and Sat.

### ARTS AND CRAFTS

▶ **Monkeybiz**
Township art, ▶ p.154

▶ **Pan African Market**
Cape Town's Africa House
▶ Baedeker Tip, p.155

▶ **Streetwires**
Township art, ▶ p.155

*Baedeker recommendation*

▶ **Whatiftheworld Gallery**
1st floor, Albert Hall, 208 Albert Road Woodstock; www.whatiftheworld.com (closed Mon). Renowned art and fashion shows located in the Old Biscuit Mill, 373–375 Albert Road, Sat–Sun 9am–2.30pm organic market along with arts and crafts and live music. Justin Rhodes and Cameron Munro also exhibit at Central, 11 Hope Street.

*Imaginative carved art*

*Strolling, people-watching and shopping at the former trade centre at the Waterfront*

## ART GALLERIES

▶ **Albie Bailey ART Gallery**
  ▶Baedeker Tip p.150

▶ **AVA Gallery**
  35 Church Street, Central
  Contemporary work, catalogues
  and art magazines

▶ **The Cape Gallery**
  60 Church Street, Central
  www.capegallery.co.za
  Contemporary Cape artists

▶ **Goodman Gallery**
  3rd floor, Fairweather House
  176 Sir Lowry Road, Woodstock
  www.goodmangallerycape.com
  Linda Given and Joe Wolpe show
  renowned South African artists
  such as Tracey Rose and Minette
  Vári, who exhibited in the Africa

Pavilion during the 2007 Venice
Biennale (closed Mon).

## BOOKS

▶ **Clarke's**
  211 Long Street, Central
  www.clarkesbooks.co.za
  Well presented contemporary literature, bestsellers and second
  hand books.

## FASHION

▶ **Africa Nova**
  Cape Quarter, 72 Waterkant
  Street, Green Point; www.africa-
  nova.co.za. Hand-woven Kente
  textiles from Ghana. Also colourful clothes, ceramics, sculptures
  and jewellery from South Africa.

▶ **Habits**
  1 Cavendish Close

Cavendish Street, Claremont
www.habits.co.za.
Award-winning fine fashions made
of linen, cotton and silk by Jenny
Le Roux

▶ **MeMeMe**
279 Long Street, Central. Show-
room for youthful fashion by Cape
Town designers, like that by co-
owners Kirsty Bannerman, Richard de Jager, Carine Terre-
blanche and David West

▶ **Skinz**
86 Long Street, Central
Handmade leather bags and belts
from springbok leather

▶ **Victoria Wharf
Shopping Centre**
V & A Waterfront
www.waterfront.co.za/shop
Top address for youthful fashion,
designer clothes and outdoor
clothing in one place

*Baedeker recommendation*

▶ **Greenmarket Square**
First choice for art and craftwork from
all over Africa with countless stalls for
wood carvings, textiles, bead jewellery
and art from recycled materials ▶ p.204

*Top place for African craftwork: Greenmarket Square*

## JEWELLERY

### ► Afrogem
64 New Church Street, Central
Watch in the workshop as diamonds, topaz, rose quartz and amethyst are set in gold and silver.

### ► Guiseppe Ciani
34 Somerset Road, Green Point
www.cianijewellers.com
Diamonds, rubies, emeralds and sapphires set in gold and silver: all choice designer pieces. Orders can be made within 24hrs.

### ► The Diamond Works
Metropolitan Life Building
7 Coen Steydtler Avenue
Foreshore
www.thediamondworks.co.za
Diamond tours including workshop visits, where tourists learn about cutting, jewellery production and gold and diamond mining. The Wall of Fame exhibits prize-winning individual pieces and the tanzanite boutique shows exquisite pieces made of this violet-blue precious stone.

### ► Philippa Green
1st floor, 51 Wale Street, Central
www.philippagreen.com
Sought-after goldsmith, who produces beautiful rings, necklaces and silver bracelets.

### ► Jewel Africa
170 Buitengracht Street
www.jewelafrica.com.
Visitors can watch goldsmiths at work and admire the rare tanzanites that are only mined in a small mine near Arusha, at the foot of Mt Kilimanjaro in Tanzania. In addition to jewellery, choice pieces of African craftwork are also on offer.

### ► Platinum Masters
5th floor, St George's House
73 St George's Mall, Central
www.platinummasters.co.za
95% pure platinum or titanium combined with jewels by Andrej Matuszewski

## MARKETS

### ► Flower market
Adderley Street, Central; Mon–Sat 9am–5pm. Proteas in all colours have been sold here, between the beach and Darling Street, for over a century.

### ► Grand Parade
Flowers, vegetable and textile market near the old City Hall
► p.203

### ► Greenpoint Market
On Sundays this is the place for haggling alongside the traffic next to the new World Cup Stadium
► p.208

## SHOPPING CENTRES

### ► Canal Walk Shopping Centre
►Durbanville
Century City, p.174

### ► Cavendish Square
1 Dreyer Street, Claremont;
www.cavendish.co.za
Opening times: Mon–Sat 9am–6pm, Fri till 9pm, Sun till 4pm. Exclusive shops in the suburb of Claremont

### *Baedeker recommendation*

### ► V & A Waterfront
Ultimate shopping destination with elegant arcades, boutiques and markets that spread all over the entertainment and leisure district at the port ► p.286

## WINE

► **Caroline's Fine Wine Cellar**
Matador Centre, 62 Strand Street;
www.carolineswine.com. Mon–Sat
daily. Tastings for the Cape's best
wines; another branch at Victoria
Wharf.

► **Winesense Mandela Rhodes**
Shop B 2 (ground floor), Mandela
Rhodes Place (corner of Wale and
Burg Street, St George's Mall,
Central; www.winesense.co.za.
Central wine bar and one of the
best places for buying your per-
sonal favourites after tasting some
of the 70 open wines. Branches at
Cavendish Square, in Kalk Bay and
in Tyger Valley.

# Sightseeing · Tours

## ► SIGHTSEEING INFORMATION

### CAPE TOWN PASS

► p.100

### CITY TOUR BY DOUBLE-DECKER BUS

► **Cape Town Explorer**
4 The Promenade
Victoria Road, Camps Bay
Tel. 021 / 511 1784
Fax 021 / 511 2401
www.hyltonross.co.za
The open-top red double-decker
buses offer a »hop on, hop off«
service. Departures from Burg
Street. The most important highlights are covered in two hours,
including the V&A Waterfront,
Kirstenbosch, Camps Bay and
Hout Bay. Get on and off as the
mood takes you. Commentary is
in English. The ride is free with a
Cape Town Pass. Hylton Ross also
runs bus tours to the Winelands
and the Garden Route.

► **Cape Town Sightseeing**
55 Auckland Street
Paarden, Eiland
Tel. 021 / 511 6000
Fax 021 / 511 2288
www.citysighstseeing.co.za
»Hop on, hop off« through Cape
Town, choosing between the blue
or red route. Ticket office and
daily departures between 9am and
5pm: Two Oceans Aquarium,
V&A Waterfront.

### BOAT TOURS

► **Waterfront Boat Company**
5 Quay, V & A Waterfront
Tel. 021 / 418 5806
Fax 021 418 5821
www.waterfrontboats.co.za

Daily boat tours and sailing trips, breakfast, champagne and sundowner cruises on motor boats, two-mast schooners or fast catamarans ► Baedeker Tip, p.289.

► **Atlantic Adventures**
Tel. 021 / 425 3785
Fax 021 / 438 3003
www.atlanticadventures.co.za
One- to two-hour boat tours on 12-seater speedboats departing from the Hildebrandt Rest at the V&A Waterfront, heading through Granger Bay via Sea Point, to the golden beaches of Clifton and Camps Bay. Other destinations included in itineraries are Robben Island, the nudist beach at Sandy Bay and the seal colony on Duiker Island.

**SIGHTSEEING TOURS**

► **Cape Excursions**
Energy Tours
Office 3, Second floor
Kenilworth Centre
Doncaster Road, Kenilworth
Tel. 083 / 777 0939
Reservations via Cape Town Tourism (►Information). Guides booked via the Cape Town Tourist Board are trained and well-informed for tours around Cape Town. They are up-to-date on the youth scene and also offer township tours. Starting point is Cape Town Tourism on Burg Street. Visitors can also be collected from hotels on request.

► **Helicopter tours**
Sport Helicopters
East Pier Road, V & A Waterfront
Tel. / fax 021 / 919 7355
www.sporthelicopters.co.za
These fantastic helicopter tours can last from 15 minutes to one hour and fly over Table Mountain, City Bowl, the two oceans, Robben Island, the Winelands and the shipwrecks along the Atlantic.

*Baedeker recommendation*

► **Andulela**
Suite 286, Private Bag X4, Hout Bay
Tel. 021 / 790 2592; www.andulela.com
Football tours including World Cup Stadium and training session of first-division club Ajax Cape Town. Other tours include jazz safaris to clubs where you can hear Cape Town musicians such as Mac McKenzie, Hilton Schilder and Robbie Jansen; also musical taster tours with drumming sessions; gospel tours and jewellery workshop visits in the townships; cooking courses and airborne tours in a Tiger Moth biplane.

# Sport and Outdoors

Cape Town's two oceans provide wonderful opportunities not only for sun seekers, but also for **deep-sea fishermen, sailors** and **surfers**, with or without sails or kites.The wind conditions on the Atlantic are best between September and May. **Sea kayaks** can be used to explore the coast. **Diving** is a common and usually affordable national sport. There are not only numerous wrecks all around the Cape Pen-

*Sporting South Africans*

insula, but also extensive seaweed forests and playful seals. Brave divers get their thrills at Gansbaai in the form of cage dives among the sharks.

**Endurance and adventure sports**

Endurance sports are very popular, and participants come from all over the world to join the 56km/35mi **Two Oceans Marathon** (▶p.87) and the 110km/69mi **Cape Argus Cycle Race** (▶p.87). Many Capetonians love to go climbing, **hiking** and **mountain biking** in the ▶Table Mountain National Park. Adventure sports such as **abseiling, sand boarding, bungee jumping, white-water rafting** and **kloofing** guarantee adrenalin rushes. Kloofing involves hiking into remote mountain ranges, swimming and jumping across ravines to reach ice-cold mountain lakes.

**National sports**

South Africa's national sports are rugby, cricket, football, horse racing and golf. **Rugby** fans should be sure to watch a game at Newlands Rugby Stadium and visit the SA Rugby Museum (▶ p.224). South Africa's **cricket** team, known as the Proteas, play at the Newlands Cricket Oval (▶p.224). **Horse races** are not just a sporting, but also a society event. The highlight of the year is the J & B Met on the Kenilworth Race Track (▶ p.86). Capetonians are also enthusiastic **football fans** and await the 2010 Football World Cup with great anticipation (▶p.207). Cape Town's best teams all play in the first division: Ajax Cape Town, Hellenic and Santos.

## Golfing Paradise

**Non-stop golfing around the Cape**

Golfing at the Cape has a tradition going back to 1885. South Africa's oldest golf course is the **Royal Cape Golf Club** founded by Sir Henry D'Oyley in Wynberg (www.royalcapegolf.co.za). The club lives up to its royal title by maintaining 18 fairways that are among the most beautiful of the **more than twenty golf courses** around Table Mountain. Compared to Europe, golfing is cheap and a national sport in South Africa. Most courses have caddies. Not even ten minutes' drive from the city centre, visitors can play at the elite **Rondebosch Golf Club** with views of Devil's Peak (www.rondebosch-golf-club.co.za. The **Clovelly Country Club** (www.clovelly.co.za), with its relatively short but challenging course, is located near False Bay at Fish Hoek. Just under 20mins drive from Cape Town, the beginner-friendly **Westlake Golf Club** is set

### Most beautiful golf courses

- Fancourt – four world-class courses at Hasso Plattner's golf Mecca
- Steenberg – genuine challenge with a lot of water and bunkers in the Constantia Valley
- Clovelly – superb location with challenging finale
- Erinvale – World Cup course at the foot of the Helderberg Mountains
- Royal Cape – flat course with narrow fairways
- Milnerton – challenging parcours by the sea with views of Table Mountain
- Westlake – beginner-friendly championship course, 20mins drive from Cape Town.

*Helpful caddies at Steenberg Golf Club*

between conifers and pines among the foothills of the Silverline Mountains (www.westlakegolfclub. co.za). Cape Town's only left-handed course is the wonderful **Milnerton Golf Club** near Blouberg-strand (www.milnertongolfclub.co.za). A top address in the Wine-lands is the **Erinvale Golf Club** in Somerset West (www.erinvalegolfc-lub.com), founded by South Africa's golfing legend Gary Player. Two more are the **Steenberg Golf Club** in the heart of the Constantia Val-ley (www.steenberggolfclub.co.za) and the wind-sheltered **Stellen-bosch Golf Club** among the vineyards of the university town (www. stellenboschgolfclub.com). The **Hermanus Golf Club** is a pleasure to play, even for less skilled patrons, but watch out: baboons live here and they often like to steal the balls! (www.hgc.co.za). The **Arabella Golf Estate** on the Bot River Lagoon, designed by Peter Matkovich, is among South Africa's top ten golf courses (www.westerncapehotel andspa.co.za/golf).

The Garden Route is considered a dream destination for all keen golfers. The **Fancourt Country Club Estate** is among the world's best golf resorts, with three championship courses and the Cape's first public golf course (www.fancourt.co.za). Wonderful fairways can also be found at the luxuriantly green **George Golf Club** at the foot of the Outeniqua Mountains, where patrons were already playing golf in 1886 (www. georgegolfclub.co.za); at the relatively hilly **Mossel Bay Golf Club** (www.mbaygolf.co.za), and at the master's course at **Oubaai (www.oubaai.co. za), designed by South Africa's golf star Ernie Els. The spectacular Pezula Championship Course** sits majestically about 70m/230ft above the sea on the eastern Knysna Head (www.pezula.-com). At the **Plettenberg Bay Country Club** with its mighty oaks and yellowwood trees, players can see monkeys and sometimes even the rare Knysna lourie (www.plettgolf.co.za). And no course short-chan-ges on the 19th hole!

**Golf courses along the Garden Route**

# ▶ SPORTS ADDRESSES

## ADRENALIN SPORTS

▶ **Abseil Africa**
Tel. 021 / 424 4760
Fax 021 / 424 1590
www.abseilafrica.co.za
Abseil 112m/367ft directly below
the Table Mountain cable car
station (▶p.277)

▶ **Bungee Jumping**
▶Garden Route, p.196

▶ **Hottentots Holland Kloofing**
Hottentots Holland
Nature Reserve, Grabouw
Tel. 021 / 659 3500
www.capenature.co.za
8-hour 17km/11mi climbing tour
through Suicide Gorge that includes jumping 3–22m /10–72ft
deep ravines into ice-cold rock
pools. Firm lightweight shoes and
a neoprene suit are essential. From
November to April only.

## CYCLE AND MOUNTAIN BIKE TOURS

▶ **Day Trippers**
Tel. 021 / 511 4766
Fax 021 / 511 4768
www.daytrippers.co.za
A tour company with an excellent
reputation that offers a variety of
trips on the Cape with and without bikes.

*Only the brave take a tour with Abseil Africa*

▶ **Downhill Adventures**
Shop 1, Overbeek Building
Corner of Kloof & Orange Street
Tel. 021 / 422 0388
www.downhilladventures.com
Half-day excursions on Table
Mountain and tours lasting several
days around the Cape and into the
Winelands. Equipment is pro-
vided, along with transport to the
destination area.

### DEEP-SEA FISHING

▶ **www.capecharters.co.za**
Shop 6, Quay 5
V & A Waterfront
Tel. 021 / 418 0782
Large tuna fish shoals come within
40 sea miles of Cape Town be-
tween September and June.

Ocean-going yachts at the Waterfront head off for four- to eight-
hour fishing tours at 10am every
morning hunting for snoek, yellow
fin and long fin tuna, sea bream
and black marlin.

### DIVING

▶ **Shark diving in the
Two Oceans Aquarium**
▶Baedeker Tip, p.290

▶ **Scuba Dive Centre**
Long Street Travel Centre
289 Long Street, Central
Tel. 021 / 424 2233,
www.scubashack.co.za
Snorkelling with seals, cage diving
with great white sharks at Gansbaai, and wreck diving all around

*Extraordinary encounters in the seas around the Cape Peninsula*

*Hot spot for kite surfers: Blouberg beach with a view of Table Mountain*

the Cape, for example in the kelp forest at Camps Bay, or around the VOC ship *Huis te Kraaiestein*, which sank in 1698. Another branch in Kommetjie:
Tel. 021 / 785 6742.

▶ **www.scuba-diving-cape-town. com**
Tel: 082 / 968 3127
A diving centre that offers taster and weekend courses, as well as whale watching, shark diving in Gansbaai, wreck and cold water coral reef dive trips.

▶ **Marine Dynamics**
P. O. Box 78, Gansbaai
Tel. 028 / 384 1005
www.sharkwatchsouthafrica.com.
Observe great whites and go cage diving around Dyer Island off Gansbaai.

## GOLF

▶ **Western Province Golf Union**
Tel. 021 / 686 1668
www.wpgu.co.za
Details of courses and green fees.

▶ **Jedek Travel**
32 Firgrove Way, Constantia 7806
Tel. 021 / 712 6055
www.jedek.com
Golf, sport and adventure trips around Cape Town.

## HORSE-RIDING

▶ **Imhoff Farm**
Two-hour rides along the 8km/5mi long beach at Nordhoek. Free to Cape Town Pass holders ▶p.220.

▶ **www.kapritt.co.za**
Horse riding trips and riding tours lasting up to eleven days.

## SANDBOARDING

▶ **Downhill Adventures**
Half-day and whole-day excursions to the 5 sq km/2 sq mi of dunes at Witsands in the Atlantic Dunes Nature Reserve, a 40min drive from Cape Town; or to Betty's Bay. Quad biking is also on offer and all equipment is supplied ▶p.125.

▶ **Gary's Sandboarding**
Gary's Surf School
34 Beach Road, Muizenberg
Tel. 021/788 9839,
www.garysurf.com
South Africa's oldest surfing school (established 1989) offers free sandboarding to holders of the Cape Town Pass. Daily 8.30am - 5.30pm setting off from Gary's Surf School. Boarding takes place at Scarborough.

## SEA KAYAK TOURS

▶ **Coastal Kayak**
179 Beach Road, Three Anchor Bay, Cape Town, tel. 082/ 439 1134
Guided tours along the Atlantic coast; kayak and canoe rentals.

## SURFING & KITE SURFING

▶ **Hotspots**
... for surfers and kite surfers are Sunset Beach, Dolphin Beach, the beaches of False Bay, Platboom in the Cape Point Nature Reserve, and the beach at Langebaan; www.wavescape.co.za

▶ **Cabrinha Kitesurfing School**
Shop 4, Marine Promenade
Porterfield Road, Table View
Tel. 021 / 556 7910
This kite »surfari« school and shop is located right on Table View Beach. Rentals and sales of equipment. Accommodation available.

# Theatre · Opera · Concerts

Cape Town's two most important stages are **Artscape** and the **Baxter Theatre**, where major operas are performed (www.capetownopera.co.za), as well as classical concerts, modern ballet (www.capetowncityballet.org.za), musicals, jazz, comedy and fashion shows. The **Cape Philharmonic Orchestra** (www.cpo.org.za) performs in City Hall and the Artscape Theatre, occasionally in the Baxter. The summer **open air concerts** held in the Kirstenbosch Botanical Garden (▶ Baedeker Tip p.223) are an unforgettable experience. Popular festivals are held at the Maynardville open air theatre, on the Spier Estate and also at Oude Libertas in Stellenbosch. The Theatre on the Bay in Camps Bay is a good small theatre. Good off-theatres are the Obz Café and Armchair Theatre in Observatory, the Little Theatre on the university campus and the Old Zoo Theatre on the Groote Schuur estate. The Spier vineyard's summer festival near Stellenbosch also includes the colourful Third World Bunfight show (www.thirdworldbunfight.co.za.). The comedian **Pieter-Dirk Uys**, a celebrated star of the Cape, performs at the Evita Se Perron Theatre in Darling. **Tickets** can be purchased at theatre booking offices or via **Computicket**.

*Curtain up!*

▶ **THEATRE**

▶ **Computicket**
Tel. 083 915 8000
www.computicket.co.za
Programme information for festivals, films, theatre, concerts and sporting events, as well as credit card reservations: dozens of Computicket outlets in Cape Town offer this service. For example, at the V&A Waterfront Shopping Centre, Shop 6182, and at Grand Parade Centre, 11 Adderley Street.

**THEATRE AND MUSICALS**

▶ **Artscape Theatre Complex**
10 D F Malan Street
Tel. 021 / 410 9838
www.artscape.co.za
The Artscape opened in 1971 – not with the scheduled *Aida*, but with a ballet, as the soprano had fallen ill. Renamed in 1999, the original name of **Nico Malan Theatre** is still in common use. The director Michael Maas is in charge of three stages, presenting everything from ballet, theatre, opera and classical concerts, to revues, art exhibitions and charity balls.

▶ **Baxter Theatre**
Main Road, Rondebosch
Tel. 021 / 685 7880
www.baxter.co.za
Musicals, comedy and theatre are presented and the restaurant hosts encounters between the public and performers late into the night.

▶ **theatre@thepavilion**
First floor, BMW Pavilion
Portswood / corner of Beach Road
V & A Waterfront
Tel. 021 / 419 7661
Music, live comedy and dinner events with South Africa's top entertainers.

▶ **Theatre On The Bay**
1a Link Street, Camps Bay
Tel. 021 / 438 3301;
www.theatreonthebay.co.za
Since 2008, Pieter Toerien has again staged the megahit *Defending the Caveman*, with Alan Committie in the lead role. Two hours before and after the show you can dine at the Act I Theatre Café on the first floor (tel. 021 / 438 8818).

*Baedeker recommendation*

▶ **On Broadway**
88 Shortmarket Street, Central
Tel. 021 / 424 1194
www.onbroadway.co.za
Entertaining dance and musical shows complete with dinner: pasta, lamb or Cape Malay curry.

# Time

South Africa is in the same time zone as Eastern Europe (GMT + 2), which means the time is the same during Central European Summer Time, while during winter South Africa is one hour ahead.

# Transport

## Road Traffic

South Africans drive on the left. The quality of roads around Cape Town meets Western standards. Side roads in the country and the mountains are often unpaved, however. Capetonians tend to drive fast. **Speed limits:** on motorways 75mph/120kmh; on country roads 62mph/100kmh; in built up areas 37mph/60kmh. Exceeding speed limits can result in expensive fines! The use of **safety belts** is compulsory, including on the back seats. Motorbike riders must wear a **helmet**. The **alcohol limit** is set at **0.5** per mille. Using mobile phones while driving is only permitted with hands-free equipment.

*Drive on the left*

Larger petrol stations are open 24hrs. Note that petrol can only be paid for **in cash**. Friendly petrol **attendants** serve and also check oil, water and tyre pressure. A tip of 3 rand is standard.

*Petrol*

In the centre of Cape Town there are supervised car parks. Official car guards for hire are identified by their yellow vests; they take the parking fee. Parking is often limited to one or two hours. In the rest of the city neighbourhoods, unauthorized car park attendants often offer their services – like the official attendants, they are always given a small tip. That way cars stay safe.

*Parking*

The Cape Town AA can be reached on tel. 021/419 6914. The AA accident emergency number is tel. 0800/010101. They arrange breakdown assistance throughout the country at no charge. They can also arrange immediate medical help at no charge: tel. 0800/033 007. If there are human casualties, the police must always be called. Even slight damage to rental cars should be reported to the rental outlet immediately.

*Accidents: what to do?*

## By Taxi

Cape Town taxis are **good value and essential at night**. Official taxis have a calibrated meter and cost around 10 rand per km/0.6mi. Taxi stands can be found at, for example, Green Market Square and Grand Parade. A trip in a **minibus taxi** is an experience – though not for the faint-hearted. There are frequent serious accidents due to speeding. Their main stand is at Adderley Street opposite the Golden Acre Shopping Centre. Regular routes include those to Sea Point and Long Street.

## By Bus

The public bus service for the metropolitan area is provided by the **Golden Arrows** company. The main terminal is at the Golden Acre

*Public bus network*

Shopping Centre on Adderley Street. Regular routes serve the Atlantic coast all the way to Hout Bay (www.gabs.co.za). The **open double-decker buses** of Cape Town Explorer and City Sightseeing, which cover the most important sights and offer a »hop-on, hop off« service (▶p.120), are a good alternative.

Airport transfers ▶ Taxi buses are responsible for the shuttle service to the airport. Among others: **City Hopper**, tel. 021 / 505 6363; **Magic Bus**, tel. 021 / 505 6300; **Way 2 Go**, tel. 021 / 934 2503, **Dumalisile**, tel. 021 / 934 1660. A good value service is also provided by the private bus companies **Backpacker Bus** (tel. 021 / 447 4991, www. backpackerbus.co.-za) and **Homeland Shuttle & Tours** (tel. 021 / 426 0294), which travel between hotels and the airport.

Long-distance buses ▶ The **Baz Bus**, which offers a hop on, hop off service for travelling all over South Africa with one long-distance ticket, is legendary among backpackers. 180 backpacker accommodations and hostels are part of the Baz Bus service with safe and comfortable transport from door to door, for example from Cape Town to Johannesburg or Durban. **Grey Hound** services the long-distance routes between Cape Town and Port Elizabeth and Durban, as well as to Johannesburg and Pretoria via Bloemfontein / Mangaung. **Intercape Mainliner** operates a comfortable bed-bus service all over South Africa from Cape Town. **Translux Express** offers high standards of comfort and security and connects Cape Town with the larger South African cities. Luxury buses by **SA Roadlink** connect 21 towns and cities all over South Africa.

## By Train

Make it first class Cape Town's **Metrorail** is a realistic choice only for destinations east of Table Mountain, such as Muizenberg, Simon's Town, Strand, Stellenbosch, and Paarl. For security reasons, the trains should be avoided at night, and it is best to travel only first class. The national railway company **Spoornet** provides long-distance services out of Cape Town and, since 2007, there has been a twice-weekly **first-class train** taking a maximum of 126 passengers from Cape Town to Johannesburg. Departures from Cape Town: Tue, Sat 8am; departures from Johannesburg: Thu, Sat 2pm (www.premierclasse.co.za).

## Hotel Trains

Blue Train This **legendary luxury train** takes its name from the deep blue colour of its carriages. The 336m/1100ft-long Blue Train has been travelling between Pretoria/Tshwane and Cape Town since 1901, and takes almost 27 hours at 90kmh/56mph to travel the 1600km/1000mi stretch. A maximum of 74 guests are transported in 37 suites, or 58 guests in 29 suites with full board, which includes an exquisite dinner. Departures from Pretoria: 8.50am, with arrival in Cape Town at noon the following day (sightseeing stop in Kimberley). Departures from Cape Town: 8.50am, with arrival in Pretoria / Tshwane at

## *Metrorail* Plan

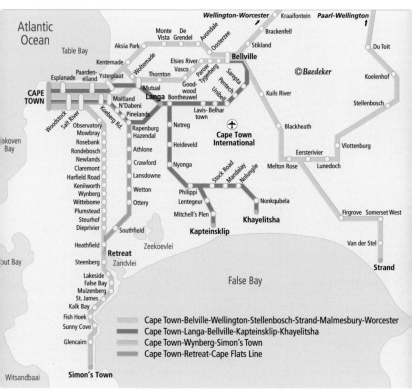

Cape Town-Belville-Wellington-Stellenbosch-Strand-Malmesbury-Worcester
Cape Town-Langa-Bellville-Kapteinsklip-Khayelitsha
Cape Town-Wynberg-Simon's Town
Cape Town-Retreat-Cape Flats Line

12.30pm the following day (safari stop in the Aquila Game Reserve
(▶p.302). Due to high demand, it is advisable to make bookings at
least six months in advance.

The ultimate train journey on the »**most luxurious train in the**    Rovos Rail
**world**« has elaborately restored carriages dating from the 1930s, including dining and bar cars and an open-air viewing platform at the
end of the train. A maximum of 72 guests are accommodated in the
spacious suites of the Rovos Rail train, which requires 48 hours for
the journey between Cape Town and Pretoria. The Old Pioneering
Trail begins at 3pm in Pretoria/Tshwane, at the Old Capital Station.
In Cape Town departures are at 11am from platform 23 of Cape
Town Station. The tour can be extended from Pretoria to include Victoria Falls. A unique experience is also the journey by Rovos Rail's
»Pride of Africa« from Cape Town to George on the Garden Route.
Departures from Cape Town Station are at 9.20am from platform 23,

# ⏵ TRANSPORT ADDRESSES

**AUTOMOBILE ASSOCIATION OF SOUTH AFRICA (AA)**

Tel. 083 / 843 22
www.aasa.co.za

**RENTAL CARS AND MOTORBIKES**

► **Avis**
www.avis.co.za
Cape Town Airport:
Tel. 021 / 934 0330

► **Budget**
www.budget.co.za
Cape Town Airport:
Tel. 021 / 380 3180

► **Europcar**
www.europcar.co.za;
Cape Town Airport:
Tel. 021 / 935 8700

► **Hertz**
www.hertz.co.za
Cape Town Airport:
Tel. 021 / 934 3913

► **Imperial**
www.imperialcarrental.co.za
Cape Town Airport:
Tel. 021 / 448 5608

► **National**
www.nationalcar.co.za
Cape Town Airport:
Tel. 021 / 934 7499

► **Tempest**
www.tempestcarhire.co.za
Cape Town Airport:
Tel. 021 / 934 3845

► **Harley Davidson Cape Town**
9 Somerset Road, Green Point
Tel. 021 / 446 2999
www.harley-davidson-cape-town.com
Rent an »Easy Rider«, set the engine roaring and get going! Special Harley tours along Route 62.

**CLASSIC CARS**

► **Motor Classic Rentals**
1 Waterloo Street
Vredejoek Central
Tel. 021 / 461 7368
Fax 021 / 461 7343
www.motorclassic.co.za
Alpha Spider, Mercedes SL, Jaguar, Austin or Morgan: ideally take an open-top on a Winelands tour or along the Garden Route.

► **Best Beetle Car Rental**
5 Staal Street, Brackenfell 7356
Tel. / fax 021 / 981 4113
www.bestbeetle.co.za
Affordable fun in historic VW Beetles – Sixties retro chic with delivery right to your door!

**TAXIS**

► **Rikkis**
Tel. 021 / 418 6713
www.rikkis.co.za

► **Marine Taxi**
Tel. 021 / 434 0434

► **SA Cab**
Tel. 086 / 117 2222
www.sacab.co.za

► **Unicab Taxis**
Tel. 021 / 447 4402

► **Touch Down Taxis**
Tel. 021 / 919 4659
Official airport taxi company

## LONG-DISTANCE BUSES

### ► Greyhound
1 Adderley Street, Central
Tel. 021 / 505 6363
www.greyhound.co.za

### ► Translux Express
Cape Town Central Station
Adderley Street
Tel. 021 / 449 6209
www.translux.co.za

### ► Intercape Mainliner
P.O. Box 618, Bellville
Tel. 021 / 380 4400
www. intercape.co.za

### ► Baz Bus
275 Main Road, Sea Point
Tel. 021 / 439 2323
www.bazbus.com

### ► SA Roadlink
### Roadforce One
Cape Town Central Station
Adderley Street
Tel. 021 / 425 0203
Tel. 011 / 333 2223
(central reservations)
www.saroadlink.co.za
www.saroadlink.co.za/rf.html

## BY TRAIN

### ► Metrorail
Tel. 0800 / 656 463 (free phone)
www.capemetrorail.co.za
Timetable info: tel. 083 / 123 7245

### ► Spoornet
Tel. 0800 / 656 463
(free phone)
www.spoornet.co.za

## HOTEL TRAINS

### ► Blue Train
Tel. 021 / 449 2672
Fax 021 / 449 3338
www.bluetrain.co.za

### ► Rovos Rail
Rovos Cape Town, Dock Road
P.O. Box 50241, Waterfront
Tel. 021 / 421 4020
Fax 021 / 421 4022
www.rovos.co.za.

### ► Shongololo Express
P.O. Box 1558, Parklands 2121
Tel. 011 / 483 0657
Fax 011 / 483 0745
www.shongololo.com

### ► Union Limited
V & A Waterfront
Tel. 021 / 449 4391
Fax 021 / 449 4395
www.transnetheritage
foundation.co.za
www.sarsteam.com.za

### ► Shosholoza Meyl
Main office in Johannesburg
Tel. 011 / 773 2992
Fax 011 / 773 2239
www.spoornet.co.za

with arrival in George the following day at 9am. Departures from George are at 1.30pm, arriving at platform 24 in Cape Town at 5pm the following day. Other journeys available are the route between Pretoria and Durban, a golfing tour around Pretoria, as well as a long-distance tour to Namibia: Pretoria – Kimberley – Windhoek – Swakopmund. There is a 9-day route departing from Pretoria to Durban – Port Elizabeth – Cape Town, and once a year Rovos Rail even travels the route between Dar Es Salaam (Tanzania) and Cape Town.

**Union Limited** For fans of **steam trains** the lovingly restored carriages and engines of the Transet Collection have two-bed and four-bed suites to explore the Western Cape and also to travel through South Africa in the direction of Pretoria and Port Elizabeth. For example, there is the Protea (1933) dining carriage or the Umtata (1942). Prices include two-course lunches and four-course dinners.

**Shongololo Express** This **cheaper and less elitist** hotel train, also known as the Safari Express, travels predominantly at night and stops during the day. South Africa's highlights are then explored in the company's own buses as day trips. Meals are made up of South African delicacies. Numerous tours are on offer throughout the nine countries of southern Africa. Departures and returns for Cape Town are at the Muizenberg station.

**Shosholoza Meyl** This **tourist train with beds and reclining seats** travels between Cape Town, Durban and Johannesburg. The name Shosholoza comes from an old song of farewell used by South African migrant workers and means »onwards!« – a phrase used to this day by sport fans urging on their teams. Meyl means train.

## Travellers with Disabilities

Many **hotels**, guest houses and lodges have adapted to the needs of disabled travellers. The larger car hire companies also rent out specially adapted vehicles. **Safaris around Cape Town** for disabled travellers are offered, among others, by Outback Africa (www.outback africa.com).

### ▶ INFORMATION FOR DISABLED TRAVELLERS

▶ **The Disabled People of South Africa**
6th Floor, Dumbarton House
1 Church Street
Cape Town 8000
Tel. 021 / 422 0357
fax 021 / 422 0389
www.dpsa.org.za

▶ **In UK: Holidaycare**
Tourism for All
The Hawkins Suite
Enham Place
Enham Alamein

Andover SP11 6JS
Tel. 08 45 124 99 71
www.holidaycare.org.uk

▶ **In USA: SATH (Society for the Advancement of Travel for the Handicapped)**
347 5th Ave., no. 610
New York, NY 10016:
Tel. (21) 4 47 72 84
www.sath.org

# When to Go

The mild **Mediterranean-type climate** means holidays at the Cape can be taken all year round, though spring and autumn are especially recommended. Being in the southern hemisphere, the seasons are exactly opposite to Europe or North America. The **show of wild flowers** during the Cape spring from early August is gorgeous; June to November is the season when **whales** congregate along the coast, returning from Antarctica to calve. The **swimming season** lasts from the end of October to April, when the water is warmer. The peak season is December, and most South Africans take their summer holidays from Christmas to mid-January. Many hotels are therefore fully booked at that time. During **high summer**, temperatures in Cape Town and near the coast rise to between 25°C/77°F and 30°/86°F. In the Klein Karoo temperatures at that time can exceed 40°C/104°F. A stiff breeze often blows along the Atlantic, even during summer. **Winter**, between mid-May and September, can be rainy, with short sharp downpours. Temperatures rarely sink below 5°C/41°F, but it is entirely possible for snow to fall on Table Mountain. Average daily maximum temperatures during winter hover between 15°C/59°F and 19°C/66°F. At this time grass is short in the bush and big game gathers at the watering holes in the national parks, providing excellent conditions for photography. Meanwhile, in Cape Town, there is a flowering of cultural life, with festivals, theatre and music.

**_i_ Weather forecasts**

- The Cape Town Meteorological Office informs on weather conditions: very important for any visit to Table Mountain. Tel. 082 / 233 9900; www.weathersa.co.za

All-year
destination

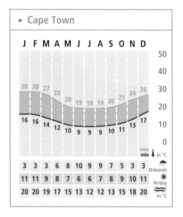

▶ Cape Town

| | J | F | M | A | M | J | J | A | S | O | N | D | |
|---|---|---|---|---|---|---|---|---|---|---|---|---|---|
| max in °C | 28 | 28 | 27 | 23 | 20 | 19 | 19 | 19 | 20 | 21 | 24 | 26 | |
| min in °C | 16 | 16 | 14 | 12 | 10 | 9 | 9 | 9 | 10 | 11 | 13 | 17 | |
| D/month | 3 | 3 | 3 | 6 | 8 | 10 | 9 | 9 | 7 | 5 | 3 | 3 | |
| Hr/day | 11 | 11 | 9 | 8 | 7 | 6 | 6 | 7 | 8 | 9 | 10 | 11 | |
| in °C | 20 | 20 | 19 | 17 | 15 | 13 | 12 | 12 | 13 | 15 | 18 | 20 | |

# Tours

A TRIP IN A TOURIST
BUS INTRODUCES
CAPE TOWN'S MOST
IMPORTANT SIGHTS, BUT IT IS MORE EXCITING TO
EXPLORE THE »MOTHER CITY« ON FOOT. READ OUR
TIPS FOR WALKING TOURS AND EXCURSIONS WITH
ENJOYABLE STOPS.

# TOURS THROUGH CAPE TOWN

Two walks through the city between Bo-Kaap and Castle of Good Hope show the entire spectrum of »South Africa's mother city«. People who are in good physical condition can complete the walks in the minimum times. But take your time, it will be worth it!

━━ **TOUR 1** **Tour 1 Classic Cape Town**
From an adobe fort to a pulsating metropolis ► **page 141**

━━ **TOUR 2** **Cultural Melting Pot**
Victorian villas, Cape Malay cuisine and great shopping adresses ► **page 142**

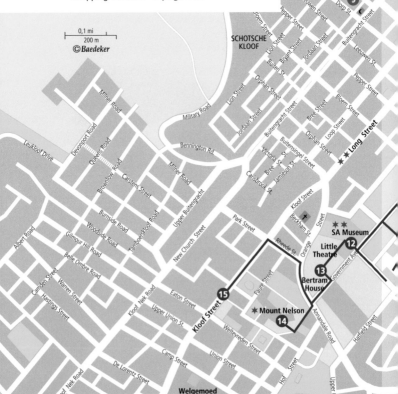

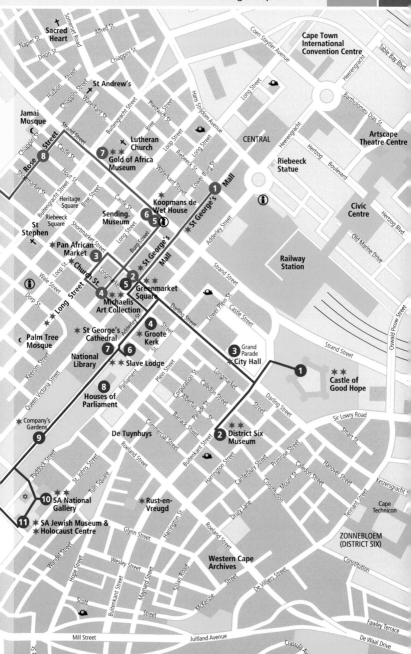

# Getting Around in Cape Town

A two-hour city tour on the open-deck **Cape Town Explorer Bus** presents a quick run-through of the highlights, from the Waterfront to Table Mountain. The sightseeing tour by double-decker bus allows visitors to hop on and off at will. As the city centre is just 4 sq km/ 1.5 sq mi in size, it is easy to **explore on foot**. Additional surface was clawed from Table Bay by land reclamation, but Table Mountain to the south prevents any further expansion. It is all the more surprising, therefore, that when the new era of the 1990s created a pulsating metropolis, there was still room left over for small shops catering to the booming art and design scene. Take **a stroll** through Bo-Kaap, to the colourful flea market at Greenmarket Square and through the fancy shopping mall of the V & A Waterfront. Feast on **fresh seafood at the harbour** and take a ride up **Table Mountain** for a sundowner. In fine weather the mountain should always be your first stop, as the »Cape Doctor« often cloaks its summit in white clouds. Uniformed car park attendants ensure the safety of **hired vehicles**. **Taxis** are relatively good value for money and absolutely essential at night. **Boat trips** departing from the V & A Waterfront are highly recommended. Hikers and mountain bikers should always travel in groups.

## ! *Baedeker* TIP

### Africa calling!

Flights and hotels for Cape Town should be booked in good time, especially during the high season and for the 2010 Football World Cup. This saves a great deal of time, money and inconvenience. All the tours suggested here for Cape Town and the Cape region can be booked via travel agents.

*Cape Town is at your feet on the summit of Table Mountain*

# Tour 1 Classic Cape Town

**Beginning and end:** From the Cape of Good Hope to the »Nellie«    **Duration:** 1 day

**This stroll traces the city's history and takes in its highlights. The beach on which the waves of Table Bay once broke now lies under the pavement of Grand Parade. Thus the city was built inland towards Table Mountain, and Cape Town's historic core developed around Jan van Riebeeck's company garden.**

The city tour begins at South Africa's oldest stone building, the ❶＊＊ **Castle of Good Hope**, where the William Fehr Collection should not be missed; changing of the guard is at noon on weekdays. The ❷＊＊ **District Six Museum** at 25a Buitenkant Street tells the story of the former multi-cultural District Six, which was forcibly cleared and demolished at the end of the 1960s. The location of the first mud-brick forts of the VOC (Dutch East India Company) are indicated in red on ❸ **Grand Parade**, which turns into one big flea market every Wednesday and Saturday. Nine days after his release, Nelson Mandela held his famous »Talk to the Nation« to an audience of hundreds of thousands from the balcony of ＊ **City Hall** opposite. The ❹＊ **Groote Kerk**, South Africa's oldest church, with a wonderful teak pulpit by Anton Anreith, can only be viewed before 2pm. Do not fail to take a detour to ❺＊＊ **Greenmarket Square**, complete with traders from all over Africa and Cape Town's most beautiful Art Deco buildings. The ＊ **Old Town House** houses the renowned Michaelis Collection of Dutch masters. The exhibition on slavery on the ground floor of the

 **Highlights of Tour 1**

- Castle of Good Hope – best preserved VOC fortress
- District Six Museum – Reminders of the legendary sixth city district
- Greenmarket Square – the heartbeat of the »Mother City«
- Slave Lodge – moving history of slavery
- South African Museum – sharks, dinos and San cave painting
- Afternoon tea at the "Nellie"

❻＊＊ **Slave Lodge** is also a must. Right behind the bend leading to Wale Street stands Desmond Tutu's »People's Church«, the Anglican ❼＊ **St George's Cathedral**. The jazz bar in the crypt is a pleasantly cool place for lunch, even on hot days. Alternatively, choose between grilled kingklip fish and tender ostrich filet around the corner in **Five Flies** at 14–16 Keerom Street. Just a few steps further, the South African parliament is in session from January to June in the ❽ **Houses of Parliament**, which can be viewed during free one-hour tours (don't forget your passport!). Mighty oaks line the pedestrian zone of Government Avenue leading through the wonderful ❾＊ **Company's Garden**, with its roses and bronze statue of **Cecil Rhodes**, diamond magnate and, from 1890 onwards, prime minister of the Cape Colony. The ❿＊＊ **SA National Gallery** presents contemporary South

African artists and imaginative township art. On the occasion of the new millennium, Nelson Mandela opened the ⑪✻ **SA Jewish Museum & Holocaust Centre**, a new cultural establishment for Jews on the Cape. Whales, giant sharks, dinosaurs and the various cultures of South Africa are introduced at the ⑫✻✻ **South African Museum**, while ⑬✻ **Bertram House** at the end of Government Avenue offers insight into the colonial lifestyle of the 19th century. Beyond the busy traffic of Annandale Road stands the high-class Art Deco ⑭✻ **Mount Nelson Hotel**; the sandwiches, cakes and pastries for afternoon tea on the terrace of the »Nellie« are without equal. There are pleasant alternatives on neighbouring ⑮**Kloof Street**: the charming Café Gainsbourg (no. 64) and Melissa's (no. 94), which also sells fantastic food souvenirs.

# Tour 2 Cultural Melting Pot

**Beginning and end:** From the railway station to Noon Gun

**Duration:** Half-day tour

**Filigree gold jewellery or charming toys made from re-cycled materials, traditional craftwork or provocative young art, Victorian villas and spicy Cape Malay cuisine: the area between Greenmarket Square and Bo-Kaap is perfect for bargain hunting, window shopping and sightseeing.**

The tour begins just a few steps from **Cape Town Railway Station**, in the pedestrian zone of ❶✻ **St George's Mall** lined by the small stands of street vendors. One of the liveliest, oldest and most beautiful places in Cape Town is the cobblestoned ❷✻✻ **Greenmarket Square**. Except on Sundays, there is always a lively trade in art and crafts from all over Africa here. Around the corner, on buzzing ✻✻ **Long Street**, there are trendy bars like the popular Mama Africa (no. 178), and the excellent ❸✻ **Pan African Market** (no. 76) with woodcarving, township art and colourful textiles on two floors. Antiques, fashionable art and flea market wares can be found on ❹✻ **Church Street**. And how about a coffee break at the charming Café Mozart (no. 37)? The ground floor of the new first-class **Rhodes Mandela Place** hotel next door also contains fancy boutiques. Return via the old vegetable market and up Burg Street to ❺**Cape Town Tourism**, where township tours can be booked. The last owners of the 18th-century ❻✻ **Koopmans-de-Wet House** were the sisters Margaretha and Marie De Wet, whose father was the first president of Cape Town's ruling

## Highlights of tour 2

- Greenmarket Square: traditional craftwork from all over Africa
- Gold of Africa Museum: gold jewellery from Ghana and the Ivory Coast
- Bo-Kaap: colourful Cape Malay quarter

*Haggling is the name of the game at Greenmarket Square*

council. The collection at the **❼ ✳ ✳ Gold of Africa Museum** is unique, and visitors can even design their own jewellery in the workshop. Imaginative township art is sold in **❿ Rose Street** at Monkeybiz (no. 65) and Streetwires (no. 79). This is where the colourful **⓫ ✳ ✳ Bo-Kaap quarter** begins, with its painted houses now protected by preservation order. The story of the Cape Malays is told in the Bo-Kaap Museum, at no. 71 Wale Street. Finally, the ascent begins to the **⓱ ✳ Noon Gun Café and Restaurant**, with its delicious Cape Malay dishes and panoramic views of Table Mountain. On the dot of noon, the daily cannon being fired above can be heard.

# Tour 3 Once Around the Cape

**Beginning and end:** Cape Town – Cape of Good Hope – Constantia

**Duration :** approx. 150km/95mi / 1 day

**Off to the world's loveliest end! Take the continent's most spectacular coastal road past colourful fynbos proteas, ostriches, baboons, penguins and wonderful beaches. The crowning finale is dinner in the renowned winery of Groot Constantia.**

Set off early in the morning, before the tourist buses head for the Cape of Good Hope. Around 20km/13mi south of **❶ ✳ ✳ Cape Town,** at **❷ ✳ Hout Bay,** the best fish and chips on the Cape can be found and the *Nauticat* sets off for the seal haunt of Duiker Island every half hour. Breathtaking views open up around almost every one of the 114 bends of the famous ❸ ✹✹ **Chapman's Peak Drive**. Stop at one of the car park and picnic spots and, with a bit of luck, you might spot whales. Be careful about leaving your car if the car park is deserted, as attacks on tourists have occurred. Buses only run

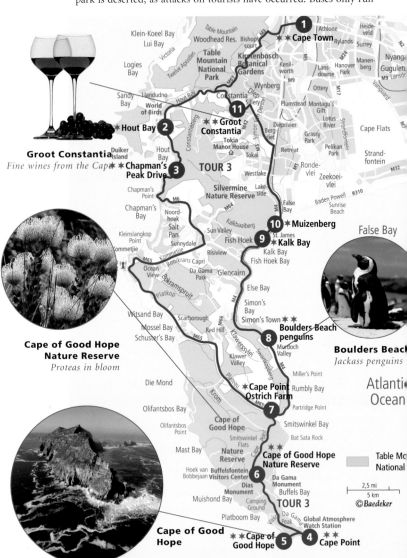

**Groot Constantia**
*Fine wines from the Cape*

**Cape of Good Hope
Nature Reserve**
*Proteas in bloom*

**Cape of Good
Hope**

**Boulders Beach**
*Jackass penguins*

on this toll route (which is often closed due to rock slides) from north to south. The route down to the Cape of Good Hope (www.capepointroute.co.za) is via Kommetjie and Scarborough on the M 65, the wonderful Cape Point Route. Except for Wild Card holders, the Cape of Good Hope Nature Reserve charges an entrance fee. The wind-battered lighthouse of ❹✶✶ **Cape Point** can be reached on foot or via the Flying Dutchman cable car, complete with terrace restaurant, souvenir shop and amazing views as far as Africa's most southerly point. Have a picnic at Cape Point or hike the 45 minutes to the ❺✶✶ **Cape of Good Hope**

*i*   Highlights of Tour 3

- Chapman's Peak Drive – legendary and spectacular Cape Town street
- Cape of Good Hope – the most beautiful end of the world!
- Cape of Good Hope Nature Reserve – great variety of flora in a small area
- African jackass penguins at Boulders Beach
- Groot Constantia – Heart of South African wine culture

to take the obligatory photo. On the return journey through the ❻✶✶ **Cape of Good Hope Nature Reserve,** which is part of ✶✶ **Table Mountain National Park**, visitors will be impressed by countless fynbos proteas, orchids and erica species. Bontebok and mountain zebra live in the southern sector of the park. Be careful with the baboons! Do not touch or feed, as they have a vicious bite. Angelika and Ernst Coelle breed up to 800 ostriches on their ❼✶ **Cape Point Ostrich Farm** north of the park gate, in the direction of Smitswinkel Bay; they also sell eggs and beautiful leatherwear (www.capepointostrichfarm.com). An entire colony of African jackass penguins can be observed from raised viewing platforms at ❽✶✶ **Boulders Beach**. Afterwards, take a stroll past the small antique shops of ❾✶ **Kalk Bay** or spend some time at ❿✶ **Muizenberg beach** with its pretty Victorian beach houses, before setting off for ❿✶✶ **Groot Constantia**, one of the oldest wineries on the Cape. Take a tour of the elegant mansion and the wine museum and spoil yourself with tasty Cape cuisine in Simon's Restaurant. We recommend the mussels in white wine or the Cape Malay lamb curry.

# Tour 4   Wine Towns for Connoisseurs

**Beginning and end :** Cape Town – Stellenbosch – Franschhoek – Paarl – Cape Town

**Duration :** approx. 180km/115mi / 2 days

**Endless oak avenues, fine parks and whitewashed mansions, choice art, classy boutiques and lovely cafés, wonderful wines and exquisite cuisine: an excursion to the Winelands is among the highlights of a holiday on the Cape.**

From ❶✶✶ **Cape Town** take the N 1 in the direction of Paarl until the turn-off for the R 304, to reach South Africa's second-oldest settlement, ❷ ＊＊ **Stellenbosch**, after just under 50km/30mi. Its particular charm lies in the juxtaposition of a lively campus atmosphere and historic ambience. Parking places can be found by the old market (braak). Take a stroll past the whitewashed Cape Dutch houses of the Rhenish Complex and to the unique museum village; wander down pretty Dorp Street and take a look at the work of contemporary South African artists in the Rupert Museum and Sasol Art Museum. The R 310 in the direction of Franschoek leads to the ❸ ＊＊ **Boschendal** Estate, founded in 1685 and a must for all lovers of wine and Cape Dutch architecture (► photo p.147). 40-minute cellar tours and one-hour vineyard walks followed by a tasting session take place daily at 10.30am and 11.30am. The restaurant offers French gourmet cuisine. Order the house shiraz with your meal – or why not have champagne with lunch, for a change? Alternatively, settle down for the »Picnic at Boschendal« (www.boschendalwines.com) under the shade of ancient oak trees.

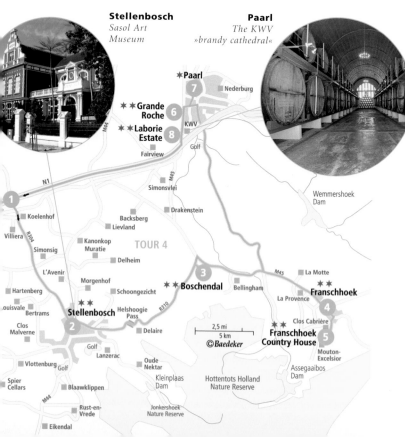

**Stellenbosch**
*Sasol Art Museum*

**Paarl**
*The KWV »brandy cathedral«*

35km/22mi further on, the enchanting wine-making town of ④ ✳ ✳ **Franschhoek** lies at the foot of the Hex River Mountains. Stroll past the little shops on Huguenot Road as far as the Huguenot memorial dedicated to the first settlers. Settle down on the terrace of the Quartier Français, which has been one of South Africa's best restaurants for years. Delights are also in store for those who stay the night at the ⑤ ✳ ✳ **Franschhoek Country House** dating from 1900, and take dinner in its prize-winning Monneaux restaurant. A former perfumery, the hotel has gorgeous suites and its own wine cellar (www.fch.co.za). The following day, at first light, it is possible to drift over the Winelands by hot-air balloon. Breakfast is then served in the beautiful ⑥ ✳ ✳ **Grande Roche** in the wine-growing centre of ⑦ ✳ **Paarl,** which is quickly reached after 30km/19mi on the R 303. Giant barrels full of renowned brands are stored at KWV on Kohler Street (tours available). The Afrikaans Museum is dedicated to the country's second official language. To round off, Hetta van Deventer serves the finest of South African country cooking at the 300-year-old vineyard of ⑧ ✳ ✳ **Laborie Estate** on Taillefert Street (www.laborie.co.za). After the meal, take a stroll on the Laborie Wine Hiking Trail before returning to **Cape Town**, a journey of just under 60km/38mi on the N 1.

# Additional excursions

Not only vineyards await visitors to the region around Cape Town. Sailors and surfers rave about the ✳ ✳ **west coast**, where Atlantic breakers crash. The ✳ ✳ **Cederberg region** contains bizarre rock formations and ancient San rock paintings. The charming Route 62 leads to the ostrich-breeding centre of Oudtshoorn and the mighty Cango Caves. Nowhere else in the world can whales be observed as easily from the mainland as in ✳ ✳ **Hermanus**, and the ✳ ✳ **Garden Route** follows one of South Africa's most beautiful coastlines, with endless dream beaches along the Indian Ocean, magical lagoons and dense rainforests.

**Top destinations around Cape Town**

# Sights from A to Z

SKYSCRAPERS, THE WATERFRONT AND VICTORIAN VILLAS; TABLE MOUNTAIN, TOP MUSEUMS AND DREAM BEACHES; A MULTICULTURAL AND VIBRANT ATMOSPHERE AND LIVELY HISTORY: WELCOME TO CAPE TOWN!

# Adderley Street

E 3

← *Sunset atmosphere at the Waterfront*

**Location:** City Bowl (Heerengracht to Government Avenue)

**Buses:** Bus Terminal, Golden Acre

**Bulky high-rise banks and insurance buildings are as much a part of the historic main street between ▶ Heerengracht and ▶ Company's Garden as the trendy shops and colourful flower stands.**

Banking and commerce

In 1849 the upper section of ▶ Heerengracht was named after the British politician **Charles Bowyer Adderley** (1814–1905), who successfully stopped a penal colony being built at the Cape. Today Adderley Street's large commercial buildings make up the **heart of the Central Business District** (CBD). Structures such as the **Colosseum Building** on the corner of Riebeeck Street – built in Art Deco style from 1900 onwards – and the First National Bank designed by Sir Herbert Baker in 1913 have received unappealing glass and concrete extensions. In front of the **Central Station**, built in 1970, the **Open Air Market** is a tempting sea of flowers, clothes, shoes and souvenirs. Next to the bus terminal stands the **Golden Acre Shopping Centre**, which was also built in the 1970s. A water reservoir dating from 1663 was revealed during building work.

! **Baedeker** TIP

**Handmade**

Since 2007, the Albie Bailey ART Gallery on the second floor of the Colosseum Building has exhibited contemporary Cape art, such as sculptures by Ronel Jordaan and colourful ceramics by the Capetonian artist Clementina van der Walt (205, The Colosseum, 3 St George's Mall, Tue–Fri 10am–5pm, Sat 10am–1pm).

✱ Groote Kerk

⊙ Opening hours: Mon–Fri 10am–2pm, Sunday services 10am, 7pm

The first version of **South Africa's oldest Christian church** was consecrated in 1678, but a new building was erected under Governor van der Stel from 1700. The clock tower was completed in 1703. In 1841 Hermann Schütte gave the »Large Church« its present form. The »mother house« of the **Dutch Reformed Church** (Nederduitse Gereformeerde Kerk, NGK) has an organ from the 1950s with 5917 pipes. The finest treasure of the church is the lion-embellished pulpit dating from 1789, which was carved from Burmese teak by Anton Anreith and Jan Graaff (43 Adderley Street, entrance on Church Square; www.grootekerk.org.za).

Church Square

The newly paved Church Square contains a statue of **»Onze Jan«** by Anton van Wouw, which honours the memory of the Boer newspaper magnate and chairman of the Afrikander Bond **Jan Hendrik Hofmeyr**, who played a key role in writing the 1909 constitution for the South African Union. A plain concrete slab on the traffic island on Spin Street marks the site of a tree under which slaves were auc-

*Benefit concert in front of Slave Lodge: Cape Town kids collect funds for their school*

tioned until 1 December 1834. A newly planted oak tree today symbolizes the **abolition of slavery**.

The **Cultural and Historical Museum** at 49 Adderley Street was founded in 1966 and renamed Slave Lodge in 1998. Its exhibition rooms on the ground floor are dedicated to the **history of slavery**. The building, which was originally built as accommodation for slaves in 1679, also served as a post office, library and law court from 1811 onwards. The most recent archaeological excavations have revealed that almost 9000 slaves lived in this building – on average 470, but sometimes up to 1000 at the same time. A sanatorium for Khoikhoi women and slaves was located in the east wing. The second floor exhibits the Egyptian collection based on finds made by Sir Flinders Petrie between 1911 and 1913. Also on view is fine European **silver tableware**, with 18th- and 19th-century teapots and jewellery boxes, as well as exquisite Chinese porcelain dating from the Tang dynasty (618–907). The Victorian **pharmacy** is also worth seeing. A statue in front of the museum entrance commemorates **Jan Christiaan Smuts** (1870–1950), who was South Africa's prime minister between 1919 and 1939.

✷ ✷
**Slave Lodge**

🕐
Opening hours:
Mon–Fri
10am–4.30pm, Sat
9.30am–1pm.

◀ www.iziko.org.
za/slavelodge

## ★★ Bo-Kaap

**Location:** Between Long Street and Signal Hill, access via Wale Street

**Internet:** www.bokaap.co.za

**Hilly Bo-Kaap is considered one of Cape Town's most atmospheric districts. Minarets, mosques and colourful houses make attractive photo motifs. Youthful boutiques and art galleries have also discovered this charming quarter and made it their own.**

History  The earliest traces of European settlement go back to Jan de Waal and his Waalendorp settlement founded in 1706, and parts of it are still criss-crossed by cobblestone lanes to this day. For centuries, Bo-Kaap was a **melting pot** for many different cultures and religions. These days it is predominantly inhabited by Muslims. The earliest of their number arrived as political exiles from 1658 onwards: slaves or prisoners from Indonesia, Sri Lanka, India and East Africa who were erroneously known as »**Cape Malays**«. The quarter was known by all

*Welcome colour: the Bo-Kaap district with its pastel houses*

# CARNIVAL IN CAPE TOWN

**Every year on 2 January thousands dance and sing and play their way through the streets of CBD and Bo-Kaap, making their hats fly and their brollies twirl. The 150 colourful floats and musical groups that participate will have spent many months preparing for this day: the highlight of the Cape Town Minstrel Carnival.**

Originally, slaves and freed men celebrated their only day off and then, from 1834 onwards, the abolition of slavery with parties and parades. The development of this colourful street parade into its present form was largely influenced by American sailors, who brought inspiration from the Mardi Gras in New Orleans in 1848. During apartheid, many participants used the carnival procession as a political vehicle. The police rarely intervened, as they hardly understood the **amusing satirical songs** performed in the Kaapse-Taal dialect.

## Kaapse Klopse

The »Voorloper« (front runner), drum major and captain of each **Cape Town Carnival club** (Kaapse Klopse) are followed by jesters known as Cape Coons, complete with parasols, garish costumes and white make-up in a parody of the former white rulers. They are accompanied by brass bands, complete with banjos, trumpets and traditional ghoema drums. Cape Town's **»Moffies«** from the city's gay scene, sporting fingerless white gloves and ladies' outfits, are also part of the show.

## »And the Winner is ...«

Countless Capetonians and tourists delight in a spectacle lasting many hours that the minstrels put on between Bo-Kaap and Adderley Street. The best groups and singers are honoured in dramatic finals. For information contact Kevin Momberg, kjmomberg@yahoo.com; www.cape townminstrels.co.za). Tickets can be booked via Computicket (see p.114). When Nelson Mandela became the carnival patron in 1998, it was official: the giant party is truly of the Rainbow Nation.

*Trendy bars, cafés and artwork: Long Street is the city's vibrant heart*

kinds of names, including Slamse Buurt, Schotcheskloof and Bo-Kaap, before it became generally known as the **Malay Quarter**, although only around 1% of the population in this neighbourhood, which is predominantly inhabited by coloureds, actually originate from Malaysia. Muslims became a majority only at the beginning of the 20th century, and it was the Group Areas Act that forced people of other ethnic and religious backgrounds to leave. The majority of the around 10,000 residents are tradesmen and artisans to this day. The **colourful little houses have preservation orders** and were built between the end of the 18th and the middle of the 19th century. Cape Town Tourism (▶p.100) offers a daily walking tour of Bo-Kaap from 9.15am to 10.30am. Two-and-a-half-hour tours with locally resident guides are also offered by **Bo-Kaap Guided Tours** (tel. 021 / 422 15 54). The spicy Cape Malay cuisine can be savoured during **cooking safaris** run by Andulela (▶ p.121).

✳
Bo-Kaap tours ▶

Charming
quarter
The best places to experience the charming atmosphere, colours, aromas and delights of Bo-Kaap are along Wale Street, Rose Street,- Leeuwen Street and Chiappini Street. Take a coffee in the **Rose Corner Café** opposite the Bo-Kaap Museum and sample a Cape Malay curry in the **Biesmiellah** restaurant at 2 Upper Wale Street. Cape Town's young middle class – the »Black Diamonds« – meet on Kloof Street in fashionable cafés such as Bardeli and Camissa. Highlight of the year is the **Minstrel Carnival** on 2 January (▶Baedeker Special, p.153).

Township art
Barbara Jackson and Matkapelo Ngaka sell beautiful glass bead works in their **Monkeybiz gallery** at 65 Rose Street. Over 450 township women are given employment in this way, and the profits go towards

Aids prevention programmes (www.monkeybiz.co.za). Almost 100 township inhabitants also work for **Art Studio Streetwires** at 77 Shortmarket Street, where creative wire art can be purchased (www.streetwires.co.za).

The museum at 71 Wale Street opened in 1978 and was originally built as a home for **Jan de Waal** in 1763–68. It has Cape Dutch origins. From 1862 the building was home to Abu Bakr Effendi, who mediated between rival Muslim factions in the service of the British. He founded an Arab school and even wrote a book in Afrikaans. Today the museum exhibits family furniture, informs on the two dozen **kramnats** (sacred burial sites) located in a ring around Cape Town, and on the history of the quarter under apartheid. The black and white photographs by George Hallet give a memorable impression of **life in Bo-Kaap**.

✱
Bo-Kaap Museum

🕐
Opening hours:
Mon–Sat 9am–4pm;
www.iziko.org.za/b-okaap

**South Africa's oldest mosque** is no more than 200m/200yd from the museum and was built on Dorp Street from 1795 (visits by appointment only). The founder Tuan Guru (»Our Teacher«) came to the Cape as a Sunni teacher in 1780. His grave is located at **Tana Baru**, the oldest Muslim cemetery.

Auwal Mosque

The over 300-year-old Long Street once marked the boundary between Bo-Kaap and City Bowl. A further nine mosques can be found in and around Long Street, including the **Hanafee Mosque** of 1881, on the corner of Long Street and Dorp Street. Cape Town's historic entertainment street is now a rendezvous for a **multi-cultural crowd** with its small cafés, restaurants and bars, as well as fashion boutiques, galleries, antique shops, music and second-hand outlets. The cast-iron balconies with their typical Victorian designs decorate the buildings of the **Blue Mountain Backpapers** at 208 Long Street, and the **Purple Turtle** hostel on the corner of Shortmarket Street. Typical African cuisine and live music is on offer at the legendary **Mama**

✱ ✱
Long Street

◄ Colonial heritage

! **Baedeker** TIP

**Pan African Market**
A large selection of traditional art and craftwork from all over Africa can be found on three floors at 76 Long Street. Apart from the obligatory masks, wood figures and jewellery, native clothing, original pictures and toys made from recycled tins are also for sale. Shopping here is not only a personal pleasure. The profits also help to support over 300 township families. (Mon–Fri 9am–5pm, Sat 9am–1pm).

**Africa** at 178 Long Street (▶p.66). The newly restored **Long Street Baths** on the corner of Long Street and Buitensingle Street offer revitalizing relaxation in Turkish steam baths originally from the 1930s. (Opening times: daily 7am–7pm). From 1820 onwards, Jan van Boughies officiated as imam at the **Palm Tree Mosque**.

**Sendinggestig Museum**

Opening hours:
Mon–Fri 9am–4pm

Four Corinthian columns adorn the façade of Cape Town's oldest slave church at 40 Long Street. Christianized slaves were given their first instruction in this **mission church**, which was built between 1802 and 1804. In those days owners refused permission for their slaves to be baptized: they feared not being able to make use of them afterwards, as Christians were not supposed to be slaves. The neoclassical pulpit is carved from South African yellowwood and stinkwood. The organ was built by Frederick Ladegast.

# Bredasdorp · Cape Agulhas

C / D 4

**Location:** 170km/105mi south-east of Cape Town

**Population:** 22,000

**Getting further south is impossible. Just 38km/24mi lie between Bredasdorp and Cape Agulhas with its red and white emblem for the end of the African continent.**

**Bredasdorp**

This quiet little town was founded by the merino sheep breeder Michiel van Breda in 1838. Visitors can marvel at beach finds and the remains of the *Arniston*, shipwrecked in 1815, in the **Shipwreck Museum** housed in the former Independent Church. (Opening times: Mon–Fri 9am–4.45pm, Sat, Sun 11am–3.45pm). Hiking paths through the **Heuninsberg Reserve**, which is up to 368m/1207ft high, begin at the end of Van Riebeeck Road. Many species of protea and erica are native here, including the »Bredasdorp lily«, which blossoms bright red in April and May.

**De Mond Nature Reserve**

In the de Mond wetland area at the mouth of the Heuningnes River there are nesting sites for black oystercatchers, Nile geese and rare Damara ocean swallows. These is also a snow-white sandy beach here.

**Arniston**

The R 316 ends at Arniston (hotel, ▶p.157) after 26km/16mi, alongside the 200-year-old **fishing settlement of Kassiesbaai**, whose photogenic thatched cottages have long since been declared a national monument. *Arniston* was also the name of the English troop transporter that sank off the coast here in 1815. 372 people drowned. The area is also known by the phrase **Waenhuiskrans** (ox-carriage cave) after a huge cave – only accessible during low tide – used by the first settlers for their ox carts.

## ▶ VISITING BREDASDORP

*Stunners: hand-painted Kapula candles*

### INFORMATION

**Cape Agulhas Tourism Bureau**
Long Street, Bredasdorp 7280
Tel. 028 / 424 2584
Fax 028 / 425 2731
www.tourismcapeagulhas.co.za

### WHERE TO EAT

▶ **Moderate**
*Blue Parrot*
Dirkie Uys Street, Bredasdorp
Tel. 028 / 425 1023
Karoo lamb and snails with bacon and cherries are cooked by Wessel van Zyl in this former stable.

### THE WARM ART OF AFRICA

Looking for one last special souvenir? Beautiful hand-painted candles with colourful African patterns can be found at the Kapula Gallery on Patterson Road in Bredasdorp. The owner Ilse Appelgryn's success story is also interesting (see www.kapula.com). She was South Africa's business person of the year in 2000.

### WHERE TO STAY

▶ **Mid-range**
*Agulhas Country Lodge*
Main Road, L'Agulhas 7287
Tel. 028 / 435 7650
Fax 028 / 435 7633
www.agulhascountrylodge.com
This building of natural stone built into the hillside has eight tasteful rooms complete with balconies and sea view. Try Sue Fenwick's Cajun shrimps.

---

At the entrance to **Struisbaai/Struis Bay** shortly before reaching the Cape stand the restored thatched cottages known as **Hotagterklip Cottages**, which have also been declared national monuments. Thanks to its 14km/9mi beach, many Capetonians have holiday homes in **L'Agulhas**. The name of the wind-battered **»Cape of Spines«** and the settlement recall the Portuguese seafarers who feared the sharp points of the protruding reefs here. The **lighthouse** was established in 1849 and is the second-oldest in the country. Here visitors can learn about the birds and plants in the car-free **Agulhas National Park**, and also enjoy panoramic views of the biotope from its viewing platform. The ground floor of the museum contains a photo exhibition with images of all South Africa's 56 lighthouses, maritime lamps and focusing mirrors. (Opening times: Mon–Sun 9am–4.30pm). The

★ Cape Agulhas

### ! *Baedeker* TIP

#### Candlelight dinner

The Arniston Spa Hotel on Beach Road not only has smart rooms with balconies and sea views and an excellent restaurant, but also offers candlelight dinners in one of the Kassiebaai cottages, where traditional dishes are cooked by fishermen's wives (www.arnistonhotel.com).

*Cape Agulhas: two oceans meet at the southernmost point of Africa*

route to Cape Agulhas, the **Southernmost Point**, is open to vehicles. The official line that marks the division between the **Indian Ocean** and the **Atlantic** is on a memorial slab at the car park.

De Hoop Nature and Marine Reserve
The 34,000ha/84,000-acre nature reserve 40km/25mi north-east of Bredasdorp is worth a visit for its species-rich fynbos vegetation and wonderful dune landscape. Between May and November southern right whales can be observed along the **Whale Trail** that runs through the nature reserve for 54km/34mi, ideally from the high dunes at Koppie Alleen. Cape zebras, Eland antelopes, bonteboks, baboons and ostriches also live here (www.capenature.org.za).

## ✷✷ Cape of Good Hope

**B 3**

**Location:** Southern point of the Cape Peninsula

**Internet:** www.capepoint.co.za; www.capepointroute.co.za

34° 21' 25'' south, 18° 28' 26'' east: a visit to the Cape of Good Hope is a must. Even today, seafarers have great respect for the »Cape of Storms«, where the Indian Ocean and the Atlantic flow into each other.

Cape Point Route
Whether by hire car or on a sightseeing bus, the »**most beautiful cape on earth**«, according to Sir Francis Drake, is the highlight of one-day and two-day tours exploring the ►**Table Mountain National Park** on the Cape Peninsula (►Tours, p.143).

## *Cape Peninsula* Map

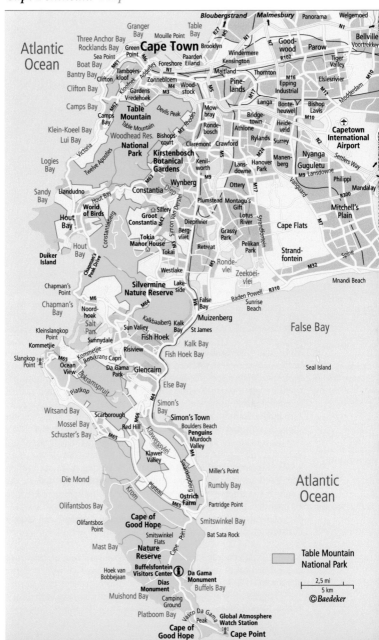

Table Mountain
National Park

2,5 mi

5 km

©Baedeker

CAPE OF GOOD HOP

**Cape of Good Hope Nature**

🕐 Opening hours:
April–Nov daily
8am–5pm, Dec &
Jan daily
7am–7.30pm, Feb &
March daily
8am–6pm

✳ More than 1200 **fynbos** species and over 250 species of bird flourish in the nature reserve founded in 1939, which has been part of Table Mountain National Park since 2004. It is also home to zebras, ostriches, rare bontebok antelopes, Chacma baboons, and turtles. Whales and dolphins play off the coast between May and November. The **Buffelsfontein Visitor Centre** with its snack bar and souvenir shop is centrally located in a farmhouse dating from the 1740s (www.tmnp.co.za). Guided tours, such as the two-day 34km/21mi circular route of the **Cape of Good Hope Hiking Trail** or the 7km/4.5mi **Shipwreck Trail** can be booked there. Hiking maps are also on sale. Furthermore, the centre rents out **Olifantsbos Cottage** in the south of the reserve, which contains three double rooms, a kitchen, an open fire and direct access to the beach. A maximum of six people each can also be accommodated in **Eland Cottage** and **Duiker Cottage**.

**Cape of Storms**

A copy of the »Padrão« with a cross and Portugal's coat of arms rises in the direction of Platboom Bay, the same as those left near Lüderitz in Namibia and Port Elizabeth by the first European to circumnavigate the Cape. It was **Bartolomeu Diaz** who initially named the Cape »Cabo Tormentoso« (Cape of Storms) in 1488. However, Portugal's

34° 21′ 25″
SOUTH LATITUDE

King João II was so thrilled by Diaz' expedition report that he confidently renamed it **Cabo de Boa Esparança** (Cape of Good Hope). Vasco da Gama is also honoured by a cross. His memorial stands in the direction of Bordjiesrief Bay. There are sheltered bays for swimming there and along **Buffels Bay** (Buffelsbaai). The **Antonie's Gat** cave is also part of Buffels Bay, to which **Lalu Abdul Kader Jaelani Dea Koasa** escaped in 1775. He had been enslaved in Indonesia three years earlier and then escaped from the dungeons of the Old Court House in ► Simon`s Town. A price was put on his head, but a local farmer helped him and he went on to become a saint to Cape Muslims. Portugal's national poet Camões was inspired in 1572 to invent the grisly **»Adamastor« Cape ghost** for his *Lusiads* (*Os Lusiadas*): complete with pitch-black jaws, yellow teeth and unkempt beard. The mythical giant succumbed to the sea nymph Thetis, according to the poet, and was turned into a mountain guarding the southern oceans. The monster frightened Vasco da Gama in the form of a terrifying

*Water, wind and the great blue yonder: the Cape of Good Hope*

### ? DID YOU KNOW ...?

- ...that the real »Flying Dutchman« was in danger of sinking off the Cape in 1641? Captain Hendrik van der Decken swore to high heaven that he would sail around the Cape if it took until Judgement Day! Some people today still think that they've sighted his ghost ship.

> ## ! *Baedeker* TIP
>
> **Round the Cape**
> Why not take a picnic to Cape Point, hike the 45 minutes to the south-west tip of Africa and take the obligatory photo at the Cape of Good Hope? A tour by rented bicycle along the 20km/13mi circular route is also enjoyable. The guided circumnavigation of the Cape by kayak from Buffels Bay to Olifantsbos Bay is no doubt unrivalled anywhere else in the world. You do need to have mastered the Eskimo roll in the waves of the ice cold Benguela Current first, however. Tel. 082 / 501 8930, www.kayakcapetown.co.za.

storm cloud over the Cape on 22 November 1497. André Brink used the ghost legend as a parable for his tragic love story *Cape of Storms: The First Life of Adamastor.*

There are several souvenir shops at Cape Point as well as the **Two Oceans terrace restaurant** with panoramic views towards False Bay (tel. 021 / 780 9200, www.two-oceans.co.za). The **lighthouse** built in 1860 at an elevation of 238m/781ft can be reached on foot via 130 steps or more comfortably via the **Flying Dutchman** cable car. Thanks to an initiative by locals in 2007, the Cape Point Old Lighthouse has been restored. 600 people per hour can be transported up by the Flying Dutchman.

**★★**
**Cape Point**

The nearby **Global Weather Station** is one of 20 around the world dedicated to studying the earth's climate.

**Africa's dangerous southern point**

Clouds and fog used to obscure the old lighthouse beacon for 900 hours each year, as during the wrecking of the *Lusitania* on 18 April 1911. Only the energetic actions of the lighthouse keeper, who swung his petroleum lamp on the beach, saved 774 people. The **new lighthouse** was built between 1913 and 1919 at a height of 87m/285ft at Diaz Point. Its light today shines as far as 63km/39mi out to sea. The Cape remains dangerous, however. In 1942, the *Thomas T. Tucker* was damaged and, in 1968, the *Phyllisia*. Officially, 26 sinkings have been recorded at the Cape and 600 along the Cape Peninsula.

# ★★ Castle of Good Hope

**E / F 3**

**Location:** City Bowl, access via Buitenkant Street

**Internet:** www.castleofgoodhope.co.za

**South Africa's oldest stone building is among the top attractions for the public. Once it lay directly by the sea, and today the pentagonal fortress is considered the best-preserved stronghold of the Dutch East India Company anywhere in the world.**

**Stronghold of the Dutch East India Company**

The fortress brochure describes all sights worth seeing in no less than seven languages. The **Casteel de Goede Hoop**, which has never been attacked, is still used by the military and was built to designs by the French architect Vauban between 1666 and 1679, on the ruins of ◄ ►3D image p.164 a wooden fort dating from 1652. Restoration work lasted almost a quarter of a century and was completed in 1993. The **five bastions** were named after Prince William II of Orange's main provinces in 1679: the Leerdam bastion to the west is followed in a clockwise direction by Buuren, Catzenellenbogen, Nassau and Oranje. The slate in the paving originates from quarries at ►Signal Hill and on ►Robben Island. Most of the beams are pine, which was shipped from the Baltic until 1679.

The main attraction is the **William Fehr Collection** of paintings, porcelain, glass and furniture once used by the **Vereenigde Oost-Indische Compagnie (VOC)** . Take a look at the Lady Anne Barnard Ballroom from the late 18th century, the Castle Military Museum, the Dolphin Fountain, the Old Smithy and »Het Backhuys« (the former bakery). Due to rising damp, the fortress basement was never used for storing gunpowder, but only served as a prison. Since 2007 it has also been possible to see **model ships and wreck finds** from the early days of sail that were transferred here from the Maritime Museum.

*Always entertaining: changing of the guard in front of the castle*

# CASTLE OF GOOD HOPE

✱✱ **A wide moat and strong walls surround South Africa's oldest stone building. The foundation stone for the pentagonal fortress of the Dutch East India Company (VOC) was laid in 1666, and the first soldiers occupied it in 1674.**

Opening times:
Daily 9am–4pm, tours: Mon–Sat 11am, noon, 2pm; www.castleofgoodhope.co.za

### ① Changing of the Guard
The Key Ceremony and the Changing of the Guard, which take place on weekdays at 10am and noon respectively, draw many tourists.

### ② William Fehr Collection
The main attraction at the fortress is the William Fehr art collection housed in the former officers' residence, built in 1695. The paintings portray Dutch merchants, Xhosa and Zulu kings, Khoikhoi and governors from the end of the 17th century to the early 19th century, among other motifs. Other exhibits include wonderful furniture made from native stinkwood and fine 18th- and 19th-century silverware; also a Ming-dynasty porcelain chandelier dating from around 1400, 17th-century Japanese vases and Dutch crystal glasses from 1745 with the VOC monogram. Oil paintings show beautiful three-masted boats once used in trading relationships that reached all the way to Asia.

### ③ Balcony
Once the bell rang every hour, and could be heard as much as 10km/6mi away. It was cast in Amsterdam by Claude Frémy in 1697 and weighs 300kg/650lb.

### ④ Clock tower
Once the bell rang every hour, and could be heard as much as 10km/6mi away. It was cast in Amsterdam by Claude Frémy in 1697 and weighs 300kg/650lb.

### ⑤ Main entrance
The gable of the classical portal of the main entrance is embossed with the Dutch coat of arms with its crowned lions and seven arrows representing the United Provinces. Underneath the coats of arms of individual Dutch cities where the VOC had major offices, such as Delft and Amsterdam, can be seen.

### ⑥ Sun dial
Time was measured with sun dials at the Cape. At night and during cloudy weather, hour glasses filled with sand were used. They were turned by a »rondeganger«, who also had to ring the bell.

### ⑦ Castle Military Museum
The former entrance from the sea now leads to the Military Museum, where visitors can admire historic uniforms and learn about the Cape regiment. An impressive exhibition on the Boer Wars on the first floor also records the role of the Khoikhoi, who served the British. The many women and children who were interned in British concentration camps are also remembered: insufficient nourishment and hygiene, and inadequate medical care cost more than 26,000 of them their lives.

### ⑧ Dolphin Pool
The fountain of »mythical sea creatures« was reconstructed in 1985, using sketches of the original Dolphin Pool made by Lady Anne Barnard in 1793.

### ⑨ Entrance arch
Wooden blocks served as cobblestones in the entrance so that people did not have to walk in the mud during the winter, and also reduced noise from passing horse-drawn carriages.

### ⑩ De Goewerneur Restaurant
South African cuisine is served under the arches next to the Boer Bastion (Mon–Sat, 10am–4pm). Requests for »breakfast on the bastion« or »dinner in the dungeon« are taken by Diana Bezuidenhout, tel. 021/787 1260.

*Cape lion: a symbol of strength*

sterdam
ours

*The Military Museum
also tells the story of life
in the concentration camps
during the Boer Wars*

*Heavy cannon secured the fortress*

© Baedeker

*The William Fehr
Collection exhibits
ric furniture and
paintings from
the Cape*

A bell from ... once rang th[e] in the tower

[Im]portant announcements were read [ou]t from the fine balcony built by the VOC in the 18th century

Cape Dutch cupboard made from native stinkwood

②

⑥

⑨

③

①

his

# ★ Company's Garden

E 4

**Location:** City Bowl, between Queen Victoria Street und Government Avenue

**Simply known as »the gardens« by Capetonians, the place where it all began just under 350 years ago is now the city's green oasis. Business people, office workers and tourists alike value this wonderful park, which is still inhabited by the squirrels whose ancestors were brought from North America by Cecil Rhodes.**

⏱ Opening hours: During summer 7am–7pm, during winter 7am–6pm

On the orders of the Dutch East India Company in 1652, Jan van Riebeeck set out to supply incoming trading ships with fresh fruit and vegetables with the help of gardener **Hendrik Boom**. The rectangular fields of the **Company's Garden** were divided into four or nine square beds each and protected from the wind with myrtles. A cleverly designed irrigation system supplied the garden with fresh water from Table Mountain. The 6ha/14 acres of the present grounds represent just a quarter of the original size. Hendrik Boom did not have to wield his spade alone. A letter from 11 April 1658 attests that 75 slaves worked for the VOC at the Cape. A third of them were allocated to cultivating plants and lived in the slave house next to the fields until 1669. Up to 1714, slaves also served as guards against plant thieves, and some later worked in accounting and in the VOC's private company houses. The **slave bell** in the park commemorates them.

**Early wine growing**

Despite initial setbacks, the Dutch trading ships were soon satisfactorily supplied with fresh produce and early attempts at wine growing were also successful. Cuttings of the French **Muscat d'Alexandrie vine** arrived at the Cape sewn into sails in 1655. Jan van Riebeeck proudly noted the first grape pressing in his diary on 2 February 1659.

**Cape Town Gardens**

⏱ Opening hours: Daily 7.30am–4pm

In 1795, the VOC's inventory for the new British authorities listed no more than four gardeners working with 534 slaves. The VOC was bankrupt and its fields lay fallow. The renamed **Government Garden** remained the preserve of the British governor until 1848. The grounds were taken over by the city in 1892, which gave free access to the public. Today people stroll between exotic plants from all over the world, admire the Japanese stone garden and are enchanted by the fragrances in the **rose garden**. A memorial to the fallen soldiers of the First World War designed by Herbert Baker can be found in the **Delville Wood Memorial Garden**. The bronze statue of diamond magnate and prime minister of the Cape Colony **Cecil Rhodes** points north, expressing his hopes for a »red line from the Cape to Cairo«. There is a café and also an occasional

*Many school excursions head for the South African Museum at the southern end of Company's Gardens*

craftwork market. Information on **open air concerts** in the park can be found in the offices of the Cape Town Gardens on Queen Victoria Street 19 (tel. 021 / 400 25 21).

At 5 Queen Victoria Street, at the northern end of Company's Garden, stands the **National Library of South Africa** – a title the former South African Library has shared with the State Library in Pretoria since 1999. In 1818 Lord Charles Somerset ordered the establishment of the first public library at the Cape, financed through a wine tax. Originally the book collection founded in 1761 was housed in the present-day Slave Lodge in 1822 (▶p.151). The new site by Company's Garden was marked out by Governor Grey in 1857, and the new library was opened by Prince Alfred in 1860. Generous donations followed, including Sir George Grey's valuable collection of medieval and Renaissance manuscripts in 1861. Among the library's treasures are newspapers from the colonial era and travel reports, old maps, descriptions of the Khoikhoi and sketches of Cape flora and fauna by Heinrich Claudius.

Still in development is the adjacent **Centre for the Book**, housed in a magnificent mansion dating from 1906 at 62 Victoria Street (www.nlsa.ac.za/NLSA/centreforthebook). It is predominantly concerned with **promoting children, young writers and small publish-**

✴

**National Library of South Africa**

🕐

Opening hours:
Mon, Tue, Thu, Fri
9am–5pm, Wed
10am–5pm;
www.nlsa.ac.za

**Centre for the Book**

**!** *Baedeker* TIP

**History close-up**

Just a few steps separate the Company's Garden from the Western Cape Archives. This giant trove of original documents on the history and daily life of Cape Town and the Cape Province can be inspected by prior appointment (72 Roeland Street, tel. 021 / 466 81 00. Opening times: Mon–Wed & Fri 8am–4pm, Thu 8am–7pm, first Sat of the month 9am–noon; free; www.national.archives.gov.za).

ers, as well as combating illiteracy, something over 8 million South Africans suffer from. For example, a successfully promoted title was *On the Road of Hope* by disabled women from Khayelitsha ►Townships. The elegant atmosphere of the building makes it popular for weddings, filming and fashion shows. Public readings are also held here during the Cape Town Book Fair. (Opening times: Mon–Fri 8.30am–4.30pm; www.capetownbookfair.com).

# ✴ Constantia Valley

Map p.159

**Location:** Southern Cape Town suburb    **Access:** M 3 to Muizenberg as far as exit 14, then the M 41 in the direction of Constantia

**A light lemon yellow or dark brick red, fresh and dry aroma or earthy – sauvignon blanc, merlot or pinotage? The Wine Route in the classy residential suburb of Constantia leads to South Africa's most historic vineyards. Savour some elegant wines during a cellar tour at the Cape.**

**✴ Alphen Country House Hotel**

Tel. 021/ 794 5011; www.alphen.-co.za ►

The country hotel on Alphen Drive in Constantia, built in 1714, provides a useful insight into **the region's wine history**. Owned by the Cloete family since 1850, their original furniture and paintings are a historic treasure. Mark Twain and George Bernard Shaw once dined in the immaculate **Cloete's Restaurant**. Take a look in the Boer 'n Brit Pub too. In the south terrace Lord Somerset once hosted hunting breakfasts and Josias Cloete duelled with Waterloo veteran **Dr James Barry** (1795–1865), who performed Cape Town's first caesareans and wine-bathing cures. After the doctor's death, it was discovered that Barry – who had had bitter arguments with Florence Nightingale in the Crimean War – was in fact a woman. She is believed to have been Margaret Bulkley from Belfast. Tip for hikers: the Alphen Hiking Trail along the Deep River and the Cecilia Forest.

**✴ ✴ Groot Constantia**

www.iziko.org.za/ grootcon/ ►

**Governor Simon van der Stel** was granted 250ha/620 acres of prime land east of Table Mountain for his private residence in 1685, and named it after Constantia van Goens, the granddaughter of a patron of the VOC. This wonderful estate is therefore one of the oldest vineyards in South Africa. The sweet dessert wines that were produced from 1778 were favoured by Bismarck, Louis XVI and Napoleon. The collapse came in the 19th century, with the arrival of phylloxera, and the property was taken over by the state in 1885. It revival began only a century later, and today Groot Constantia is an outstanding **tourist attraction** where 90ha/222 acres annually produce over 550,000 bottles of pinotage, shiraz, merlot, cabernet sauvignon, chardonnay and sauvignon blanc.

An avenue of great oaks leads to the **mansion in the Cape Dutch style**, which is now a museum with elegant 18th-century furniture. Take a look in the study, dining room, kitchen and copper smithy. A superb view of the garden and vineyard can be enjoyed from the bedroom in the east wing. In the **wine museum**, whose decorative gable was fashioned by Anton Anreith, barrels, wine glasses and decanters dating from classical antiquity to the early 20th century can be admired. The carriage stables by the Jonkershuis display mill carts, six-horse carriages and Vortrekker wagons. The **Iziko Orientation Centre** in the former slave quarters tells the story of the San's forced labour and that of other slaves. The first were brought from Angola and Benin in 1661; later arrivals came from Madagascar, Mozambique and South-East Asia. Also featured are Hendrik Cloete's butler August van Bengale and the chambermaid Sabina van de Kaap.

🕐
Opening hours:
Daily 10am–5pm;
daily wine-tasting
and cellar tours

*National heritage: the manor house at Groot Constantia is now a museum*

*Constantia Valley: the cradle of South African wine*

**Klein Constantia**

www.klein
constantia.com ▶

🕐
Opening hours:
Mon–Fri 9am–5pm,
Sat 9am–1pm, daily
wine-tasting

✳ When Constantia was divided into three parts in 1716, this smaller vineyard was created; it too has a pretty 18th century mansion. The kramat (shrine or holy place) at the entrance gate honours Sheik Abdurachman Malebe Shah, who was banished to the Cape from Sumatra in 1661 and meditated in the Constantia Valley. Of the grape varieties grown here, 70% are white and 30% are red. Any tasting should definitely include the aromatic sauvignon blanc and the barrel-aged red Marlbrook. A half-litre bottle of the legendary **Vin de Constance** makes an appealing souvenir. This honey-coloured sweet dessert wine with a hint of muscatel was already appreciated by Frederick the Great and Napoleon. It is complemented by the *Vin de Constance Recipe Book* published in 2006, by star chef Michel Roux Jr.

**Gourmet temple
Constantia Uitsig**

www.constantia
uitsig.co.za ▶

✳ A visit to the Constantia Uitsig vineyard is rewarded by top-class cuisine and prize-winning wines. Frank Swainston seduces guests with his delicious Mediterranean dishes in the Uitsig Restaurant, while Frank Dangereux serves Provençal cooking of the first order in the award-winning restaurant **La Colombe**. Lunch and breakfast can be savoured on the sun terrace of the Spanschemat River Café (tel. 021 / 794 3010; opening times: Mon–Fri 9am–5pm, Sat, Sun 10am–5pm).

**Buiten-
verwachting**

✳ The history of the Klein Constantia vineyard began in 1793, when 80ha/200 acres of Groot Constantia land went to Cornelius Brink. 90,000 vines were then planted by Ryk Arnoldus Cloete from 1825, thereby inaugurating the tradition of wine-growing here. From 1866 the new owner was the legendary Oom Danie Lategan, who sported a freshly picked camellia on his lapel each day. The neglected estate was bought in 1980 by Christine and Richard Müller, who restored it and planted new vines. Their revival already brought in 100 tons at the first harvest, and thus the estate easily lived up to its name, which means »Beyond all Expectation«.

! **Baedeker TIP**

**»Beyond all expectation ...«**
Caramelized quail saltimbocca with green asparagus, delicate springbok filets or a light raspberry soufflé – the Austrian Edgar Osojnik is among South Africa's top ten chefs. Why not book a table with views onto the vineyards in the Buitenverwachting's winter garden? Tel. 021 / 794 3522.

Today, its **award-winning wines** are the feisty Buiten Blanc and the Bordeaux-style ruby red Christine, which has been served to first-class passengers on South African Airways since 2007. The Café Petite offers irresistible Austrian pastries and cakes. Picnic lunches are taken under a shady oak in front of the elegant **Manor House**. (Opening times: Mon–Fri 9am–5pm, Sat 9am–1pm, daily wine-tasting; picnic lunches Nov–April, Mon–Sat from 12.30pm; www.buitenver wachting.co.za).

The **oldest vineyard** is Steenberg Farm, which was founded in 1682. Its prize-winning wines are its sauvignon blancs and merlots. (Opening times: Mon–Fri 8.30am–4.30pm, Sat 9am–1pm; daily wine-tasting). Stunning accommodation is available at the **5-star Steenberg boutique hotel** with its exquisite restaurant and wonderful **18-hole golf course** (www.steenberghotel.com). The nearby **Tokai Forest Arboretum** has been in existence since 1694. South Africa's oldest forest park, with oaks and Californian redwoods, is ideal for hikers and mountain bikers.

*Steenberg Vineyards*

★
◀ *Steenberg Hotel*

★ ★ # District Six Museum

E 4

**Location:** 25a Buitenkant Street, Zonnebloem

**Internet:** www.districtsix.co.za

**Almost every company that offers ▶ Township Tours includes the Apartheid Museum in its itinerary. Here photos, old street signs, images from everyday life and eye-witness reports record Cape Town's legendary District Six.**

When the allocation of farmland plots below Devil's Peak began in around 1800, it also heralded the early history of District Six, also simply known as **D 6**. 3000 people already lived here in neat, usually two-storey houses in 1840, when Cape Town was divided into twelve

*District Six Museum tells a vivid story of the legendary sixth district*

🕐
Opening hours:
Mon 9am–3pm,
Tue, Sat 9am–4pm,
Sun by
appointment,
tel. 021 / 462 4050

districts. In 1860 **Zonnebloem College** moved to this area, where the sons and, more rarely, daughters of Xhosa chieftains were brought up to be black ladies and gentlemen. In 1867 the Municipal Act then divided the city into six districts, and the **Sixth Municipal District** was born. At that time, according to the 1865 census, Cape Town had 28,400 white inhabitants, as well as 13,300 »Hottentots and Kaffers«. The statistics further stated there were 9000 workers, 1400 traders, 3200 craftsmen and 2300 domestics.

**Vibrant neighbourhood**

The majority of the working class lived in the poor **District Six**, which from 1880 onwards also served as a first home for new arrivals. **Immigrants** of all colours and religions came from all over the world and settled around **Hanover Street**, which no longer exists. Within a short time they had turned the neighbourhood into a **cultural melting pot**. The parades with their unusual costumes held for the New Year carnival from 1870 marked the birth of the **Minstrel Carnival** (▶Baedeker Special, p.153). The roots of South African **jazz** also lie in this »fantastic town within a town«, according to Abdullah Ibrahim( ▶p.46). The inhabitants worked in textile and tobacco factories in Woodstock and the port. The public wash house on Hanover Street was known as Cape Town's laundry, and crinoline and shirts were diligently ironed there. After the smallpox epidemic of 1882 and the bubonic plague outbreak in 1901, fear of infection led to the expulsion of all blacks from District Six that same year. Well-heeled whites moved away, and coloureds and immigrants were soon in the majority. During 1914 TB raged in D6, and four years later the Spanish flu killed almost 6400 Capetonians.

**Forced resettlement**

But it was not until the **apartheid regime** that the quarter's fate was sealed: District Six was declared a **whites-only area** on 11 February

1966. The official justification for forced resettlement to the inhospitable **Cape Flats** was that the »people in D6 were criminal and dangerous and that the district had become a slum and hotbed of gambling, drunkenness and prostitution«. Almost 60,000 coloureds were relocated to the ►townships 25km/16mi further south between 1968 and 1982, their houses bulldozed to the ground. D6 was officially renamed **Zonnebloem** (Sunflower) in 1985. From then onwards, around 3500 whites lived there, most of them civil servants. The **district's reconstruction** has been going on since 2003, and the keys to the first 24 houses were given to former inhabitants, including the 87-year-old Ebrahim Murat and the 82-year-old Dan Ndzabela, by Nelson Mandela himself on 11 February 2004. Up to 4000 families are set to return in the coming years.

The derelict land in D6 is witness to the work of demolition balls and bulldozers to this day. Only because of loud international protests were the mosque on Muir Street and the **Holy Cross Church** near Keizergracht Street (the successor of the one on Hanover Street) preserved. A mural there entitled *The Earth Cries Out* by Peggy Delport recalls the Hendricks family, who were the last to vacate their home. A plaque installed on the Moravian Church in 1989 honours the action group HODS (Hands Off District Six), whose successor organization built the District Six Museum after 1994. The church is now located on the campus of the **Cape Peninsula University of Technology**, which with almost 26,000 students is the largest university in the Western Cape Province (www. cput.ac.za).

**Hands off? Hands on!**

The District Six Museum is housed in the 170-year-old **Methodist Mission** on Harrington Street, which was considered the freedom church during the campaign against apartheid. Today former D6 inhabitants manage the museum, in which the **multimedia exhibition »Digging Deeper«** brings to life the legendary atmosphere of District Six with photos, paintings, street signs and stories of everyday life (►photo p.36). The museum's stock includes over 14,000 historic images by renowned photographers such as Jackie Heyns, Jimi Matthews and Cloete Breytenbach. The sound archive compiled by the jazz fan Ants Kirsipuu is also unique. Books on the subject of District Six are available in the Little Wonder Bookshop, which is also the starting point for guided **tours through District Six** (reservations: tel. 021 / 466 7200). Menisha Collins tells anecdotes from the district in the **museum café**.

**Digging deeper ...**

**! Baedeker TIP**

**D 6 on Tour**
Richard Rive captured the old neighbourhood with sensitivity and tremendous humour in his novel *Buckingham Palace* (New Africa Books, 2002), whose title is a synonym for Eaton Place in D 6. The rhythm & blues musical *District Six* penned by David Kramer and Taliep Petersen in 1986 is touring the world and enjoying great success (www.musicals.co.za).

# Durbanville

**Location:** 23km/14mi north-east of
Cape Town (N 1, exit 23, R 302)

**Internet:** www.durbanville.info

**Fancy shopping, surfing, art and craftwork and fine wines: a tour of Cape Town's northern suburbs includes beautiful beaches and a wine route through the Durbanville Hills.**

✳
Century City

🕐
Opening hours:
Daily 9am–9pm

The excursion could easily end as soon as exit 10 on the N 1, where Cape Town's largest **shopping mall** was built at the turn of the millennium. All national and international brand names are represented along **Canal Walk** (www.canalwalk.co.za). **Shuttle buses** ply the route between the large hotels in Cape Town's centre, Green Point and Seapoint several times a day. Public buses depart for the 12km/8mi to Century City between Monday and Saturday from the corner of Golden Acre and Adderley Street. Right in the centre, at 407 Canal Walk, the **MTNScienCentre** welcomes children with a fascinating multi-media display and interactive experiments. (Opening times: Sun 10am–6pm, Mon–Thu 9.30am–6pm, Fri, Sat 9.30am–8pm; www.mtnsciencentre.org.za). Further attractions are the 16ha/40-acre **Intaka Island** wetland and the **Ratanga Junction** theme park, complete with rollercoaster, crocodile alley and cabaret. (Opening times: daily 10am–5pm; www.ratanga.co.za).

🕐

🕐

✳ ✳
Bloubergstrand

The **most beautiful panoramic view** of Cape Town's emblem can be found 15km/9mi north of the city, at the endless white Bloubergstrand (▶photo p.136–137). The roaring waves of the Atlantic break

*Shop, eat and admire: Century City*

on the rocks right by the car park. It is usually too windy and cold for swimming, but instead visitors can watch **kite surfers** with the spectacular backdrop of Table Mountain, which is frequently hidden by a blue haze – hence the name Blouberg, »Blue Mountain«. Major international surfing championships are held at Bloubergstrand, where the bay makes a small bend that allows the south-easterlies to blow sideways to the shore.

✷
◄ Surfing

Driver further along the coastal road, which provides an endless succession of wonderful views, to reach the dune landscape of the broad Melkbos beach, where there is a large **golf course** among wonderful fynbos vegetation and also one of the few camp sites in the greater Cape Town area.

Melkbosstrand

Before the end of the 20 minutes' drive to Durbanville north-east of Cape Town, the N1 passes the **Tygerberg Centre**, a mega shopping venue with its own waterfront. Durbanville itself celebrated its 200th anniversary in 2006 and is today part of the City of Tygerberg. Afrikaans is still the predominant language in the Tygerberg Valley. In former times, the region's farmers congregated at the Pampoenkraal (»pumpkin kraal«) beneath the Durbanville Hills. The settlement was originally named Johannesfontein after »Jan« Jacobus Uys, the great-grandson of the first Uys at the Cape. It was renamed Durbanville in honour of the Cape governor Benjamin D'Urban (1834–38). The restored windmill of **»Onze Molen«** goes back to Uys' times. The locals also take pride in the **rose garden** on Durban Road, which contains over 500 species of roses. The 18-hole **golf course** is considered the most beautiful in the area. Historic 19th- and early 20th-century buildings under preservation orders include the Dutch Reformed Church on Weyers Avenue and the Edwardian residence of Kings Court on Church Street.

Durbanville

> **!** **Baedeker TIP**
>
> ### Ceramics, varnished crafts and ethnic jewellery
>
> On every first Saturday of the month (as well as Sunday during December), the Durbanville Craft Market is held under the ancient oaks in the garden of Rust en Vrede (8.30am–2pm), where more than 200 artisans exhibit. Night markets are also held on the last Friday of November and the last Friday before Christmas (5pm–10pm; www.durbanvillecraftmarket.co.za.

The cultural centre at 10 Wellington Road houses **Tygerberg Tourism**, a **pottery museum** and the **Rust-en-Vrede Art Gallery** for contemporary art. (Opening times: Mon–Fri 9am–5pm, Sat 8.30am–12.30pm). The official administrator's residence of **Rust-en-Vrede**, built in 1840–50, was a police station until 1856, and later a school and a law court. Poetry readings are held in the Gallery Café and advertised at www.litnet.co.za.

✷
◄ Rust-en-Vrede
Cultural Centre
🕐

Grape vines have been cultivated on the hills around Durbanville since the 18th century. The present wine route connects **seven vine-**

◄ Durbanville Wine
Route

**yards** that predominantly produce cabernet sauvignon, shiraz and merlot, but also chardonnay and sauvignon blanc. For daily tours and wine-tastings visit the wine-maker Martin Moore on the M13, a little beyond the crossroads with the Contermanskloof Road (www.durbanvillehills.co.za).

**Tygerberg Zoo** Continuing on route N1 in the direction of ▶ Paarl, exit 39 leads to the Cape Province's only zoo. Tigers, lions, zebras, cheetahs and monkeys can be seen on the 24ha/60-acre grounds. (Opening times: daily 9am–5pm; www.tygerbergzoo.co.za).

## ＊＊ Franschhoek

**C 3**

**Location:** 85km/53mi east of Cape Town; access via route N1 to Paarl, then follow the R 45

**Population:** 4000

**It is not just the name of this wine village that is French – a franco-phone culture of savouring wonderful wines and enjoying gor-geous food is also second nature here. Follow the Franschhoek Wine Route to famous wine cellars at the Cape.**

*The elegant gable of the town hall is in typical Cape Dutch style*

## Franschhoek *Map*

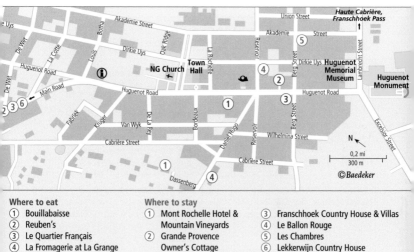

Akademie Street · Borra · Oak Ridge · Dirkie Uys · La Rochelle · Akademie Street · Union Street · Berg Street · Dirkie Uys · **Haute Cabrière, Franschhoek Pass** · Lambrecht Street

a Uys · De Wet · La Corte · Louis · Huguenot Road · Main Road · De Wet · Fabriek · Kruger · Van Wyk · De La Rey · Cabrière Street · Bordeaux · Daniel Hugo · Dassenberg · NG Church · Town Hall · Huguenot Road · Reservoir · Reservoir · Wilhelmina Street · Cabrière Street · Berg Street · Huguenot Road · **Huguenot Memorial Museum** · **Huguenot Monument** · Excelsior Street

N    0,2 mi    300 m    ©Baedeker

**Where to eat**
① Bouillabaisse
② Reuben's
③ Le Quartier Français
④ La Fromagerie at La Grange

**Where to stay**
① Mont Rochelle Hotel & Mountain Vineyards
② Grande Provence Owner's Cottage
③ Franschhoek Country House & Villas
④ Le Ballon Rouge
⑤ Les Chambres
⑥ Lekkerwijn Country House

Franschhoek's story began in 1688 with the arrival of 277 **Huguenots** who had fled their homeland after they were denied all religious and civil rights through the revocation of the Edict of Nantes. At that time they were not only granted religious freedom at the Cape, but also given land in what was then known as **Oliphantshoek** (Elephant Corner). The elephant herds were quickly decimated, the last of their number killed in 1847. Wine-growing began with the first Huguenot immigrants, of whom at least three are known to have been vintners. Today numerous **vineyards in the Franschhoek Valley** can be visited for cellar and wine-tasting tours, and Franschhoek, where first-class restaurants, fashionable boutiques and small art galleries line up on **Huguenot Street** next to the Cape Dutch **town hall**, is considered a **mecca for gourmets** at the Cape.

**✶ ✶**
Charming
»French Corner«

◄ Wine and food capital of the Cape

The **Huguenot Memorial** at the southern end of Huguenot Road was designed by C. Steynberg in 1938, on the occasion of the wine village's 250th anniversary. The Huguenot Cross on the four arches of the monument and the central figure of a woman holding a Bible and broken chain symbolize the new beginning. The museum documents the history of Franschhoek and the genealogy of important family names. For a break try the freshly baked scones in **Café Antoinette**. (Opening times: Mon–Sat 9am–5pm, Sun 2pm–5pm).

Huguenot
Memorial
Museum

◄ www.museum.
co.za
⊙

A multimedia presentation in the wine cellar presents the history, typical for the Drakenstein Valley and Franschhoek, of the **Solms-Delta** estate, which was founded in 1740. It lies on the R 45 in the

Museum
van de Caab

# ▶ VISITING FRANSCHHOEK

## INFORMATION

**Franschhoek Wine Valley Tourist Association**
29a Huguenot Road
Franschhoek
Tel. 021 / 876 3603
Fax 021 / 876 2768
www.franschhoek.org.za;
www.tourismfranschhoek.co.za

## WAFER THIN

Huguenot Fine Chocolates at 62 Huguenot Road has fine pralines made to Belgian recipes. Try the chocolate truffles with South African Amarula liquor.

## WHERE TO EAT

### ▶ Expensive

**① Bouillabaisse**
38 Main Road
Tel. 021 / 876 4430;
Watch Camil Haas as he prepares fresh oysters, kingklip and giant gambas. His wife and sommelier Ingrid can help with choosing wine.

**② Reuben's**
9 Huguenot Road
Tel. 021 / 876 3772
Reuben Riffel, South African Chef of the Year 2005, serves veritable delights in his top-class brasserie. Our tip: tandoori gambas and caramelized lemon tart. The bar was made from the wing of an old DC 10.

**③ Le Quartier Français**
16 Hugenot Road
Tel. 021 / 876 2151
www.lqf.co.za (reservations essential!).
Grilled scallops, marinaded warthog or wild berry soufflé? This gourmet restaurant has been one of the best in South Africa for years. 4–8 courses are served in the Tasting Room; the bistro Ici, which has a garden terrace, is less expensive. The winning team is made of by the owner Susan Huxter, director Linda Coltart and chef Margot Janse. They also offer 15 luxurious double rooms and three suites. The ladies are also socially committed and support KUSASA, which runs educational and Aids projects in the townships (www.thekusasaproject.org).

### ▶ Moderate

**④ La Fromagerie at La Grange**
13 Daniel Hugo Street
Tel. 021 / 876 2155
This 200-year-old barn is a popular meeting place for lunch. Afterwards you can choose from 40 different varieties of South African cheese. The owner, jazz pianist Derk Blaisse, and his band play every Friday from 5.30pm between November and Easter.

## WHERE TO STAY

### ▶ Luxury

**① Mont Rochelle Hotel & Mountain Vineyards**
Dassenberg Road
Franschhoek 7690
Tel. 021 / 876 2770
Fax 021 / 876 3788
www.montrochelle.co.za
This 5-star boutique hotel re-opened in 2006 to offer wine lovers the

*Fine living in the villas of the Franschhoek Country House*

ultimate experience. The Cape Dutch manor house has 16 gorgeous rooms and six high-class suites, and two restaurants treat guests to Provençal haute cuisine. Visitors can create their own blends from the wine cellar's barrels.

② *Grande Provence Owner's Cottage*
Main Road
Franschhoek 7690
Tel. 021 / 876 8600
Fax 021 / 876 8601
www.grandeprovence.co.za
Stylish colonial and designer furniture ensure a wonderful atmosphere in this romantic luxury villa on the Grande Provence vineyard. Allow chef Peter Tempelhoff to spoil you with his light cooking and try prize-winning wines during a cellar tour (tours daily 11am, 3pm, wine-tasting daily 10am–6pm). Young sculptors like Jacques Dhont and Angus van Zyl Taylor exhibit their work in the sculpture garden.

► **Mid-range**
④ *Le Ballon Rouge*
7 Reservoir Street East,
Franschhoek 7690
Tel. 021 / 876 2651, fax 021 / 876 3743
www.leballonrouge.co.za; 10 rooms.
Lovingly restored Victorian guest house with pool, Provençal cooking and crisp croissants for breakfast.

⑤ *Les Chambres*
3 Berg Street
Franschhoek 7690
Tel. 021 / 876 3136
Fax 021 / 876 2798
www.leschambres.co.za
Elegant town house with four romantic rooms in Victorian style.

► **Budget**
⑥ *Lekkerwijn Country House*
Groot Drakenstein 7680
Tel. 021 / 874 1122, fax 021 / 874 1465
www.lekkerwijn.com
Wendy Pickstone welcomes visitors in a Cape Dutch country house built by her grandfather and set at the foot of the Groot Drakenstein Mountains. B&B or holiday cottage, wine-tasting and lunch.

# BARON OF BUBBLY

**The success of the Haute Cabrière vineyard in Franschhoek began very low key in 1982. At that time, Achim von Arnim still worked as cellarer in Boschendal. From 1994 onwards, however, the »Baron of Bubbly« caused a sensation with South Africa's first sparkling wine, Pierre Jourdan.**

A bright red 2 CV bounces along the steep vineyard slopes above **Haute Cabrière** before tracing a loop around a building set into the hillside – the prize-winning **gourmet restaurant** where star chef Matthew Gordon and his wife Nicky are energetically making their preparations. It passes the visitor centre in the neo-Gothic vaults and, with a gentle jerk, finally comes to a standstill at the visitors' car park. **Achim von Arnim**, a tall man in his early sixties, emerges from the door of his 1967 Citroen 2 CV. This descendant of an ancient aristocratic line from Brandenburg in Germany sets no store by titles, but he is very keen on good humour. His media title, »**Baron Bubbly**«, pays homage to the success of South Africa's first sparkling wine – Pierre Jourdan. Teasing at his expense means nothing to a marketing professional like von Arnim. The view across his 11ha/27 acres of vines above the wine press is more important to him. The favourable site on the slopes of the Franschhoek Pass allows a wine harvest that easily fills his stores to the roof.

»10,000 vines per hectare, just like in Burgundy«, muses the baron, »all worked by hand!« The visitor centre displays the very shoes in which von Arnim once discovered the soil above an old gravel pit in Franschhoek. It was the same clay earth that stuck to the soles of his shoes as in Burgundy – perfect for **pinot noir** and **chardonnay**! Thus, when many were turning their backs on South Africa, he dared to pursue his dream. Around 2 million euros were invested before the big move from Burgundy to Haute Cabrière took place. It was a memorable date: 300 years earlier, on 22 December 1694, the Huguenot Pierre Jourdan had been given this land on the banks of the Franschhoek and had named the estate Cabrière, after a place near Avignon.

## »Sun, earth, wine and people...«

Thus the credo of the successful winemaker, who has elevated wine-making to an art. Von Arnim's career began with the oenologist Karl Werner in Cape Town, followed by a year with

Karl-Josef Hoch on the Germany Wine Road, before moving on in 1967 to the vintners' academy in Geisenheim, where he studied wine-growing and wine production. He met a wine-maker's daughter on the banks of the Moselle, and Hildegard von Arnim has now been his wife for almost forty years. They have four children. Achim von Arnim is proud that his family is the fifth generation that can claim both a German and South African parent. He claims he inherited his love of art from his mother and his sense of humour from his father.

## »Sabrage« on Saturdays

Of course, von Arnim is not allowed to call his sparkling wine »champagne« even though it is produced strictly according to traditional champagne methods, using either the blanc de blanc method exclusively with chardonnay, or the cuvée brut method that adds pinot noir. For tastings under the von Arnim coat of arms, crowned by two buffalo horns, **Pierre Jourdan** brut is used. It contains 60% chardonnay and 40% pinot noir. Von Arnim always invites a lady to join him during the »sabrage«: the opening of the bottle. French cavalry officers once opened bottles with their sabres when corks were stuck or broken. The officers, says von Arnim

with a twinkle, may have willingly died for their fatherland any time, but never thirsty! Decanting with a perfectly aimed chop of the sabre against the bottle neck completely separates the cork from the bottle top, and a net catches any glass shards.

## »Find yourself ...«

... is the message of Achim von Arnim's exhibition catalogue *Naked*, published in 2005. It contains his poems, prose and around 60 paintings chosen from a period of four decades. His project followed in the footsteps of his forebears. His ancestor Ludwig Achim von Arnim was a major proponent of the German Romantic movement who published a songbook entitled *Des Knaben Wunderhorn* and whose wife Bettina became famous through her exchange of letters with Goethe. Paintings by von Arnim decorate the arches at Haute Cabrière and, of course, his bright red 2 CV is also included. *Red Deux Chevaux* from 2004 can be seen projected onto a screen. **Cellar tours with wine-tasting and sabrage**: Sat 11am–1pm, tel: 021/876 2630; www.cabriere.co.za. **Wine sales**: Mon–Fri 8.30am–4.30pm Sat 11am–2pm. A reservation in the Haute Cabrière cellar restaurant to experience a veritable marriage of wine and food is a pure delight: tel. 021/876 3688; www.hautecabriere.com.

*The Huguenot Memorial recalls French immigrants fleeing religious persecution*

direction of ► Paarl. At present an archaeological excavation of a Stone Age Khoisan settlement is taking place here. (Opening times: daily 9am–5pm; www.solms-delta.co.za).

**★ ★**
**Franschhoek Wine Route**

Over two dozen **vineyards** offer wine-tastings and sales in and around Franschhoek (www.franschhoekwines.co.za). At **La Motte** on the R 45 in the direction of ► Paarl, vines were planted for the first time in 1752, the year when the pretty manor house was built. The passion of Jacques Borman's wine-making team centres around the brick-red shiraz that once again won awards in 2007. (Wine-tasting: Mon–Fri 9am–4.30pm, Sat 9am–3pm; www.la-motte.com).

At the **Dieu Donné** estate in the foothills of the Franschhoek Mountains (www.dieudonnevine yards.com), wine-maker Stephan du Toit creates white wines that also win international awards.

The **Grande Provence** estate not only has fine wines, but also choice cooking and contemporary Cape art (► p.179). World-

! **Baedeker TIP**

**Forest and valley**

The Huguenot Jean Le Long founded the beautiful Boschendal vineyard near the R 310 in the direction of ► Stellenbosch over 350 years ago. Wine-tastings are held in the La Rhône manor house built in 1812, complete with yellowwood floors and original 19th-century furniture. Try the ruby-red, faintly chocolatey shiraz, which is aged in French oak. The gourmet restaurant spoils visitors with the finest of Provençal cooking and also offers picnic lunches. (Opening times: daily 8.30am–4.30pm, cellar tours 10.30am and 11.30am by appointment, tel. 021/870 4272; www.boschendal.com).

class wines are also produced by **Graham Beck** (www.grahambeckwines.com), who learned his trade on the Haute Cabrière estate (►Baedeker Special p.180). A specialty of the **Chamonix** wine estate is their Swedish Bitter herb schnapps. Beautiful accommodation and good food is also available (www.chamonix.co.za). A must for grappa fans is a visit to South Africa's distilling star **Helmut Wilderer**. His place is on route R 45 in the direction of ►Paarl (www.wilderer.co.za).

**★ ★**
**Four Pass Tour**

Fans of the outdoors can combine top vineyards with superb panoramic views during a day's tour over the 701m/2300ft-high **Franschhoek Pass**. The route circles the 25ha/60-acre **Hottentots Holland Nature Reserve**, where antelopes, springboks, lynx, jackals and leopards live. Hikers can also explore the reserve on the **Boland Hiking Trail**. The renowned vineyards of **Thelema** (www.thelema.co.za) and **Tokara** can be reached via the R 310, which turns off shortly before ► Stellenbosch and leads over the 336m/1102ft **Helshoogte Pass**. Why not book a table with star chef Etienne Bonthuys (tel. 021 / 808 5959; www.tokararestaurant.co.za). The route continues on the N 2 over the spectacular **Sir Lowry's Pass** (402m/1319ft) until the turn-off to Grabouw on the R 321. Return to Franschhoek via the 525m/1723ft-high **Viljoen Pass**.

*The breathtaking panorama from Franschhoek Pass*

# ✶✶ Garden Route

**Location:** 430–640km/270–400mi east of Cape Town

**Internet:** www.tourismgardenroute.co.za

**The Garden Route between Mossel Bay and the mouth of the Storms River encompasses one of South Africa's most beautiful stretches of coast, a Garden of Eden on the Indian Ocean, with white dream beaches and enchanted lagoons, luxuriant rainforests and majestic mountains, fertile valleys and sleepy villages.**

## ✶ Mossel Bay

**Historic capital of the Garden Route**

Mossel Bay (pop. 90,000) is half way between Cape Town and Port Elizabeth. It has a picturesque harbour, **miles of sandy beaches** and sunshine 300 days of the year. Bartolomeu Diaz was the first European to set foot on South African soil at **»Mossel Bay«** in 1488, after having circumnavigated the ▶Cape of Good Hope . He was followed ten years later by Vasco da Gama, who initiated peaceful trading with the Khoikhoi. The big Diaz Festival is celebrated in February, and July is the month of the Super Splash Water Festival.

**✶✶ Bartolomeu Dias Museum**

The museum on Market Street exhibits a replica of the tiny **medieval caravel** used by Diaz to sail around the Cape. It was reconstructed in Portugal for the 500th anniversary of the famous seafarer's landing

## *Garden Route* Map

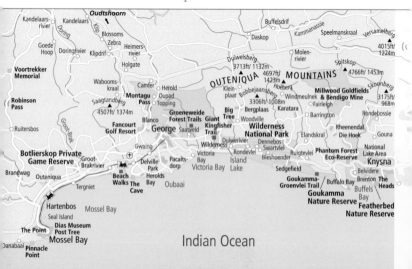

and then sailed from Lisbon to Mossel Bay on the original route taken by Diaz. Oysters and other mussels can be handled at the »touch tank« installed at the **Shell Museum & Aquarium**. A boot among the branches of the mighty **Post Office Milkwood Tree** once served as a post box for seafarers, and it was here that Pedro de Alaide left a warning of disturbances in Calcutta in 1500. Today, visitors can deposit postcards in a stone boot that is emptied twice daily. The spring christened »Aguada de Sao Bras«, where ships once replenished their drinking water, is still bubbling. A cross

*Replica of the small caravel with which Diaz rounded the Cape of Good Hope in 1488*

recalls South Africa's oldest Christian chapel, erected by the Portuguese Admiral da Nova in 1501. The Ethnobotanic Garden contains medicinal plants used by the San. The whitewashed Munrohoek Cottages were built by Alexander Munro in around 1830. His son was granted the first whaling permit. (Opening times: Mon–Fri 9am–4.45pm, Sat & Sun 9am–3.45pm).

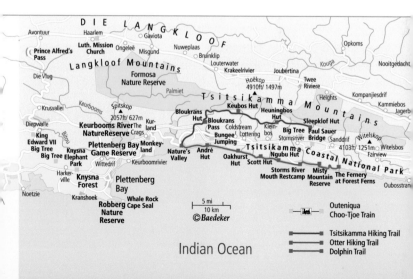

## *Highlights* Highlights of the Garden Route

**Seal Island**
Tour boats depart from the harbour at Mossel Bay to off-shore Seal Island, where thousands of **seals**, penguins, gannets and cormorants live. Sharks are often spotted on the way out there too.

**Cape St Blaize Lighthouse**
Since 1864 a **lighthouse** has been flashing east of Mossel Bay on the spit of land known as **The Point**. Majestic humpback and southern right whales can be observed from here. The **St Blaize Trail** leads from The Point Hotel (with its own natural tidal pool) 15km/9mi along the coast to Dana Bay.

**Prehistoric finds**
At **Pinnacle Point** 13km/8mi west of Mossel Bay, in 2007, fossilized bones, stone knives and the remains of shellfish were exposed during excavations in a cave that once lay 15m/50ft above today's sea level, proving that early man lived here and used the sea as a source of food 164,000 years ago. At **Blombos Cave**, 20km/13mi east of Still

## ! *Baedeker* TIP

**Botlierskop Private Game Reserve**
Take a malaria-free no more than 20km/13mi north of Mossel Bay, at the Botlierskop Game Reserve. 2500ha/6000 acres of former farmland is today home to lions, elephants, rhinos, zebras, buffaloes and black impalas. Safaris are possible by jeep, on foot, on horseback or even on the back of an elephant. 19 luxury tents in old-time colonial style by the river, complete with wood decks and four-poster beds. (Little Brak River, Mossel Bay, tel. 044/696 6055, fax 044/696 6272, www.botlierskop.co.za).

# ▶ VISITING MOSSEL BAY

## INFORMATION
### Mossel Bay Tourism
Market Street, Mossel Bay
Tel. 044 / 691 2202
www.visitmosselbay.co.za

## GARDEN ROUTE VARIETY
Those who don't wish to drive
themselves can also enjoy the Garden
Route's highlights on one of the
organized tours offered by many
travel agents (www. tourismcape
gardenroute.co.za).

## WHALE ENCOUNTERS
The sailing ship *Romonza* sets off
from Vincent Quay between July and
October and approaches to within
50m/50yd of the whales (www.mos-
selbay.co.za / romonza). Roy and Jacky
Portway offer pure adrenalin rushes in
the form of cage dives from their
15m/50ft catamaran to see great white
sharks (www.sharkafrica.co.za).

## WHERE TO EAT
### ▶ Moderate
### Café Gannet
Market Street
Mossel Bay
Tel. 044 / 691 1885
www.oldposttree.co.za
Whether he is cooking shark steak,
kingklip or fresh mussels, Cuan Payne
is well known for his excellent
seafood. The restaurant by the Dias
Museum is part of the elegant Mossel
Bay Protea Hotel, in a former trading
post of 1846, complete with views of
Santos Bay.

## WHERE TO STAY
### ▶ Mid-range
### Eight Bells Mountain Inn
On the R 328 going out of Mossel Bay
in the direction of Oudtshoorn

Tel. 044 / 631 0000
Fax 044 / 631 0004
www.eightbells.co.za
Jean and Peter Brown's guest house
(restored in 2008) offers a cosy
atmosphere, an enchanting garden
with pool and horse riding and tennis,
35km/22mi north of Mossel Bay, at
the foot of the Robinson Pass.

### Bay Lodge On The Beach
29 Bob Bouwer Crescent
Bayview Mossel Bay
Tel. 044 / 695 0690
Fax 044 / 695 1711
www.bay-lodge.co.za
Jan und Lydia Kruger have eight
beautiful rooms right by the sea.
Breakfast includes views of the end-
less sandy beach.

### ▶ Budget
### Allemans Dorphuis
94 Montagu Street
Mossel Bay
Tel. 044 / 690 3621
www.mosselbay.co.za/allemans
Lovingly restored Victorian house
with six rooms near the harbour.

Bay, there was another find of spearheads 77,000 years old and a Stone Age necklace made of snail shells and animal tendons that is among the oldest items of human artwork ever found. Today they are kept at the ►South African Museum in Cape Town.

## George

**★ ★**
**Golfing mecca**

With a population of 140,000, George is the **largest town on the Garden Route**. Founded in 1811, it was named after King George III and occupies a plateau at the foot of the Outeniqua Mountains. The author Anthony Trollope described George as »the world's loveliest village« over a century ago. Today its significance lies more in being the terminus of the **Outeniqua Choo-Tjoe** train route and a golfing mecca that draws sports enthusiasts.

**George Museum ►**

The museum is housed in the **Old Drostdy** on Courteney Street, built in 1811, and is dedicated to regional history. It includes an exhibition of pieces collected by the publisher of the George and Knysna Herald, Charles Sayer: for example mechanical musical instruments and typewriters. (Opening times: Mon–Fri 9am–4.30pm, Sat 10am–12.30pm).

*South Africa's no. 1: guest players are also welcome at the championship courses of the Fancourt Hotel and Golf Estate*

# ► VISITING GEORGE

## INFORMATION

**Garden Route
Regional Tourism**
34 York Street, George
Tel. 044 / 873 6314
www.tourismgardenroute.co.za

**The City of
George Tourism**
124 York Street, George
Ttel. 044 / 801 9295
www.tourismgeorge.co.za

## OUTENIQUA
## CHOO-TJOE TRAIN

**Full steam ahead!**
The popular historic steam train was
in operation between the railway
stations of George and Knysna until
the autumn of 2006, when a landslide
close to George forced a change of
course onto the route Diaz Museum–Mossel Bay–George Railway
Museum. Departures: April–Aug
Mon, Wed, Fri; Sep–March Mon–Sat
10am from George, 2.15pm from
Mossel Bay; mid Dec–mid Jan also at
10.10am from Mossel Bay and 2pm
from George.
Timetable information:
Tel. 044 / 801 8288
www.onlinesources.co.za/chootjoe

## WHERE TO EAT

### ► Expensive

**The Conservatory
at Meade House**
91 Meade Street, George, tel. 044 / 874
1938; www.meadehouse.co.za. Darren
Roberts, who used to be head chef at
the Fancourt Hotel, creates wonderful
dishes such as trawlerman's pie with
mussels, fish and crabs in one of the
oldest and most beautiful buildings in
town.

*Baedeker recommendation*

THE GOLFER

**Top-class putting**
Is a visit to South Africa's
number one golf course on
your list of things to do?
According to *Golf Digest* that
would be Montagu Place
at the Fancourt Hotel.
World-class standards
are also maintained
by the Fancourt-
Outeniqua Golf
Course and
the left-
handed course designed by Gary Player, on
which you can easily get the impression of
playing on a Scottish coast. Bramble Hill is a
public pay-for-play course. Non-residents
are also welcome to play here (Fancourt
Hotel & Country Club Estate, see below).

## WHERE TO STAY

### ► Luxury

**Fancourt Hotel,
Country Club & Golf Estate**
Montagu Street, Blanco, George
Tel. 044 / 804 0000
Fax 044 / 804 0700
www.fancourt.com
Without doubt one of the world's top
golf resorts with three high-quality
championship courses. Added to this
are refined rooms with panoramic
views of the Outeniqua Mountains,
gourmet restaurants and, for relaxation, Roman baths, a Jacuzzi and pool.

**Serendipity Guesthouse**
Freesia Avenue
Wilderness
Tel. 044 / 877 0433
Fax 086 / 671 7992
www.serendipitywilderness.com

Lizelle Stolze spoils her guests with haute cuisine at her stylish guest house on the lagoon. All four rooms have direct access to the sea.

▶ **Mid-range**
*The Dune Guest Lodge*
31 Die Duin, Wilderness
Tel. / fax 044 / 877 0298
www.thedune.co.za
Gary and Melisa Grimes' beautiful lodge stands on the dune at Wilderness. All four rooms offer superb views to the sea.

*The Waves*
6 Beach Road, Victoria Bay
Tel. 044 / 889 0166

An ideal location on the enchanting Victoria Bay. The charming little house built in 1906 has three rooms and two holiday apartments and is reached via a wooden jetty.

▶ **Budget**
*Land's End*
The Point, Victoria Bay
Tel. 044 / 889 0123
Fax. 044 /889 0141
www.vicbay.com
Only patrons of the B&B are allowed to park in tiny Victoria Bay. The last house at the end of the bay has four comfortable rooms right by the beach.

**Dutch Reformed Church** ▶
The Dutch Reformed church on Meade Street was built in 1842 and contains a pulpit carved of stinkwood. The pillars and dome are made of yellowwood. South Africa's oldest Catholic church is the church of **St Peter und Paul**, consecrated in 1843.

✳
**Outeniqua Railway Museum** ▶
It is worth casting an eye into the railway museum before making a nostalgia trip on the **Outeniqua Choo-Tjoe narrow-gauge railway** (▶ p.189). 13 engines and old-time carriages can be admired there, including the Royal Train of 1947 and Paul Kruger's private carriage.
🕐 (Opening times: Mon–Sat 8am–5pm).

✳
**Outeniqua Hiking Trail**
It takes seven days to walk the **108km/67mi-long hiking path** through the mountains known to the Khoikhoi as the »honey carriers«. The route passes from Beervlei in the Bergplaas State Forest all the way to Harkerville Forest near Knysna (www.tiscover.co.za/outeniqua-nat urereserve). As an alternative to the N2, the partly unpaved **Seven Passes Road** goes from George through dense forest and past green meadows and historic farms to Knysna. Like so many others, the valleys and gorges of the »seven passes« of Swart River, Kaaimans, Touw River, Hoogekral, Karatara, Homtini and Phantom were surveyed by **Thomas Bain** from 1867.

! *Baedeker* TIP

**Through the wilderness by canoe**
Paddle from Wilderness all the way to the end of the calm Touw River, which is 10–15m (35–49ft) wide. A good half-hour's walk through the rainforest then leads to a waterfall and a swim, before heading back. Eden Adventures hires out canoes, and also offers guided tours (Eden Adventures, tel. / fax 044 / 877 0179; www.eden.co.za).

Pink flamingoes, storks and kingfishers – the wonderful lake landscape 15km/9mi east of George is a **paradise for water fowl**. Six hiking paths cover »The Lakes«. For example, the 10km/6mi-long **Pied Kingfisher Trail** is a circular route leading from the Ebb & Flow Visitor Center along the Serpentine River and the sea. During the season, whales and dolphins can be spotted along the miles and miles of often untouched sandy beaches.

★ ★
Wilderness
National Park

The adjacent dune landscape to the east, between Sedgefield and Buffels Bay, is also a **paradise for birds**, with 14km/9mi of beaches. The freshwater **Groenvlei** lake is home to otters and green meerkats.

★
Goukamma
Nature Reserve

Shortly before reaching Knysna, it is worth making a detour to the ghost town of Millwood. Gold was found in the forests here in 1876, causing a regular **gold rush**. Almost 1000 gold miners lived in the camps at Millwood in around 1885, but when gold was discovered at the Witwatersrand in Transvaal in 1886, most of them moved there and the last gold mine here was closed in 1924. These days the gold rush is relived in the Materolli Museum and on tours through the Bendigo Mine. (Opening times: Tue–Sun 10.30am–4pm).

Millwood
Goldfields &
Bendigo Mine

🕐

## ★ ★ Knysna

With its wonderful lagoon at the foot of the Outeniqua Mountains, Knysna – pronounced »nicenah« – is a veritable **holiday-maker's paradise**. Over 200 species of fish and even seahorses live in saltwater lakes and swamps that have been declared a **national natural heritage**.

Lagoon town on
the Indian Ocean

*Freshly caught Knysna oysters at Oystercatcher on the waterfront*

## ⓞ VISITING KNYSNA

### INFORMATION
**Knysna Tourist Centre**
40 Main Road, Knysna
Tel. 044 / 382 0303
www.tourismknysna.co.za

### FIT FOR FUN?
Boat tours, sailing trips and sundowner cruises with champagne and oysters can be booked directly on the waterfront. Take a quad bike into the hills, a canoe through the lagoon or brave the spectacular abseil from the 121m/397ft-high Western Head. Seal Adventures at the waterfront run exciting trips (tel. 044 / 382 5599; www.sealadventures.co.za). At Eastern Head there is also the option of driving out to the *Paquita* wreck, which lies at a depth of 15m/50ft (www.headsadventurecentre.co.za).

### WHERE TO EAT
#### ▸ Moderate
*34° South*
Knysna Quays
Waterfront
Tel. 044 / 382 7268
www.34-south.com
The shop sells seafood delicacies and choice wines, while the terrace serves up fresh seafood and oysters.

*The Dry Dock*
Waterfront Shop 1
Tel. 044 / 382 7310
Chef Rudy's specialties are grilled giant crayfish and catch of the day with lemon, pineapple and chilli.

### WHERE TO STAY
#### ▸ Luxury
*The St. James of Knysna*
The Point
P.O. Box 1242
Knysna 6570

Tel. 044 / 382 6750
Fax 044 / 382 6756
www.stjames.co.za
Superb 5-star hotel with gourmet restaurant and a large garden on the shore of the lagoon. Book a room in the main building with view out to sea.

---

### *Baedeker recommendation*

**Phantom Forest**
**Eco Reserve and Lodge**
Phantom Pass Road
7km/4.5mi before Knysna
Tel. 044 / 386 0046
www.phantomforest.com
This prize-winning eco-lodge above the Knysna River serves delicious African menus in the Forest Boma, which is designed as a traditional round hut. The Moroccan dinner gives guests the feeling of being in the *Arabian Nights*, the ten tree suites with panoramic views bed them in silk and satin, while a massage by the pool promises rejuvenation in harmony with nature.

---

#### ▸ Mid-range
*Leisure Isle Lodge*
87 Bayswater Drive
Leisure Isle
Knysna 6570
Tel. 044 / 384 0462
Fax 044 / 384 1027
www.leisureislelodge.co.za
An oasis of peace with 11 tastefully decorated rooms on the lagoon island of Leisure Island. Hear the ocean waves during dinner at the Daniela Restaurant on Bollard Bay and pamper yourself at the spa with an Indian massage.

Hotels, holiday houses and pensions line the 21ha/52-acre lagoon, whose mouth to the river is guarded by two giant sandstone rocks: the **Knysna Heads**. Tour boats, the floating restaurant *John Benn* and the *Rivercat* paddle steamer all travel to the Knysna Heights from the lively **waterfront** with its fish restaurants, souvenir shops and small boutiques. The boat tours take four hours to reach the Featherbed Nature Reserve and its huge milkwood trees and »blue duikers«, South Africa's smallest antelope species (www. featherbed.co.za). The famous **Outeniqua Choo-Tjoe** steam train, which used to run between George and Knysna, now connects George and Mossel Bay (►p.189).

**Knysna National Lake Area**

◄ Featherbed Nature Reserve

Knysna's history begins with **George Rex** (1765–1839) in 1803. His lavish lifestyle underlined the suspicion that he was, in fact, an illegitimate son of George III who had been forced to leave England. Officially, however, Knysna was not founded until 1825, by the Cape governor. The places for up-market **shopping** are the Woodmill Lane Centre and the lively **Main Street**. **Millwood House** on Queens Street contains an exhibition on George Rex and the 19th-century gold rush, and was originally located at the Millwood gold prospectors' camp (► p.191 Opening times: Mon–Fri 9am–4.30pm, Sat 9.30am–12.30pm). The region's **young artists** exhibit in the Knysna Fine Arts Gallery next door (no. 45, www.finearts.co.za). The small **Mitchell's Brewery** on Vigilance Drive brews four types of beer (tours Mon–Fri 10.30am & 3pm; www.mitchellsknysnabrewery.com). Over 100 fynbos species are displayed and described north of the town centre, at **Pledge Park**.

**Relaxing and bathing**

## ! *Baedeker* TIP

### Knysna Oysters

World-class oysters are produced in the lagoon. The **Oyster Festival** in July lasts ten days and draws tens of thousands of visitors every year. Be sure to try the »wild coastal oysters« that are harvested from the rocks between Riversdale and Tsitsikamma.
Fresh gourmet oysters served in a fun atmosphere can be enjoyed at the **Knysna Oyster Company** (tel. 044 / 382 6941) on Long Street on Thesen Island, at the **Oystercatcher** (tel. 044 / 382 9995) on the waterfront and at **Paquita's** (tel. 044 / 384 0408) on George Rex Drive near the Knysna Heads.

**Brenton-on-Sea**

A branch road turns off for Brenton-on-Sea at the north-western end of the lagoon, passing the **Belvidere Estate** and its private chapel, constructed in 1855 by the son-in-law of the legendary George Rex. The mansion dates from 1849 and is now a 4-star hotel (www.belvidere.co.za). Enjoy the sunset after a day of swimming on the **wonderful sand** of Brenton Beach.

**Prince Alfred's Pass**

A spectacular though occasionally very rough road leads north through the Outeniqua Mountains via the Prince Alfred Pass, built between 1864 and 1867, to **Avontuur** in the Langkloof Valley. This pass is another of **Thomas Bain's** amazing achievements.

✳
**Knysna Forest**

www.
knysnaforesttours.
co.za ►

The best way to explore **South Africa's largest forested area** (80,000ha/200,000 acres), which spreads between Knysna and Plettenberg Bay, is one of the three **Elephant Walks** that start at the Diepvalle Forest Station: access via the R 339 in the direction of Uniondale. Guided tours last 3–4 hours. The route leads past the **King Edward VII Tree**, a 46m/151ft-high yellowwood tree that is at least 600 years old. This is the only place where the light green parrot, the **Knysna loerie** (Tauraco corythaix) is native. It is best spotted during flight, as the underside of its wings are a bright carmine red ► (image, p.113). The challenging 9km/5.5mi circular **Kranshoek Walk** follows the dramatic cliff coast in the direction of Plettenberg. The **Perdkop Tough Nature Walk** requires fitness and a permit from the forest station. It begins at the Harkerville Forest Station and leads 10km/6mi through forest and gorges. An easy 6km/4mi circular route for hikers and mountain bikers covers the coastal region around **Harkerville Lodge** (www.harkerville.co.za).

✳
**Knysna Elephant Park**

🕐

The elephant park, 9km/5.5mi before reaching Plettenberg Bay, is an amazing experience for all the family. At the beginning of the 19th century there were still 600 elephants in the Knysna Forest. Today just six elephants live in the park, and they came from the Kruger National Park. A tour takes around two hours and includes **feeding and a hands-on experience**. The museum in the main building has more information on the elephants. (Opening times: daily 8.30am–4.30pm; www.knysnaelephantpark.co.za).

## ✳ Plettenberg Bay

✳ ✳
**Dream beaches along the Indian Ocean**

The turquoise sea and endless white sandy beaches make Plettenberg – affectionately known as »Plett« by the locals – one of the **most popularseaside resorts** along the Garden Route. There are numerous hotels, fancy **shopping malls** and three outstanding **golf courses**. Anyone who is anybody has a holiday house in »South Africa's St Tropez«, and there are prices to match. It also means that during the holiday season the population jumps from 10,000 to 80,000. The sun shines on average 320 days per year here, and the water temperatures

*Endless beautiful white sand: Plettenberg's beaches on the Indian Ocean*

are usually above 20ºC/69ºF. The Portuguese seafarer Mesquita da Perestrolo already recognized the advantages of this »wonderfully beautiful bay« in 1576 and christened it the **»baia formosa«**, but it received its present name at the end of the 18th century, when it was named after Governor Joachim von Plettenberg. Today, the **All That Jazz Festival** in September is famous. At Easter and during December, Plett is a rendezvous for the jet set, when it becomes South Africa's **polo town**.

8km/5mi south of Plett, Robberg Peninsula and its **seal colony** that lives at the »Mountain of the Seal« can be explored during 1–4-hour **hiking tours** (www.robbergwalks.homestead.com).

✳ **Robberg Nature Reserve**

5km/3mi north of Plett, a popular region for **canoe trips** is the Keurbooms River, which can be paddled in two days. Boat hire is available from the Angling Club (tel. 044 / 535 9740).

**Keurbooms River Nature Reserve**

On no account pass up the chance to take a tour through Monkeyland – a 12ha/30-acre forest in which lemurs, squirrel monkeys, baboons, gibbons and guenons (meerkats) saved from zoos, private owners and experimental laboratories enjoy their freedom. The 128m/420ft-long swinging bridge is a highlight. Another excursion

✳ ✳ **Monkeyland**

# ► VISITING PLETTENBERG BAY

## INFORMATION

### Plettenberg Bay Tourism
Main Street, Shop 35
Melville's Corner Centre
Plettenberg Bay
Tel. 044 / 533 4065
www.goplett.co.za
www.tourismplettenbergbay.co.za

## »FATBOYS«

... is a popular phrase for whales in
Plett and that is precisely the name
Ocean Safaris (Hopwood Street, tel.
044 / 533 4963; www.oceansafaris. co.-
za) chose for their largest boat for
whale charters. Southern right whales
and humpback whales can be seen off
the coast, while bottlenose dolphins
play near Arch Rock and thousands of
seals can be spotted at the Robberg
Peninsula. Ocean Adventures' boats set
off for whale charters from Central
Beach (tel. 044 / 533 4897; www.ocea-
nadventures.co.za).

## PURE ADRENALIN

The Bloukrans River Bridge marks the
border between the Eastern and
Western Cape and, according to the
Guinness Book of Records, this is also
where you can take the world's highest
commercial bungee jump from a
height of 216m/709ft. Alternatively,
you can whiz alongside the bridge arch
on a 200m/650ft-long cable in the
Flying Fox (www.faceadrenalin.com).

## WHERE TO EAT

### ► Moderate
### Cornuti al Mare
1 Perestrella Street
Plettenberg Bay
Tel. 044 / 533 1277
The place to be and be seen in Plett!
Excellent pizzas, juicy tuna and cous-
cous, beer on tap and good wines.

### Nguni
The White House
6 Crescent Street
Plettenberg Bay,
Tel. 044 / 533 6710
The specialties here are grilled kudu,
springbok salad and braised leg of
lamb.

## WHERE TO STAY

### ► Luxury
### The Plettenberg
Look-out Rocks, P.O. Box 719
Plettenberg Bay 6600
Tel. 044 /533 2030
Fax 044 / 533 2074
www.plettenberg.com
This 5-star Relais & Chateaux Hotel
with 38 rooms shines in white on a
rock promontory with breathtaking
views of the sea. Try the delicious fish
dishes in the Sand Restaurant and treat
yourself at the Carchele Spa.

## Baedeker recommendation

### Tsala Treetop Lodge
P.O. Box 454, Plettenberg Bay 6600
Tel. 044 / 501 1111
Fax 044 / 501 1100
www.hunterhotels.com. 10km/6mi west of
Plettenberg, this spectacular lodge is set in
the crowns of trees, deep in the twilight
world of the Tsitsikamma National Park.
Wooden walkways wind 6m/20ft above the
forest floor to ten extravagant suites built of
stone, wood and glass that make for an
unusual and romantic holiday experience.
Delicious pan-African cuisine and top
service.

### ► Mid-range
### Southern Cross Beach Hotel
1 Capricorn Lane

*Stylish gourmet dining and sleeping: The Plettenberg ticks all the boxes*

Plettenberg Bay 6600
Tel. 044 / 533 3868, fax 044 / 533 3866;
www.southerncrossbeach.co.za
This elegant colonial-style villa is set right on the beach and its five rooms were designed in the colours of sand, sky and sea.

### Tsitsikamma Lodge
P.O. Box 10, Storms River 6308
Tel. 042 / 280 3802
Fax 042 / 280 3702
www.tsitsikamma.com
An award-winning location 75km/ 47mi west of Plettenberg with 30 block cabins, all complete with jacuzzi, their own veranda and grill area. A cosy restaurant serves South African home cooking.

### ► Budget
### Dolphins' Playground B & B
3 Tillamook Avenue
Plettenberg Bay 6600
Tel. 44 / 5333654
www.dolphinsplayground.co.za
Pleasant rooms with sea views at Robberg Beach.

could be a stroll through one of the largest aviaries in the world: Bird of Eden, 16km/10mi east of Plettenberg on the N 2, exit Forest Hall. (Opening times: daily 8am–6pm, www.monkeyland.co.za).    ⊙

The small village of Nature's Valley is still an insider's tip. It lies off the N 2, along the R 102 that winds its way down the Groot River gorge, where the river forms a paradisiacal lagoon. Hike along the **endless white sandy beach** where, with a bit of luck, otters can be spotted in their natural habitat. Alternatively, walk the 6km/4mi circular **Kalanderkloof Trail** through dense coastal forest to giant yellowwood trees.    ★ Nature's Valley

# »LAND OF MUCH WATER«

... »Tsitsikamma« – this name was given to the mouth of the River Storms delta by the Khoisan over 2000 years ago. Today, the national park founded in 1964 protects an 80km/50mi stretch of largely untouched coastline that contains one of South Africa's last rainforests: a dream for all nature lovers and hikers.

Plentiful water from rivers and 1200mm/50in of annual rainfall sustains a luxuriant fynbos vegetation in wild craggy mountains and coastal landscape, which attracts hikers in particular, but also kayakers, mountain bikers and other adventure sports enthusiasts. The **Tsitsikamma Coastal National Park** is a paradise for birds and home to green guenons, baboons, fish otters and small antelopes. Divers can discover fantastic ocean fauna, and there are regular sightings of dolphins and whales off the coast. The park is open all year round and there are some wonderful places to stay (p.196). Most visitors choose the short route from the Storms River Mouth Restcamp to the mouth of the river, where they cross the **Storms River Mouth Bridge** (completely renewed in 2006) to reach an ocean viewpoint. Signs along the path describe the unique plant world, including giant ferns, orchids and centuries-old, 40m/130ft-high yellowwood trees. Those with steady nerves can take boat rides up the Storms River. The three-hour **Treetop Canopy Tour** in the rainforest is a unique experience. Secured in a seat attached to a steel cable, visitors speed through the tree tops at a height of 30m/100ft to reach ten viewing platforms (www.treetop tour.com).

## On the Otter Trail

Three of South Africa's most beautiful hiking routes explore the national park (p.185). Due to its popularity, the strenuous 42km/26mi **Otter Trail**, from the mouth of the River Storms to Nature's Valley via the coastal cliffs, has to be booked a year in advance (www.sanparks.org; www.footprint.co.za/otter.htm). The less frequented **Tsitsikamma Trail** follows a 64km/40mi route in the opposite direction inland (MTO Ecotourism George, tel. 044 874 4363; www.mtoecotourism.co.za; www.tsitsikamma.info). The Otter Trail and Tsitsikamma Trail can both be completed in five days. The 17km/11mi **Dolphin Trail** is easier. It goes from the Storms River to the Sanddrift River and includes luggage transport and two nights in beautiful lodges (www.dolphintrail.co.za).

1km/0.5mi east of the Storms River by the **Tsitsikamma Coastal National Park**, near the N 2, stands the **Big Tree** (Groot Boom): a giant yellowwood believed to be over 800 years old. It is 37m/121ft high and it takes eight people to embrace the trunk, which has a diameter of 8.5m/28ft. The eastern boundary of the Garden Route is marked by the **Paul Sauer Bridge**. Its 130m/427ft-high arch spans the **Storms River**. The viewpoint at the west side of the bridge offers superb views of the **Tsitsikamma State Forest** to the north of the N 2, with its dense rainforest and many jungle trees higher than 50m/160ft. Mushrooms, mosses and lichen indicate the high rainfall here. A 4km/2.5mi hiking track to the Big Tree begins at the Paul Sauer Bridge.

**Rainforest giants**

## ! *Baedeker* TIP

### Take a walk on the wild side

7km/4.5mi north-west of Plettenberg, it is just a quarter of an hour's drive to the 2000ha/5000-acre Plettenberg Bay Game Reserve, a private reserve near Wittedrift. During two-hour safaris on horseback, on foot or in open jeeps, rhinos, lions, buffaloes, zebras, gnus, hippos, springboks, impalas and giraffes can be spotted. Those who want to stay overnight can book the Uur Baroness Game Lodge, which has five luxury suites and two pretty cottages (Uniondale / Wittedrift Road, tel. 044/535 0000; www.plettenbergbaygamereserve.co.za).

## »Big Five« without Malaria

Many visitors to South Africa combine the Garden Route with a safari in the malaria-free **game reserves of the Eastern Cape Province**, located between **Port Elizabeth** and Grahamstown. In recent years, more and more farmers have given up animal husbandry in favour of creating private game reserves in which large animals such as elephants, lions and giraffes now roam.

**»Out of Africa« feeling**

The state-run Addo Elephant Park 75km/47mi north of Port Elizabeth guarantees fascinating wildlife viewing. At 164,000 ha/630 sq mi it is South Africa's third-largest national park and was founded in 1931. It is not only home to over **400 elephants**, but also to buffaloes, rhinos, antelopes, lions, leopards, hyenas, and countless bird species. By 2010, the National Park is due to be extended to almost 360,000 ha/1400 sq mi, which will include a marine reserve on the Indian Ocean and then make it home to the world's largest popula-

**✶ ✶**
**Addo Elephant National Park**

◄ www.sanparks.org/parks/addo

*Stars of the steppe: elephant families in the Addo Elephant Park*

tion of Cape gannets, as well as whales and great white sharks, not to mention the big game on land. It will be a unique place to see the **Big Seven**! Trained **»Eyethu Hop-on« guides** who advise on the latest locations of game can be booked in the park and join visitors in their own vehicles.

★ ★
Shamwari
Game Reserve

The **private reserve** halfway between Port Elizabeth and Grahamstown is also home to big game. Adrian Gardiner realized his dream to turn a 25,000ha/100 sq mi former farm on the Bushman's River into a reserve for the **»Big Five«** and built six luxury suites in ethnic style. An open overland vehicle is used for two daily safari drives to seek out rhinos, giraffes, , elephants, zebras, lions, leopards, buffaloes, antelopes and waterbucks (www.sham wari. com).

The entrance to the 7500ha/18,000-acre **private Lalibela game reserve** is barely 15km/10mi to the east, on the N 2, and is home to cheetahs, giraffes, hippos, gnus, elands, kudus and

! **Baedeker TIP**

**African Dream**

Gorah Elephant Camp, with its 11 thatched-roof colonial style luxury tents, in the southern part of Addo Park was the first lodge to get a private license. Watch animals from the elegant restaurant and the terrace by the pool as they come to the nearby watering hole. Unforgettable: candlelight dinner (www.hunterhotels.-com). The nine suites of the Nguni River Lodge, which opened in 2006, are also on 5-star level. It is located above the plains and offers a wonderful view (www.ngunilodges.co.za). The nostalgic Elephant House has nine comfortable rooms ans is located 7 km outside of the park – Tip: book an elephant ride through the Zuurberg Mountains (www.elephanthouse.co.za).

bushbucks. There are three romantic lodges as well as a pool, viewing deck and delicious African cuisine. Why not book the eight-room Tree Tops Lodge on wood posts, set among the rainforest canopy? (www.lalibela.net).

**★ ★**
**Lalibela**
**Game Reserve**

# ✳ Government Avenue

E 3 / 4

**Location:** City Bowl, between Adderley Street and Orange Road

**Mighty oaks line Cape Town's major promenade – the city's cultural heart. This is the seat of parliament and the state president, and also where you will find the ▶South African Museum, the ▶Jewish Museum and the ▶South African National Gallery.**

From January to June, **South Africa's parliament** is in session at the northern end of Government Avenue. The free tours last one hour.

**Houses of**
**Parliament**

*Nelson Mandela held his inaugural speech as president of the new South Africa at the Houses of Parliament*

! *Baedeker* TIP

**Tea time at the »Nellie«**
According to the London Sunday Times, the Mount Nelson Hotel on Orange Road serves the best tea in the world. Treat yourself to a break on the lovely garden terrace of this luxury hotel or order some salmon sandwiches, South African cheese, the irresistible petit fours or the famous scones with strawberry jam. Afternoon tea is served from 4.30pm to 5.30pm; www.mount nelson.co.za.

Tours:
Mon–Fri 8am–noon;
www.parliament.
gov.za

Bookings can be made at the **Tours Office**, tel. 021 / 503 2266. Meet 15 minutes beforehand at 90 Plein Street and don't forget your passport. Attending parliamentary debates is only possible via the Public Relations Office (tel. 021 / 403 2460). The foundation stone was laid by Sir Henry Barkly in 1875, and the neo-classical building with Corinthian pillars was then inaugurated amidst controversy in 1885. It was completed by Henry Greaves. A statue of Queen Victoria adorns the garden. The debating chamber was the scene of a violent political event on 6 September 1966: Hendrik Verwoerd, state president and chief architect of apartheid, was murdered by the parliamentary employee Demitrios Tsafen, who stabbed him four times.

**De Tuynhuis**

The **state president's residence** can be visited. Initially built as a guest house in 1701, the »garden house« was extended in 1751 and gained its present form in 1795, the work of Louis Thibault. Anton Anreith designed the decorative arches with Neptune, Mercury and the insignia of the VOC – the world's oldest company logo.

**Bertram House Museum**

Opening hours:
Tue–Thu
10am–4.30pm;
www.iziko.org.za/
bertram

Bertram Museum, at the southern end of Government Avenue, offers an insight into **19th-century colonial lifestyle**. The oldest documents relating to this late Georgian brick building go back to 1794, when Andreas Momsen was granted the land. The present estate is believed to have been built from 1839 by the notary John Barker, who named it after his wife Ann Bertram Findlay. A spiral staircase leads to the museum, which was opened in 1984, and whose heart is the Lidderdale donation of furniture from the second half of the 18th century, as well as valuable English and Chinese porcelain. During summer, chamber music is played on the piano dating from 1906. Just a few steps further, at 37 Orange Street, stands the **Michaelis Art School** (www.michaelis.uct.ac.za), which is the top place in the Cape to study the arts. Next door to the Hiddingh Campus, the creative **Little Theatre** celebrated its 75th jubilee in 2006.

# Grand Parade

E 3

**Location:** between Darling and Castle Street, City Bowl

**The old parade ground has linked the ►Castle of Good Hope with ►Adderley Street since 1710, and every Wednesday and Saturday this giant square is transformed into a colourful flea market.**

The colourful **flower market** of Trafalgar Place opens the way from ►Adderley Street to the Grand Parade, on which a big **clothes and food market** is held every Wednesday and Saturday. On other days up to 600 cars can park here. Red lines along the Plein Street side outline the site of the first earth and wood fort built by Jan van Riebeeck. The Grand Parade still serves for political announcements and major events, such as the 4th Homeless World Cup football championship, held here in 2006: President Mbeki and thousands of fans cheered over 1800 goals scored by 48 participating national teams.

Parade square and flea market

*Markets instead of military: the Grand Parade square becomes a flea market on Saturdays*

*
**City Hall**

On 11 February 1990 over 100,000 people listened to Nelson Mandela's famous Freedom Speech from the balcony of **City Hall**, shortly after his release. »Madiba« demanded freedom and universal suffrage for the black majority. The town hall on Darling Street was completed in 1905 and built from Table Mountain sandstone in a neo-Renaissance style. Its interior contains fine mosaics, marble stairs and an organ built by Norman Beard with no less than 3165 pipes that was dedicated to King Edward VII and Queen Alexandra. The 60m/200ft clock tower is modelled on Big Ben and its chimes have been playing since 1923. The **Cape Town Philharmonic Orchestra (CPO)** puts on excellent classical concerts in City Hall every Thursday and Sunday, and the ambitious Cape Town Philharmonic Youth Orchestra has been promoting young musicians of all races since 2003.

Ticket service: tel. 021 / 465 2029; www.cpo.org.za ►

**Nelson Mandela Library**

The municipal library, which used to be housed in City Hall, was moved to the neighbouring **Old Drill Hall** in 2007. The building was restored thanks to a US$ 2 million donation from the New York Carnegie Foundation.

## ★ ★ Greenmarket Square

E 3

**Location:** City Bowl

**Cape Town's most beautiful Art Deco buildings are on Greenmarket Square, the vibrant heart of the »Mother City«. One big flea market from Monday to Saturday, this is the place to bargain for wood carvings, jewellery, leather and recycled art.**

★ ★
**African craftwork**

The scene at **the country's oldest market square** is lively. The cobbled Greenmarket Square takes its name from an earlier vegetable market. **Traders from all over Africa** offer their wooden masks, colourful necklaces, textiles and township art here – often with contemporary themes, such as the 2010 Football World Cup. The Christmas tree decorations of wire and beads are very pretty. The entertaining **»Eggie Man«** with his headdress made of hollowed-out eggs a metre high is happy to have his photo taken in return for a small gratuity.

Opening hours: Mon–Sat 10am–4pm

*
**Old Town House**

The **Old Town House** was built in Cape Rococo style between 1755 and 1761 under the aegis of the popular governor Rijk Tulbagh and initially housed the city watch, then also the magistrate's offices, the law courts and the police. Since the completion of the new City Hall on the ► Grand Parade in 1905, however, it has been home to Cape Town's oldest art collection. **Sir Max Michaelis** is honoured by a bronze bust by Moses Kottler above the fountain in the courtyard. He is well known in Cape Town as the sponsor of a hospital, libraries

★ ★
**Michaelis Art Collection ►**

*There is everything here: wood carvings, bead jewellery, soapstone eggs …*

and the Michaelis School of Fine Arts. Cape Town owes its development as a centre for the arts to Lady Florence Philipps, who inspired the British collector Sir Hugh Lane to buy Dutch old masters, and also to donate them to the South African nation in 1914. Thus two floors of Dutch and Flemish 16th- and 18th-century painters can be viewed, including studies by **Rembrandt van Rijn** for a self-portrait, dating from 1639. Also exhibited are *Return of the Prodigal Son* and *Dutch Ship in a Foreign Bay* by Ludolf Bakhuizen (1631–1708); an *Old Man* from the Rembrandt school; *Portrait of a Lady* by **Frans Hals** (1583–1666); *Dancing Dog* by **Jan Steen** (1623–67), and a portrait of *Johan Oxenstierna* from the workshop of van Dyck (1599–1641). The concerts and changing exhibitions of contemporary art staged here also enjoy a good reputation.

🕐
Opening hours:
Mon–Fri
10am–5pm, Sat
10am–4pm;
www.iziko.org.za/
michaelis

**Antiques** and **contemporary South African art** are sold in the small shops and art galleries of Church Street, such as the AVA Gallery (no. 35), The Cape Gallery (no. 60) or »art 1« (no. 66; ►p.117). During the summer, a daily **street market** sells antiques, kitsch and second-hand goods (during winter Thu–Sat 8am–2pm). An ideal place for a break from shopping is **Café Mozart**, which plays classical music (►p.99).

✷
Church Street

Cape Town's nucleus was Riebeeck Square, where the city father once set up his first tents (►Famous People). **St Stephen's Church**, dating from 1799, first served as a theatre, opera and school before being transformed into the United Reformed Dutch Church in 1839.

Van Riebeeck Square

**Heritage Square** Only vigorous public protest in the mid-1990s prevented the demolition of the buildings opposite, at Heritage Square. Today it is lined with bars and small cafés, such as the popular **Africa Café** in the bright yellow 18th-century Cape Georgian house on the corner of Shortmarket Street (▶p.96).

## ★ Green Point

C / D 1

**Location:** North-west of the V & A Waterfront

**The Waterfront bus departs every 15 minutes from Victoria Wharf, travelling via Green Point to the sea promenade at Sea Point. Green Point is ideally suited for Sunday excursions or a stroll along the sea, and of course football fans must also take a look at the new World Cup stadium.**

**Cape Medical Museum**

🕐 **Opening hours: Tue–Fri 9am–4pm**

This museum at the western end of the ▶ V & A Waterfront on Portswood Road is dedicated to Western and African medical history.Herbal knowledge and San healing dances, Ngoni and Muti Xhosa medicine and Zulu sangomas, as well as the Asian healing traditions of the Cape Malays are introduced alongside a recreated Victorian hospital room and dental practice. Catastrophic epidemics and Aids are also covered (www.museums.org.za/cmm).

**Breakwater Lodge**

www.bwl.co.za ▶

The **Breakwater Prison** once stood opposite, but today the building is part hotel and part the Graduate School of Business. The first prison was built with 60-bed dormitories for convicts commandeered to build the port in 1859. This is also where the San prisoners whom Dr Wilhelm Bleek (▶ Famous People) once brought to his home were locked up. As freed domestic staff they later advised him on their language and culture. The present building dates back to 1902, when prisoners were already being sorted according to their skin colour. From 1926 onwards, coloured port workers lived here. At the end of the solitary cells at the upper car park stands a **treadmill**, used from 1890 onwards to punish prisoners for minor offences.

**The Foundry** Interesting **designer shops** and the top-class **Beluga restaurant** (▶ p.83) can be found in the century-old brick building of the former foundry on Preswick Street.

★
**Greenpoint Stadium**

An **arena of superlatives** will be completed at Green Point Commons by autumn 2009, in good time for the **2010 Football World Cup** and complete with a retractable roof and 68,000 seats. It replaces the old Greenpoint Stadium, which was pulled down in 2007. At around 350 million US$, this is the most expensive construction taking place for the World Cup. From 2011 the stadium is to be used

*Nelson Mandela was thrilled to hold the FIFA trophy in 2004 – South Africa's ex-president (who was already 85 years old) had tirelessly campaigned for his country's nomination to host the World Cup.*

# FOOTBALL WORLD CUP 2010

**The eyes of millions of visitors and billions of TV viewers will be on the southern tip of Africa in June 2010, when 32 nations compete in the 19th Football World Cup: the world's second-largest sporting event.**

The opening game will take place on 11 June, and the final will be played on 11 July 2010. Qualifying matches for the World Cup will take place up to the end of 2009, and the championship itself will then be played out at **nine South African venues**. Five games from the first round of the World Cup, one second-round game, one quarter-final and a semi-final will be held in Cape Town's new central **Green Point Stadium**. And the »Mother City« is certainly a suitable venue, with outstanding additional cultural programmes, top hotels and gourmet restaurants. All over the Cape so-called »cool off areas«, for public viewing on 100 solar-powered large screens, are springing up, so that those who don't even own a television can watch the championships. Sports-crazy South Africa is renowned as a fair host that will not only cheer its own national team of **»Bafana Bafana«** (boys, boys), but all teams. Nevertheless, the South African government is playing it safe: by 2010, the National Police Force alone will have 190,000 trained men at its disposal. Over 10 million visitors are expected, and South Africa's airports will be expected to deal with 22 million arrivals. There are feverish expansion programmes everywhere. With the completion of Green Point Stadium in 2008, the country was even ahead of the prescribed FIFA schedule, but as before there continue to be shortfalls in beds, transport and energy supplies. For Capetonian football fans – whether supporters of Ajax Cape Town or its rival Santos – the **vuvuzela** is an essential item. This plastic trumpet designed after a kudu herder's horn emits an ear-splitting sound akin to an approaching herd of elephants. Two colour combinations from Soweto should be avoided in Cape Town, however: the black and white used for the vuvuzelas of the Orlando Pirates, and the yellow used by the Kaiser Chiefs. The ideal solution for the World Cup is to have a vuvuzela in South Africa's national colours.

## FIFA Worldcup 2010

www.southafrica.info/2010
www.worldcup2010southafrica.com
www.fifa.com/worldcup
www.swc2010.com

for football games by Cape Town's premier league teams **Ajax Cape Town** and **Santos**, as well as for rugby matches. Twenty large screens are being installed around Cape Town for the World Cup. On Sundays and holidays there is a **flea market** between the stadium and Western Boulevard from 8.30am to 5pm.

**Fort Wynyard**  In 1861, General Robert H. Wynyard (1802–64), commander of the British troops in South Africa, set 100 prisoners to earth-moving and brick-laying duties on the artillery position known as **Kyk in die Pot**. 68-pounders were directed towards Table Bay for defensive reasons and Kyk in die Pot was then renamed Fort Wynyard. Today it stands guard over the yacht and motor-boat harbours of **Granger Bay**.

**Mouille Point**  The 20m/65ft-high red and white striped **lighthouse** at Mouille Point was built by Hermann Schütte in 1824. A fog horn was added in 1926. The lighthouse shines 55km/35mi out to sea, yet it was unable to prevent the sinking of the steamer *Athens* in 1865, nor could it save the freighter *Seafarer* from running aground off Green Point in 1966.

✱
**Sea Point**  During apartheid Sea Point was a strictly white neighbourhood, but today this densely populated area is in transition. Its **ocean promenade**, over 10km/6mi long and lit up colourfully at night, is now a popular run for inline skaters and joggers. Tourists from all over the world mingle with street musicians, wealthy retired persons and Cape Town's tramps, known as »Bergies«. Instead of braving the ice-cold Atlantic, visitors can bathe at Beach Road in the 24ºC/75ºF heated saltwater pool of the **Sea Point Pavilion**. On Sunday mornings, long-distance swimmers train here for swimming tours to ► Robben Island (Opening times: mid-Oct to mid-April 7am–7pm, mid-April to mid-Oct 8.30am–5pm; www.capeswim.com/seapointpool.htm).

! **Baedeker** TIP

**Jazz wanted**
Not just jazz fans like to come for brunch at Harvey's when Amanda Tiffin, Zelda Benjamin or Sylvia Mdunyelwa are playing. Sunday papers and a glass of sparkling wine are on the house. The terrace restaurant belonging to the Winchester Mansions Hotel is right by the beach promenade at Sea Point (Beach Road 223, tel. 021 / 434 2351, buffet: Sun 11am–2pm; www.winchester.co.za).

✱
**Camps Bay, Clifton Bay**  South of Sea Point lie Cape Town's **exclusive suburbs** of Camps Bay and Clifton. Both seaside resorts are also popular bases for European holiday-makers and immigrants. The Round House on Kloof Street in Clifton Bay once served as Lord Charles Somerset's hunting lodge. Pieter Toerien presents international artists at the Camps Bay **Theatre on the Bay** (►p.128). The massive summits of the **Twelve Apostles** (►photo  p.16) tower above Victoria Road (M 6). Exclusive villas also line the hillsides of **Llandudno** further south, and nudists meet there at **Sandy Bay**.

*Sand and the city: Clifton and Camps Bay are renowned for white beaches and smart fashionable bars*

# Heerengracht

**Location:** City centre: between Adderley Street and Foreshore, corner of Riebeeck

**Buses:** Bus Terminal (Golden Acre), water taxi (Roggebaai Canal)

**Cape Town's oldest street between the ▶ V & A Waterfront and City Bowl was turned into a palm-fringed boulevard with flower beds and lawns when the International Convention Centre and the Roggebaai Canal were opened in the summer of 2003.**

Heerengracht once ran from the old pier at the harbour up to the Mount Nelson Hotel. Bridges crossed the **canal** between ▶ Company's Garden and the port, which was filled in in the 19th century. The upper section was later renamed ▶ Adderley Street and ▶ Government Avenue and, until 1940, the lower section remained the most direct connection to the port, before **land reclamation** in the Foreshore district also resulted in a new role for the Heerengracht. The start of the summer season and the lighting of the Christmas illuminations are celebrated with music and processions by the **Heerengracht Fountain**.

*From the canal to the boulevard*

◀ City of lights

At Hans Strijdom Street, two bronze statues recall the first landfall made by the city father on 6 April 1652. John Tweed's statue of **Jan van Riebeeck** (▶ Famous People) was a gift to the city from Cecil Rhodes. Riebeeck's wife Maria de la Quellerie was honoured in 1952 with a statue by the Dutchman Dirk Wolbers, commissioned by the van Riebeeck Society on the occasion of the city's 300th anniversary.

Van Riebeeck statues

Alongside the traffic leading to Coen Steytler Avenue, a statue commemorates the first European to circumnavigate the Cape, **Bartholomeu Diaz** in 1488. Since 2003, the Heerengracht, which was extended

Cape Town International Convention Centre (CTICC)

as far as Duncan Dock for the millennium, is completed by the **International Convention Centre**, which has two auditoria with 2000 seats, as well as over 10,000 sq m/110,000 sq ft of exhibition space. The large ballroom can accommodate up to 2000 guests for dinner. Art related to the Cape is the aesthetic centrepiece, and there are views of Table Mountain from the roof terrace. The foyer opens onto **Convention Square**, the Westin Grand Cape Town Arabella Quays Hotel and the **Roggebaai Canal**, which leads to the ▶V & A Waterfront.

www.capetownconvention.co.za, www.cticc.co.za ▶

**Desmond Tutu Peace Centre**

www.tutu.org ▶

Peace Museum ▶

The city of Cape Town responded to Archbishop Desmond Tutu's (▶Famous People) suggestion for a **Peace Centre** in 2005 by setting aside just under 4000 sq m/43,000 sq ft at the Convention Centre. The Peace Centre was designed by Van der Merwe, Miszewsky and Luyanda Mpahlwa. Once completed, it will be dedicated to the global **peace movement**. Training programmes and university-level study programmes are envisaged, alongside room for exhibitions, conferences, theatre, and a library and bookshop. Among other things, the exhibition *The Hands that Shape Humanity*, which has been touring the world since 2007, is also set to find its permanent home at the planned **Peace Museum**. The Desmond Tutu Peace Trust is housed in the nearby ABSA skyscraper on Thibault Square (www.tutufoundation-usa.org).

# ★ ★ Hermanus

**Location:** 110km/70mi east of Cape Town

**Population:** 13,000

**The so-called champagne breeze at Walker Bay was already recommended by London's lung doctors over 80 years ago. However, Hermanus is not only the most exclusive seaside resort along the ▶Overberg coast, but also – most importantly – the »world capital of whales«. Nowhere else can these ocean giants be observed so well from land.**

> ## ! Baedeker TIP
>
> ### There she blows!
>
> For observing the gentle giants close up, two charter boats are permitted to make 2-hour tours to within 50m/50yd of the whales. Southern Right Charters, The Whale, The Whale Shack, New Harbour, tel. 028/316 3154; Hermanus Whale Cruises, New Harbour, tel. 028/313 2722; www.hermanus-whale-cruises.co.za.

The whale capital owes its name to the wandering preacher Hermanus Pieters, who settled here in 1830, while Walker Bay was named after an illustrious Royal Navy officer in 1904. One of the first spa visitors was **Sir William Hoy**, director of the South African railways. As a nature enthusiast, he successfully prevented a connection to the national rail network, so there has never been a track leading to the railway station on Mitchell Street. Hoy and his wife are buried at the town's most beautiful viewpoint, at **Hoy's Koppie**.

All around the old harbour there is a choice of excellent restaurants and small cafés, such as Cubana or the Mugg & Bean. Restored fishing boats from 1855–1961 are moored in front of the **Old Harbour Museum**, while the **Fisherman's Village Photo Cottage** tells of life at sea with historic black-and-white photographs. (Opening times: Mon–Sat 9am–1pm, 2pm–5pm). Be sure not to miss the film on the life of whales and dolphins at the new **Whale Museum** at the market square (shows: daily 10am and 3pm) before joining the whale crier for the **Whale Walk** (start: 10.40am, 3.40pm).

★
**Old Harbour**

## Hermanus *Map*

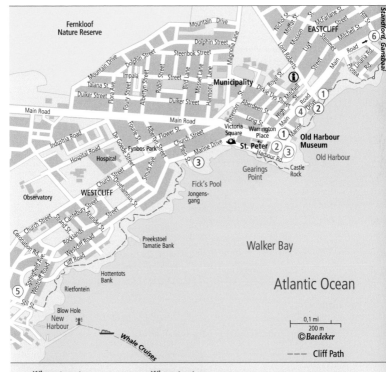

**Where to eat**
1. Burgundy
2. Bientang's Cave
3. The Harbour Rock

**Where to stay**
1. The Marine Hermanus
2. Auberge Burgundy
3. Harbour House
4. Misty Waves
5. Whale Rock Lodge
6. Walker Bay Lodge

# ▶ VISITING HERMANUS

## INFORMATION
### Hermanus Tourism
Old Station Building
Mitchell Street, Hermanus
Tel. 028 / 312 2629
www.hermanus.co.za
www.hermanus.com

## WHALE WATCHING & FESTIVAL
The »whale crier« (► Baedeker Special, p.214) tells you where whales can be spotted between June and the beginning of December at Walker Bay, or phone the Whale Hotline on 028 / 312 2629. The arrival of the whales is celebrated by all Hermanus with the »Kalfiefees« festival, complete with exhibitions, theatre and music; festival office tel. 028 / 313 0928; www.whale festival.co.za.

*Thatched idyll:*
*Harbour House above the old harbour*

## WHERE TO STAY
### ▶ Luxury
#### ① The Marine Hermanus
Marine Drive, P.O. Box 9
Hermanus 7200
Ttel. 028 / 313 1000
Fax 028 / 313 0160
www.marine-hermanus.co.za
Listen to whale song from your bed!

Just the location high above the ocean cliffs is spectacular. The elegant building dating from 1890 has 43 beautiful rooms and suites. The Pavilion restaurant provides culinary delights, while Seafood at the Marine is a good place to order curries.

#### ② Auberge Burgundy
16 Harbour Road, Hermanus 7200
Tel. 028 313 1201, fax 028 / 313 1204
www.auberge.co.za
Not Burgundy but Provence comes to mind in this magical villa. There are 17 luxurious rooms and the penthouse is a dream for six people. The shady courtyard has a pool and there are wonderful views over the bay from the balconies.

### ▶ Mid-range
#### ③ Harbour House
22 Marine Drive, Hermanus 7200
Tel. 028 / 312 1799
www.harbourhuse-hermanus.co.za
An enchanting thatched oasis above the old harbour, with five stylish rooms, a pool and garden.

#### ④ Misty Waves
21 Marine Drive, Hermanus 7200
Tel. 028 / 313 8460, fax 028 / 312 1755
www.hermanusmistybeach.co.za
Romantic boutique hotel by the sea with 24 tasteful rooms, a pool and garden. Candlelight dinners are served at the Waves Restaurant with views over Walker Bay.

#### ⑤ Whale Rock Lodge
26 Springfield Ave, Hermanus 7200
Tel. 028 / 313 0014
Fax 028 / 312 2932
www.whalerock.co.za
Pristine white thatched cottage with 11 pretty rooms, open fire and pool.

## ► Budget
⑥ **Walker Bay Lodge**
323 Main Road
Hermanus 7200
Tel. 028 / 312 2585
www.thevillage-collection.co.za
Feel right at home: familiar atmosphere with three enchanting rooms and a superb view over the bay.

## WHERE TO EAT
### ► Moderate
② **Bientang's Cave**
Marine Drive
Tel. 028 312 3454
www.bientangscave.com; open daily 11.30am–4pm, dinner by appointment.
The »world's best whale-watching restaurant« serves delicious seafood

near the cliffs, a short walk from the old harbour.

### ► Inexpensive
③ **The Harbour Rock**
New Harbour
Tel. 028 / 312 2920
www.harbourrock.co.za
Brilliant views over Walker Bay and towards the mountains. Try the grilled salmon, mussels in coconut cream or sushi at the bar.

### ► Expensive

*Baedeker recommendation*

① **Burgundy**
Marine Drive
Tel. 028 / 312 280
www.burgundyrestaurant.co.za
The two cottages dating from 1875 at the old harbour are considered the best place for fish, but the beef with caramelized onions is also a dream. Book a terrace table with bay view.

## Around Hermanus

Paragliders take advantage of the constant up-draughts at Kleinriver Mountain, where the 1800ha/4500-acre Fernkloof Nature Reserve also lies. The 12km/8mi-long **cliff path** leading from the new harbour to Grotto Beach is also part of the reserve. Due to the difference in elevation from sea level up to 842m/2763ft, over 1000 different **fynbos** species such as erica and protea flourish here, as well as the hardy white milkwood tree. The star attraction, however, is undoubtedly the world's largest carnivorous plant: the **flybush** (vlieëbos), which grows up to a height of 2m/7ft. It has hairy leaves that are in perfect symbiosis with the Pameridea miridae beetle and as part of the Cape flora only exists here. The more than 90 bird species include the royal eagle and the **blue crane**, South Africa's national bird. Hiking paths over 50km/30mi long provide opportunities to spot deer, klipspringers, porcupines and rabbits (visitor centre and picnic places tel. 028 / 313 8100).

✱ **Fernkloof Nature Reserve**

✱ ✱ ◄ Cliff Path

🕑 Opening hours:
Daily 7am–7pm
www.fernkloof.com

*Whale crier Zolile Baleni knows where the gentle ocean giants come up for air*

# »WHALE IN SIGHT!«

**There are many rare and strange jobs, but Hermanus – the world's self-appointed capital of whale watching and one of the best places anywhere on the globe to observe the grey giants from land – has the world's only »whale crier«. The present incumbent is Zolile Baleni, whose surname, amazingly, is almost identical to »balena«, which means »whale« in many Romance languages.**

Cheerful calls of »boerwors« – »Boer sausage«, the South African equivalent of saying »cheese« – are heard in the background as a European couple at Hermanus' new harbour have their photo taken with the whale crier. Zolile Baleni, the world's only whale crier, breaks into a broad smile. Since 2006 this charming man in his mid-forties has had what is probably one of the best jobs Hermanus has to offer. The town's first whale crier in 1992 was Pieter Classen, who passed the job on to Wilson Salukusana in 1998. Since the latter retired, Zolile Baleni has strolled along the beach promenade of Hermanus daily between 10am and 4pm – much like a beachcomber – spying out approaching whale pods to announce to visitors.

## Frisch aus dem Meer

Whenever whales are in sight, Zolile toots his **kelp horn** which, along with his leather hat sporting a stylized whale fin as a feather and his board explaining the signals, is his trade mark. The horn, modelled on ancient instruments, was built by Brian Alkatel. A veteran of the environmental Walker Bay Action Group, this seventy-year-old contributed towards ensuring that the »Walker Bay Whale Sanctuary« was established in 2001. Ever since, fishing and boat traffic from the vessels heading out for whale watching tours has been strictly regulated. Brian signed the end of his kelp horn »fresh from the sea«, in white paint. He personally harvested the saltwater kelp, which can grow up to 6m/20ft long, on the rocky shore, and then dried it in the famous »champagne air« of Hermanus, before finally painting and varnishing it. As in Morse code, Zolile toots long and short horn signals, the significance of which visitors can read on the explanations on the sandwich board that he carries. For example, one long tone following by a short one signifies whales in front of the new harbour; one long tone, followed by a short one, followed by another long blast indicates whales sighted off the old harbour; and three short blasts is the signal for whales off Roman Rock.

## Hot spots

In truth, the whale crier should be keeping an eye on the entire 15km/10mi cliff path along the coast encompassing New Harbour and Siever's Point, Preekstoel and Old Harbour, Kwaaiwater and Roman Rock, Fick's Pool and Vöelsklip. But that is hardly practical. Thus Zolile Baleni is constantly up-dated on whale movements in Walker Bay via mobile phone. According to him, the **best places** to observe whales are Old Harbour, Roman Rock and Siever's Point. There is also a whale telephone hotline: 028/ 312 2629. Or just call Baleni himself on 079/ 854 0684. His job brings around US$300 plus tips into the family coffers, which pleases his wife Ruth, a primary school teacher. He finds it very appropriate that Ruth means »friendship« in Hebrew and likes to point out that his daughter's name, Inga, means »yearning« in Xhosa, and that his son's name Sandile stands for »we are together«.

## Whale Watching

The first sighting is the most difficult. Very often whales are positioned in the bays alongside each other, rather like submarines, without a visible fin. The eye adjusts only gradually to distinguish between their giant bodies and dark shadows cast by clouds or sudden depths in the green ocean. According to Zolile, it is possible to see up to 20 southern right whales at Siever's Point, and these giants, which are up to 18m/60ft long, can even be seen near beaches. Zolile learnt his craft of spotting southern right whales, Bryde's and humpback whales, as well as dolphins and killer whales, from the experience and knowledge of his predecessor, and he has also studied many books. He is guided less by the tail fins than by the jets of water sprayed when the whales come up for air. Since the whales swim into Walker Bay to calve, it is his special delight to spot baby whales. After a gestation period of 13 months, they are already 6m/14ft long at birth. In 2007, there was even an albino. This is in fact not rare: 4% of all southern right whales are born albino, though hardly any depart from the bay as the new **Moby Dick** because their skin darkens rapidly. Zolile Baleni's seasonal whale work lasts from June to November. During the rest of the year, he gives talks in schools and in Hermanus, and studies his whale books. In the meantime, Baleni's profession has also been recorded in literature. Zakes Mda's novel *The Whale Caller* tells of the love between the whale crier of Hermanus and a female southern right whale called Sharisha (Picador, 2005).

*The whales swim very close to shore at Walker Bay*

**Hemel en Aarde Valley Wine Route**

The five vineyards in »heaven and earth valley« enjoy an excellent reputation. Try the gold chardonnay and the oak-aged pinot noir on the **Hamilton Russel** estate on the R 320, in the direction of Caledon. (Wine-tasting: Mon–Fri 9am–5pm, Sat 9am–1pm). In 2007, the cuvée Galpin Peak pinot noir from **Bouchard Finlayson** was the only South African pinot noir wine to be awarded five stars. (Wine-tasting: Mon–Fri 9am–5pm, Sat 9.30am–12.30pm; www.bouchardfinlayson.co.za).

**Stanford**

In 2007, this tranquil village 24km/15mi east of Hermanus celebrated its 150th anniversary. The founder was **Captain Robert Stanford**, who is inseparable from the events that took place in 1849, when the British planned to turn Cape Town into a penal colony. Charles B. Adderley represented Cape Town's citizens during a disagreement over the provisioning of prison ships. Stanford, who was still an army officer, finally caved in and supplied the prison ships, thereby losing his good reputation at the Cape. Damned as a collaborator, he was forced to sell everything, but the Crown let him down too and he died completely impoverished in Manchester, in 1877. Those who enjoy hunting for **antiques** should have a look in the New Junk Shop on Queen Victoria Street 11. The copper vats at the **Birkenhead Micro Brewery** contain four types of beer: try Black Snake (tours daily 10am–6pm).

**Gansbaai**

Fans of **great white sharks** meet at the south-eastern end of Walker Bay, at **De Kelders**, and also in the nice fishing village of Gansbaai. Diving charters with shark cages set off to **Dyer Island** at

7.45am from the harbour at Kleinbaai, where whale watching is also on offer (www.dive.co.za; www.whalewatching.co.za). The rocks at **Danger Point** have always been a threat to boats: in 1852, for example, the British troop carrier *Birkenhead* sank with the loss of 445 lives. When the captain called out the command, »all those who can swim, jump overboard and make for the boats«, his soldiers nevertheless waited until all seven women and 13 children were in the lifeboats. Thus a new emergency order was coined for the high seas: **»women and children first!«**. Also on board were three tons of gold which, but for a few gold coins, disappeared without trace. The lighthouse was only erected in 1895.

◄ Whale watching, white shark tours

At Kleinmond, on the **Hangklip Coast**, 23km/14mi west of Hermanus, active holiday-makers can choose between mountain biking trails, the Klippspringer hiking path or kayak, fishing and diving tours. The **wild horses** living by the Bot River Lagoon are unique at the Cape. Fish restaurants, art and curio shops line Harbour Road, and the best steak is served at the restaurant The View, at 2 Main Road (tel. 028 / 271 4937). The **Toy Museum** at 93 2nd Ave shows its collection of toy cars and dolls by appointment (tel. 028 / 271 3798).

**Kleinmond**

To the north-west of Kleinmond, South Africa's first **Unesco Biosphere Reserve** harbours over 1600 species of **fynbos**. There are giant protea bushes here as well as yellowwood trees. Falcons and ospreys circle above the jagged mountains, on which mountain goats and leopards live. Mountain bikers can choose between the Kogelberg Route or the valley route along the Palmiet River, and between June and September kayak tours are also available on the river (www.capenature.co.za).

**★
Kogelberg
Biosphere
Reserve**

During spring, species-rich fynbos vegetation blossoms at the **Harold Porter National Botanical Garden** on the R44 (opening times: daily 8am–4.30pm). A small colony of **jackass penguins** has been living at neighbouring **Stoney Point** since 1982.

**Betty's Bay**
⊙

# Hout Bay

Map p. 159

**Location:** 20km/13mi south of Cape Town

**Welcome to the »Republic of Hout Bay«! The harbour of this wonderful »wood bay« is the perfect place to buy seafood fresh off the boat or order some lobster or snoek in one of the fish restaurants.**

Jan van Riebeeck recorded the bay's former wealth of forest in his diaries of 1652, and named it »Houtbaai« or **»Wood Bay«**. It provided building material for Riebeeck's ships and the fort. The

**Local history**

# ► VISITING HOUT BAY

## INFORMATION

### Tourist Information
4 Andrews Road, Hout Bay
Tel. 021 / 791 8380
www.houtbayholiday.co.za

## SNOEK DERBY

The winner of the Snoek Festival, the lively harbour festival in August, is the person who catches the largest snoek, a kind of ocean pike.

## WHERE TO EAT

### ► Moderate
**The Wharfside Grill**
Mariner's Wharf, Harbour Road
Tel. 021 / 790 1100
This popular restaurant by the harbour prepares delicious meals from the catch of the day.

### Comida
Main Road, tel. 021 / 791 1166
Crispy duck and Thai vegetables with lemon grass are among the specialties of chef Sue, along with the best pizza on the Cape! Beer on tap and panoramic views of the local Sentinel Mountain.

## WHERE TO STAY

### ► Luxury
**Hout Bay Manor**
Baviaanskloof, Off Main Road
Hout Bay 7872
Tel. 021 / 790 0116, fax 021 / 790 0118
www.houtbaymanor.com
A riot of colours surprises guests behind the Cape Dutch façade of 1871 in a 5-star hotel that was totally revamped in 2007: contemporary Cape artists, Xhosa masks and Zulu jewellery are on show. Top chef Alexander Müller serves up kingclip with mielie pap soufflé at the elegant restaurant Pure.

### ► Mid-range
**Amblewood Guest House**
43 Skaife Street, Hout Bay 7806
Tel. 021 / 790 1570, fax 021 / 790 1571
www.amblewood.co.za
June and Trevor Kruger have three lovingly decorated double rooms. Relax by the pool with a spectacular view of the bay.

### Victoria Views
94 Victoria Avenue, Hout Bay 7806
Tel. 021 / 790 0085, fax 021 / 790 4591
www.victoriaviews.co.za
Four beautiful double rooms, pool and view of the mountains. Breakfast includes crispy croissants!

### Butterfly Haven Castle
Blackwood Drive
Constantia Nek, Hout Bay
Tel. 021 / 790 0276, fax 021 / 790 7940
www.capestay.co.za/butterflyhaven
Looking for something out of the ordinary? How about a magical castle with an enchanted garden and adventure playground and a spa? Profits also go towards supporting the children's charity Kids Can (www.freethe children.com).

## Baedeker recommendation

### DUIKER ISLAND CRUISES

Boat tours to Duiker Island are popular. Over 6000 seals live on the cliffs of this tiny island, and glass-bottomed boats and catamarans depart every half-hour from Hout Bay: Circe Launches
Tel. 021 / 790 1040, www.circelaunches.co.za
Drumbeat charters
Tel. 021 / 791 4441
Nauticat Charters
Tel. 021 / 790 7278
www.nauticatcharters.co.za.

*The Nauticat sets off for the seal island of Duiker Island every half an hour*

cannons among the ruins of **East Fort**, erected in 1795–1802, are testimony to colonial rivalries. The local history and the construction of the spectacular Chapman's Peak Drive are documented at the **Hout Bay Museum** at 4 St Andrews Road (opening times: Tue–Fri 8.30am–4.30pm, Sat 10am–3.30pm). Enjoy fresh oysters and smoked snoek at **Mariner's Wharf** by the harbour, where boat tours set off for the seal colony of Duiker Island (▶ p.218). The **SA Fisheries Museum** on Harbour Road presents the development of fishing methods (opening times: Mon–Fri 8am–4pm).

> ## ! *Baedeker* TIP
>
> ### Simply the best!
> Capetonians agree: the best fish and chips at the Cape are in Hout Bay, at the end of the Harbour Road, at Fish on the Rocks, daily 10.30am–8.15pm.

At 4ha/10 acres, the giant aviaries in which visitors can wander, north of the Valley Road, add up to **Africa's largest bird park**, and children adore the dwarf marmosets in the Monkey Jungle. (Opening times: daily 9am–5pm; www.worldofbirds.org).

★
World of Birds
⏲

The guided walks run by **Township Tours SA** (tel. 083 / 719 4870, www.suedafrika.net/imizamoyethu) through the township on Main Road last two hours. Along the way, visitors meet a sangoma and try traditional dishes. Evening tours including meals, dancing and choir singing are organized by **Dinner at Mandela's** (tel. 021 / 790 5817, www.dinneratmandelas.co.za).

Imizamo Yethu Township

*Blasted out of the rock: the famous Chapman's Peak Drive*

**⋆ ⋆**
**Chapman's Peak Drive**

www.chapmans peakdrive.co.za ▶

At the southern end of Hout Bay begins **the world's most spectacular coastal road**. Italian convicts spent seven years up to 1922, blasting it out of the mountain. The name of the panoramic road comes from the English seaman John Chapman, who made land here in 1607. This dream route, **a toll road**, ascends up to 150m/500ft above the sea and runs 9km/5.5mi to **Noordhoek**, a **surfer's paradise** with pretty little shops, restaurants and 5km/3mi-long beach. Near the beginning of Chapman's Peak Drive, Ivan Mitford-Barberton's **bronze leopard**, made in 1963, gazes out to Flora Bay from a rock. The last leopard was killed here in 1930. Breathtaking views, which are popular with the makers of car advertisements, open up beyond almost every one of the 114 bends in the road. The highlight of numerous park bays is **Chapman's Point**. Despite landslide nets and restoration work in 2003 and 2007, rock slides and bad weather regularly result in road closure. Sections of Chapman's Peak are also used for the annual **Two Oceans Marathon** and the **Cape Argus Cycle Tour**, the largest cycle race in the world.

**Kommetjie**

Baron Gustav Wilhelm van Imhoff, the VOC's special governor, left the region of Kommetjie to his capable wife Christina Rousseau in 1743. She had had great success supplying the VOC from her farm Zwaansweide. Today, the **Imhoff Farm** on Kommetjie Road is a good place to eat and buy regional art, as well as for horseback rides along the beach or even for excursions by dromedary. Shaun and Tracey lead tours to snakes and reptiles. (Opening times: Tue–Sun 10am–5pm; www.imhoff farm.co.za).

# ★ ★ Kirstenbosch National Botanical Garden

F 9/10

**Location:** Rhodes Drive, Newlands (Cape Town)

**Internet:** www.sanbi.org/frames/ kirst-fram.htm

**Kirstenbosch is one of the most beautiful botanical gardens in the world, a must-see not just for nature and plant lovers. It is also a »gene bank« for the protected Cape flora and was added to the Unesco list of Natural Heritage in 2004.**

Golden Arrow buses (www.gabs.co.za) depart from the terminal (corner of Golden Acre and Adderley Street) three times daily between Monday and Friday. The journey to the botanical gardens takes 70 minutes, and the last bus leaving Kirstenbosch for the city centre departs at 4.30pm. The **»hop on-hop off«** open double-decker buses of Cape Town Explorer (www.the capetownpass.com) and City Sightseeing (www.citysightseeing.co.za) stop at the garden's main entrance several times a day.

*Access by bus*

## *Kirstenbosch National Botanical Garden*

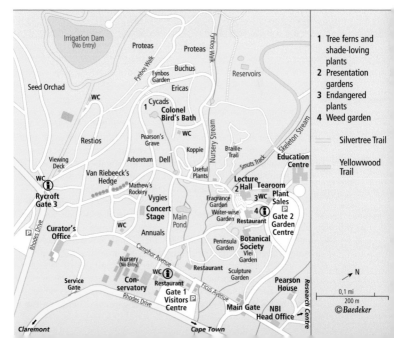

*In a sea of colours: guinea fowl love the Botanical Gardens*

**★ ★**
**Amazing gardens**

🕐
Opening hours:
Sept–March daily
8am–7pm,
April–Aug daily
8am–6pm.
Tours: Tue 10am &
11am, Wed, Thu,
Fri, Sat 10am

The borders of the small Cape Colony were demarcated by a hedge of wild almond bushes in 1660. Remains of this hedge, which is known as the **van Riebeeck Hedge**, now form the oldest section of the spectacular park. The area known as **The Dell** is where Colonel Christopher Bird's enchanting bird bath of 1811 can be seen. It was designed in the shape of a bird; an otter pond and the Cycad Amphitheatre with the oldest botanical plantings are also in The Dell. The true foundation of the garden was not until 1895, however, when Cecil Rhodes purchased the terrain. In 1898, in honour of Queen Victoria, the governor commissioned Rhodes Avenue (to the north of the present **visitor centre**), which was planted with rare trees from all corners of the British Empire. Today it is known as **Camphor Avenue**. After Rhodes' death in 1902, the 528ha/1305-acre area became state property and Harold Pearson was the first director to develop the garden. His grave in The Dell carries the epitaph »If ye seek his monument, look around you«. His garden legacy can be explored with an **audio guide**, as part of a **tour**, or even via golf cart. Take **at least half a day** to explore the wonderful gardens. They are **a sea of**

**colourful blossoms** almost all year round, but especially during spring. There is a **Braille Trail** and a **scented garden** with aromatic plants. The most famous plant of the Cape**fynbos** flora is the **protea**, which is also South Africa's national flower. They come in all shapes, sizes and colours here, from pink, white and red to silver and yellow. The **Erica Garden** contains over 600 different heathers, while the **Stone Garden** has shrubs from the country's dry areas. Raised wooden walkways lead through the natural **wetland area**, and the **arboretum** introduces South Africa's 450 tree species. The **domestic garden** is planted with Cape flowers.

For refreshment try the first-class **Silvertree restaurant** (tel. 021 / 762 9585) or the **Kirstenbosch Tea Room** (tel. 021 / 797 4883). Caffe Botanica (tel. 021 / 762 6841) in the visitor centre also contains a sculpture gallery, bookshop and souvenir shop.

Karoo lamb and rooibos tea

Plant lovers can find fynbos varieties and **rare seeds**, which can also be dispatched by post, at the Botanical Society of South Africa's Garden Centre (www.botanicalsociety.org.za). How about the blue and orange Mandela's Gold strelitzia? The annual **Garden Fair** is held in February/March, and during summer the Protea Village holds an **arts and crafts market** on the last Sunday of the month, from 9am to 3pm.

Kirstenbosch
Garden Centre
⏲
Opening hours:
Daily 9am–5pm

## Around Kirstenbosch Gardens

By prior appointment, it is possible to visit for free the world's third-largest brewery, **South African Breweries** at 3 Main Road, tel. 021 / 658 7386. Of course you also get to try a Castle beer. On 29 October 2007, thousands of enthusiastic fans welcomed the triumphant

Newlands

! **Baedeker TIP**

**Summer Sunset Concerts**
The famous open-air concerts are staged from the end of November to the beginning of April, every Sunday at 5.30pm. Usually they are classical concerts, but sometimes jazz or township music is performed. The audience can also bring picnics to relax on the immaculate lawns. Between July and the beginning of September, the Kirstenbosch Tea Room also puts on the pick'n pay chamber music concerts each Sunday morning. The latest programme is available from tel. 021 / 761 2866; www.sanbi.org/frames/whatsonfram.htm.

World Cup-winning Boks at the **Fedsure Park Newlands Rugby Stadium** on Boundary Road. Cape Town's bastion of rugby has been hosting games since 1890. In addition to regular rugby games, Ajax Cape Town football club also plays here (www.wp.rugby. com).

Rugby Museum ►

Just a touch-down sprint away, the Rugby Museum at the South African Sports Sciences Institute tells of famous players such as Naas Botha, Joel Stransky and Frik du Preez. Of course there is also an exhibition on the **2007 World Champions**, and the hero of Paris, captain Percy »U Beauty« Montgomery. (Opening times: Mon–Fri 10am–4.30pm; www.sarugby.co.za). Newlands Tours offers trips to sporting venues and to the Newlands Cricket Ground, where the South African »Proteas« play test matches. Tours end with lunch at the **Josephine Mill**, Cape Town's oldest water mill, which also hosts classical open-air concerts during the Cape summer (www.newlands tours.co.za).

Claremont

At the studios of the **Montebello Design Centre**, 31 Newlands Avenue, more than 50 artists and craftsmen produce musical instruments, ceramics and jewellery. (Opening times: Mon–Fri 9am–5pm, Sat 9am–4pm; www.montebello.co.za). Fancy shopping seven days a week is also possible at the fashion boutiques around **Cavendish Square** (www.cavendish.co.za).

# Muizenberg

**B 4**

**Location:** 35km/22mi south of the city, via M 3 and M 4

**Victorian villas from around 1900 along the beach promenade recall a golden era when wealthy Capetonians made Muizenberg a fashionable seaside resort. The colourful huts along the endless broad sandy beach became a local emblem, and Muizenberg is still a top destination, especially for surfers and sun worshippers.**

Joan St Leger
Lindbergh
Arts Centre

The architecture of the sea-front villas was largely the work of Sir Herbert Baker, who lived at House Sandhills at 18 Beach Road. One of four houses designed by him in 1899, it is today part of the **Joan St Leger Arts Centre** (she was publisher of the *Cape Times*. House Swanbourne is now home to the foundation set up by Joan St Leger's great-granddaughter. **Swanbourne House**, **Rokeby House** and **Crawford-Lea** House accommodate exhibitions, concerts, a library and a café. (Opening times: Mon–Fri 9.30am–4.30pm, Sat 10am–1pm).

Beaches along
False Bay

The colourful Victorian **bathing huts** are very photogenic. They recall a time when mining magnates from Witwatersrand invested in Muizenberg (►photo p. 226).

# ▶ VISITING MUIZENBERG AND FALSE BAY

## INFORMATION

*False Bay Tourism Association*
P.O. Box 302
Muizenberg 7950
Tel. 021 / 788 8048
www.muizenberg.info

### THE PERFECT WAVE

The surfing scene meets up in Gary Kleinhans' surf school shop in Muizenberg, at Beach Road 90 (www.garysurf.co.za).
The neighbouring Roxy Surf Club is only open to women; monthly membership is possible (www.roxysurfschool.co.za).

### KALK BAY QUARTER

Colourful ceramics, maritime souvenirs and hand-painted candles by the region's craftspeople can be found at 58 Main Road, in Kalk Bay (tel. 021 / 788 6312).

---

Long in decline, the late 19th-century villas along **Beach Road** are now gradually being restored so that the glory of days gone by can be revived. **Het Posthuys** (no. 180) was a look-out and staging post for changing horses in 1673. 70 years later, the military post of Muysenburg was founded here by the officer Wynard Muijs.

**Historic mile**

The pink villa at 192 Main Road was built in 1930 for the Italian diplomat Prince Natale Labia (1877–1936) and his wife Ida Louise. His son Count Natale Labia turned the Venetian mansion into a museum, complete with its original furniture from Europe, in 1985 (view by appointment only, tel. 021 / 788 4106).

**Natale Labia Museum**

The thatched country house at 246 Main Road was bought by **Sir Cecil Rhodes** three years before his death, and he died here on 26 March 1902. His furniture, personal items and his carriage can be inspected. The **Rust-en-Vrede** villa planned for Rhodes at 232 Main Road was completed by Sir Herbert Baker in 1905 and purchased by the art patron Sir Abe Bailey. (Opening times: Mon–Sat 10am–3.30pm).

**Rhodes Cottage Museum**

🕐

Cape Town's mayor Helen Zille inaugurated the restored cannons between Main Road and Boyes Drive in 2006, just one day before the anniversary of the legendary **Battle of Muizenberg**, fought between 1600 British and 800 Dutch soldiers on **7 August 1795**. (Opening times: Sun 9am–3pm and by appointment, tel. 021 / 788 1069).

**Battle of Muizenberg Open Air Museum**

🕐

*The Victorian beach huts at Muizenberg glow yellow, red and blue*

## Around False Bay

❋ False Bay
The almost 40km/25mi-wide bay is famous as the home of large **colonies of sea lions and seals** and for **white sharks** that can be safely eye-balled during cage dives. A boat trip to **Seal Island** is an unforgettable experience: over 50,000 seals live here. Between May and November, **whales** also congregate in the waters of False Bay, which are warmed by the Agulhas Current. False Bay takes its name from early navigators who mistakenly thought they were already in Table Bay past the Cape of Good Hope.At the end of the 17th century,

❋ Kalk Bay
3km/2mi south of Muizenberg, the small whaling station of Kalk Bay was named after the many wood-fired ovens here in which shell limestone was once burned to make building material for Cape Town. The **fish market** by the harbour is a good place to buy the catch of the day directly from the boats each afternoon. A great view of False Bay can be enjoyed from the **Harbour House Restaurant**. Why not try champagne oysters or West Coast steamed mussels in white wine (tel. 021 / 788 4133; www.harbourhouse.co.za)? Take time for a leisurely stroll along Main Road to see its **antique shops** and small art galleries.

❋ Rondevlei Nature

www.
rondevlei.co.za ▶
A 220ha/550-acre wetland area of the Zeekoevlei marshes was officially protected in 1952, and lies just 5km/3mi north-east of Muizenberg. The saltwater lagoon surrounded by sand and dunes is a **bird sanctuary** in which visitors can observe ibis, weaver birds and white

pelicans from two viewing towers. The natural stars, though, are the **hippos**, which were introduced in 1981 and, with any luck, can be admired at the Hippo Crossing. (Opening times: March–Nov daily 7.30am–5pm, Dec–Feb daily 7.30am–7pm). ☉

The nature reserve to the west of Muizenberg, which includes the 756m/2480ft-high Noorhoek summit, owes its name to the fruitless mining efforts that took place here during the years 1675–85. Today, the 2158ha/5332 acres are part of the ► Table Mountain National Park. Archaeological finds from **Peers Cave** prove that the Khoisan already inhabited the Cape Peninsula 10,000 years ago. Footpaths all around the Silvermine water reservoir, built in 1898, offer chances to encounter antelopes, gazelles, wart hogs and desert lynx. Access: from Kalk Bay or via Ou Kaapse Weg/M 64. (Opening times: April–Sep daily 7am–6pm, Oct–March 8am–5pm).

**Silvermine Nature Reserve**

◄ www.tmnp.co.za

> **!** *Baedeker* TIP
>
> **In the middle of the bush**
> Imvubu Tours has been organizing tours with bird watching, fishing and overnight stays in bush camps on a lagoon island in the Rondevlei Reserve since it founded a community project here in 2002. (Tel. 021/706 0842, www.imvubu.co.za).

# Observatory and Woodstock

H–K 4/5

**Location:** Cape Town, eastern suburbs

**Trendy bars, junk shops, cabaret and a colourful alternative scene characterize the multi-cultural student quarter of »Obs«, east of the city centre. The media and designer world has also discovered this former industrial area.**

The district owes its name to the **South African Astronomical Observatory** on Observatory Road, installed in 1828, which is used to study the skies of the southern hemisphere and ensure that the cannons on ► Signal Hill are fired on time. (Tours: Mon–Fri 10.30am, 2.30pm, Sat 11.30am, 2.30pm; Mon, Wed, Fri & Sat during winter also 6pm, during summer also 8pm; www.saao.ac.za). The busy core of this neighbourhood is the narrow **Main Road** with its tiny Victorian town houses, in which many students live today and which also house bars, cafés and small arts venues such as the Independent Armchair Theatre. The most fashionable meeting spot is the **OBZ Café** at 115 Lower Main Road (tel. 021/448 5555).

**Observatory**

☉

The museum in the Groote Schuur Hospital was opened on 3 December 2007, the 40th anniversary of the first heart transplant operation, which was conducted here. **Professor Christiaan Barnard**

★
**Heart of Cape Town Museum**

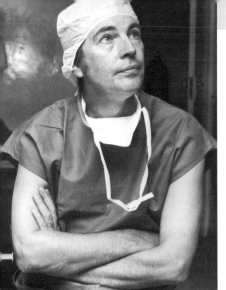

*Chris Barnard completed the first successful heart transplant in 1967*

(► Famous People) performed the first successful transplantation of a human heart in 1967. His operating theatre has been recreated true to the original. (Opening times: Mon–Sat 8am–5pm, tours: 9am, 11am, 1pm, 3pm; www.heartofcapetown. co.za).

The art market is booming in **Woodstock**. Justin Rhodes and Cameron Munro have expanded their **Whatiftheworld Gallery**, and also host entertaining art events in the Albert Hall (► p.116; www.whatiftheworld.com). The renowned **Goodman Gallery** on Sir Lowry Road belonging to Linda Given and Joe Wolpe celebrated its 40th anniversary in 2008 (► p.117; www.goodmangallerycape.com). If you are interested in young contemporary art at the Cape, check the award-winning internet magazine **ART THROB**, created by Sue Williamson, Michael Smith and Tavish McIntosh in Woodstock (www. artthrob.co.za).

# ＊ Overberg

C/D 4

**Location:** 110–240km/70–150mi east of Cape Town

**The farming region of Overberg, »over the hills«, is reached via the spectacular Sir Lowry's Pass. Africa's southernmost region, once just a dirt carriage track, now offers a host of attractions: green hills and thatched cottages, whale watching, wild flowers and wonderful hiking routes.**

＊＊
**Whale coast**

Overberg's coast is famous for the whale centre of ►**Hermanus** and for **Cape Agulhas** (► Bredasdorp), the southernmost point of the African continent, where the Indian Ocean and the Atlantic meet. The tranquil little town of Caledon (www.tourismcaledon.co.za) was founded in 1708 in the heart of this agricultural region, by the side of **medicinal springs** that were already highly valued by the San. 900m³ (240,000 US gallons) of mineral-rich water at temperatures up to 50ºC/122ºF bubbles each day from seven springs that are used in the elegant **Caledon Hotel, Spa & Casino** and in the Victorian bath

# VISITING OVERBERG

## INFORMATION

**Overberg Tourism**
22 Plein Street, Caledon
Tel. 028 / 214 1466
www.tourismcapeoverberg.co.za
www.viewoverberg.com

## WHERE TO EAT

### ► Moderate

**Roosje van de Kap**
5 Drostdy Street, Swellendam
Tel. 028 / 514 3001
www.roosjevandekaap.com
Evenings only, closed Mon. Ilzebet
and Nick spoil their guests with Cape
Malay and French cuisine. Book a
spot in the »Geselskamer« for a
romantic candle-lit dinner by an open
fire. There are also charming garden

rooms, a wedding suite and a family
apartment.

## WHERE TO STAY

*Baedeker recommendation*

### ► Luxury / Mid-range

**Klippe Rivier Cape Country House**
2km/1mi north-west of Swellendam
Tel. 028 / 514 3341, fax 028 / 514 3337
www.klipperivier.co
An enchanting Cape Dutch estate from the
era around 1820, set in the middle of
vineyards by the Klippe Rivier. This jewel
was once the family seat of the Boer
presidents Steyn and Reitz. First-class
seasonal cuisine and choice regional wines.

---

house. Modern corn silos on Mill Street contrast with the Victorian architecture. The story of the earliest settlers is told in the local **Caledon Museum** at 22 Plein Street. (Opening times: Mon–Fri 9am–4pm). A large wild flower exhibition is held at the **Wild Flower Garden** in September. (Opening times: daily 8am–5pm).

The white-washed thatched houses shaded by mighty oak trees give this farming village founded in 1860 its particular charm. The 15km/9mi-long **Boesmanskloof Trail** to De Galg begins in Greyton and leads over the fynbos-covered **Riviersonderend Mountains**. **Greyton**

Just 3km/2mi west of Greyton, Georg Schmidt of the Moravian Brethren founded the country's oldest mission station, at **Genadendal**, in 1738. **Nelson Mandela** honoured the services of the mission to South Africa in 1995, when he paid a visit and also renamed Westbrooke, Cape Town's presidential seat, as Genadendal. Schmidt taught and christened the Khoisan, who were already under threat,

**! Baedeker TIP**

### Genadendal hiking trail

Fit hikers take two days to complete the 25km/16mi challenging circular route from Genadendal through the wonderful Riviersonderend Mountains. A maximum of 24 participants set off from and return to the Mission Church in Genadendal (get there early). Reservations: Cape Nature, tel. 028 /425 5020; www.capenature.org.za.

thereby making enemies of the farmers, who were illiterate themselves and supporters of the conservative Dutch Reformed Church. He was expelled in 1744 and the mission was abandoned until 1792. In 1838, Genadendal opened South Africa's first teacher training college, but it fell victim to apartheid policies in 1926. Today, the **Moravian Mission Museum** exhibits the country's oldest organ, a printing press from 1859, and also the bible that Schmidt gave to the Khoisan woman Vehettge Tikkuie in 1744 as a parting gift. (Opening times: Mon–Thu 9am–1pm, 2pm–5pm, Fri 9am–3.30pm, Sat 10am–2pm). Officially protected 18th- and 19th-century houses survive all around **Church Square**. The choir at the **Moravian Church**, built in 1795, is worth hearing.

**Salmonsdam Nature Reserve**

The attractions of the 839ha/2073-acre nature reserve 40km/25mi south-east of Caledon are fynbos vegetation, antelope herds and blue cranes. (Opening times: daily 8am–6pm).

**Elim**

The quiet rural village of Elim is also a **Moravian Mission**, founded in 1824. Its thatched cottages are today protected monuments. The

*Nature up close: just one national park protects the rare bontebok antelope*

water mill built in 1833 for the village bakery has the largest wooden waterwheel in the country. Despite prohibitions, Elim's school taught without racial divisions during apartheid.

The third-oldest European town at the Cape lies at the foot of the Langberg Mountains and was founded as a VOC post in 1745 (www.swellendamtourism.co.za). This pretty town with many **Cape Dutch buildings** takes its name from Governor Hendrik Swellen and his wife Helena ten Damme. Evidence of the settlement of the Khoikhoi tribe of Hassekwa around Swellendam can be found in Bontebokskloof, where the graves of the last two chieftains lie: Klaas and Markus Shababa. Today a museum, the whitewashed **Drostenhof** at 18 Swellengrebel Street was the seat of the Cape government's local representative, Theophilus Rhenius, from 1747 onwards. The openair section of the museum also includes the former prison, a workshop and Mayville, a residence dating from 1853. (Opening times: Mon–Fri 9am–4.45pm, Sat & Sun 10am–4pm; www.drostdymuseum.com). Wonderful hikes can be made through wild-flower meadows and a fynbos paradise at the foot of the Langberg Mountains, in the **Marloth Nature Reserve**. To complete the 81km/50mi **Swellendam Trail**, visitors need to plan for six days, staying overnight in cabins (www.footprint.co.za/ swellendam.htm).

 **Swellendam**

 ◄ Drostdy Museum

🕐

Until the late 18th century, when they were almost entirely wiped out, large herds of **Bontebok antelopes** grazed along the Breede River to the south of Swellendam. To protect these animals, the 3000ha/ 7500-acre national park was established. Around 200 bonteboks now live there once more.. Mountain zebras, springboks, duikers and 200 bird species are also found in the park (entrance 7km/4.5mi southeast of Swellendam; www.sanparks.org/parks/bontebok).

✱ **Bontebok National Park**

🕐 Opening hours: Daily 7am–6pm/ 7pm

# ✱ Paarl

B / C 3

**Location :** N 1, 56km/35mi north-east of Cape Town    **Population:** 117,000

**With its endless main road Paarl, a centre of wine-making and the home of Afrikaans, is much less attractive than ►Stellenbosch and ►Franschhoek. Yet Paarl also has famous vineyards, first-class restaurants and elegant places to stay.**

Abraham Gabbema came to the Berg River Valley in 1657 in search of the legendary Monomotapa treasure. He did not find it, though the glittering pearls of water on granite rocks here inspired him to christen the area **Perlenberg**. 18,000 Khoi of the Cochoqua tribe once lived here, but had long been reduced to the status of labourers

**Paarl Mountain**

# VISITING PAARL

## INFORMATION

**Paarl Tourism**
216 Main Street, Paarl 7600
Tel. 021 / 863 4937
www.paarlonline.com

**Paarl Wine Route
and Paarl Vintners**
86 Main Street, Paarl 7600
Tel. 021 / 863 4886
www.paarlwine.co.za
www.paarlvintners.co.za

## WINE & AFRIKAANS

Paarl celebrates the Shiraz Festival and its heritage with its Afrikaans Week. Wine is also the theme of the Culti-varia Festival in September (www.cultivaria.com), the Horse & Wine Festival in October, and the Olive & Wine Festival in November.

## UP, UP AND AWAY ...

Carmen and Udo Mettendorff's hot-air balloon sets off with the first rays of the sun to drift over the Berg River Valley with views of the majestic Hottentot Holland Mountains. In good weather, the balloon sets off every morning between November and April. Breakfast is served at the Grande Roche Hotel after the one-hour flight (Wineland Ballooning, 64 Main Street, tel. / fax 021 / 863 3192; www.kapinfo.com).

## WHERE TO EAT

► **Expensive**

① *Bosman's*
Grande Roche, Plantasie Street, tel. 021 / 863 5100; www.granderoche.co.-za. Chef Frank Zlomke treats guests to first-class Cape Malay and South

*Breakfast at the Grande Roche after a hot-air balloon tour*

African cuisine in the elegant manor house of the 5-star Grande Roche Hotel (▶Where to Stay).

② *Laborie*
Laborie Estate
Taillefert Street
Tel. 021 / 807 3095
www.gloriousfood.co.za
Daily 10am–5pm, evenings by appointment
Hetta van Deventer has been serving the best of South African home cooking at this old Cape Dutch estate, which is over 300 years old. Try top wines in the Tasting Room and explore the Wine Hiking Trail.

▶ **Moderate**
③ *Marc's Restaurant*
129 Main Street
Tel. 021 / 863 3980
www.marcsrestaurant.co.za
The herbs and fruit used in Marc and Maya Friedrich's Mediterranean and Lebanese cuisine come from their own garden and they have a prize-winning wine list. Morne Meyer plays jazz on Saturday nights.

④ *The Goatshed*
Fairview Estate
Sud Agter Paarl Pad
Tel. 021 / 863 3609
www.fairview.co.za. Freshly baked bread, leg of lamb and springbok chops are served under a rustic wooden ceiling, together with house wines and 25 different kinds of homemade cheese.

## WHERE TO STAY
▶ **Luxury**

*Baedeker recommendation*

① *Grande Roche*
Plantasie Street, Paarl 7646
Tel. 021 / 863 5100
Fax 021 / 863 2220
www.granderoche.co.za
Legendary top-class hotel with beautiful terrace suites and a magnificent main house in Cape Dutch style. The old slave chapel is popular for weddings. The Bistro Allegro offers light meals by the pool and the prize-winning Bosman's is the only Relais & Gourmand-listed restaurant in Africa.

② *De Oude Paarl*
132 Main Street, Paarl
Tel. 021 / 872 1002
Fax 021 / 872 1003
www.deoudepaarl.com
This charming boutique hotel, which spreads over two historic buildings of the late 18th century, has 26 rooms with lovely interiors. Try the cardamom chicken with caramelized apricots in the Gabbemma Restaurant. An affordable alternative is the tented Moroccan buffet. Hand-rolled cigars of the Montecristo no. 5 brand are offered in the Cuba Lounge.

▶ **Mid-range**
③ *Lemoenkloof*
*Guest House*
396a Main Street, Paarl
Tel. 021 / 872 3782
Fax 021 / 872 7532
www.lemoenkloof.co.za
20 pretty rooms behind a Victorian façade. The lounge and wedding suite still have the original yellowwood ceilings and stinkwood beams.

## *Paarl* Map

**Where to eat**
① Bosman's
② Laborie
③ Marc's Restaurant
④ The Goatshed

**Where to stay**
① Grande Roche
② De Oude Paarl
③ Lemoenkloof
   Guest House

for new farmers or driven away towards the Orange River by 1687, when Governor van der Stel granted the first plots of farmland to freemen. The Khoi called the local 729m/2392ft mountain »Turtle Mountain«. One of the largest vineyards in the world, the **Kooperatieve Wijnbouwers Vereniging van Zuid-Afrika (KWV)**, has been based at La Concorde, one of Paarl's oldest farms, since 1918. The wine-making association with its 6000 members is responsible for around 70% of South African wine exports. The five **largest wine barrels in the world** can be seen at Kohler Street, in the giant wine cellars. They were made from huge sequoia trees. (Tours: Mon–Sat 10am, 10.30am, 2.15pm, Sun 11am; www.kwvwine emporium.co.za). At just under 11km/7mi, the oak boulevard of Main Street, laid out in 1720, is **South Africa's longest high street**. **Strooidak Kerk**, the thatched church at the crossing of Main Street and Lady Grey Street, was built in 1805. The **Paarl Museum** housed in the former parish building of 1787 at 303 Main Street contains Cape Dutch antiques, silver, glass and historic photographs (Oude Pastorie, opening times: Mon–Sat 9am–1pm).

✳ **Afrikaans Language Museum (Taal Monument)** ⏲ The museum in Gideon Malherbe House at 11 Pastorie Avenue is dedicated to **Afrikaans**, which was first written down in 1875. »Taal« means »language« in Afrikaans. The printing press that printed the first Afrikaans newspaper in 1876 can be viewed on the ground floor. (Opening times: Mon–Fri 9am–4pm, Sat 9am–1pm; www.taalmuseum. co.za). The three pillars of the **Taal Monument** symbolize the roles of Africa, England and Holland in the development of the Afrikaans language, which became South Africa's second official language, after English, in 1925. The monument was designed by Jan ⏲ van Wyk in 1975. (Opening times: daily 8.15am–5pm).

**Nelson Mandela** ended his long road to freedom in the prison at Jan van Riebeeck Road in 1990. The old farmhouse recalls that era in the **Madiba House Project**.

Paarl's signposted Wine Route leads to South Africa's largest vineyard at **Nederburg**, which produces over 10 million bottles per annum. The estate, founded in 1791, has an elegant mansion dating from 1800 in which Sotheby's hold an annual wine auction for South Africa's top wines each March. (Wine-tasting Mon–Fri 8am–5pm, Sat & Sun 10am–4pm; cellar tours: Mon–Fri 10.30am, 3pm, Nov–March also at 11am on Sat & Sun; www.nederburg.co.za). Although the private vineyards produce quality wines, they are often overshadowed by the giants of KWV and Nederburg. Historic vineyards include **Laborie** (▶ p.233) and the **Fairview Estate**, where vines have been grown since 1699 and Charles Back now produces a wonderful shiraz. (Wine-tasting: Mon–Fri 8.30am–5pm, Sat 8.30am–1pm; The Goat Shed, p.233; www.fairview.co.za). The Finlayson family at **Glen Carlou** on the northern reaches of the Simonsberg serve top wines and exquisite cuisine in the Zen Restaurant. (Wine-tasting: Mon–Fri 8.30am–4.30pm, Sat & Sun 10am–3pm; www.glencarlou.co. za). Exclusively kosher wine is produced at **Zandwijk** (www.zandwijk.co.za).

Drakenstein Prison

** **
Paarl Wine Route

◀www.
paarlwine.co.za
🕓

🕓

🕓

*Giant wine barrels are stored at the cellars of the KWV*

**Pure nature**  Nature fans can observe 140 bird species at the **Paarl Bird Sanctuary** at Drommedaris Street. Hiking paths of 3–10km/2–6mi length are part of the Klipkershout Walking Trail in the **Paarl Mountain Reserve**. Free climbers meet at Bretagne Rock and Paarl Rock. The **Limietberg Trail** goes from the foot of Du Toitskloof to Tweede Tol via Bainskloof and covers a distance of 36km/23mi.

**Wellington**  This small town 20km/13mi north of Paarl is the centre of dried fruit
www.  and brandy production. Wellington also has its own wine route. Try
wellington.co.za ▶  the prize-winning pinotage from **Diemersfontein**. (Wine-tasting dai-
⏰  ly 10am–5pm; www.diemersfontein.co.za). The **Wellington Museum** on Church Street contains ethnic jewellery and Egyptian finds from the Akhenaten era. The museum also tells how Andrew Geddes Bain and Andrew Murray conquered the Limiet Mountains. The fantastic **Bain's Kloof Pass** on the R 303 in the direction of Ceres was named
⏰  after Bain. (Opening times: Mon–Fri 9am–5pm).

## ★ ★ Robben Island

**B 3**

**Location:** Island in Table Bay          **Internet:** www.robben-island.org.za

**Seven sea miles off Cape Town, the former prison island is a memorable, if sobering, testimony to South Africa's history. Robben Island is a national memorial and has been a Unesco World Heritage Site since 1999.**

⏰
**Ferries:**
Daily from the V & A
Waterfront at 9am,
10am, noon, 1pm,
2pm and 3pm, Dec
and Jan also at
4pm.

For South Africans, Robben Island is primarily a **symbol of freedom**: it recalls the brutality with which the racist apartheid regime crushed resistance and also the victory over that inhuman state terror. South Africa's first black president, **Nelson Mandela** (▶Famous People), was imprisoned here for almost two decades. Robben Island – also known as »Mandela's University« at that time – is where Mandela became »Madiba«, father of the South African »Rainbow Nation«. This is also where the first part of his memoirs *The Long Road to Freedom* was written. In 2008, the government passed a resolution for a five-year plan to renovate the island museum.

**On Nelson**  **Guided island tours** can be booked at the ▶V & A Waterfront, in the
**Mandela's tracks**  Nelson Mandela Gateway Centre of the **Robben Island Museum (RIM)**. Due to the high demand, advance booking is advisable: tel. 021 / 413 4200; www.robben-island.org.za. The 4-hour tour includes a crossing in the ferry *Sikhululekile* (»we are free«) launched in 2008, which takes half an hour. The last ferry departs from the island at around 6pm. Ferry traffic is cancelled when there are strong winds. After arrival, visitors take a minibus from the island harbour. The old guards' motto in Afrikaans, »we serve with pride«, stands

*Remembering the past for the sake of the future:*
*today ex-prisoners guide visitors around the former prison for anti-apartheid activists*

above the gates to the prison. The tour includes a visit to **Mandela's solitary cell**, which measures just 6 sq m/64 sq ft, where visitors can see his cutlery and blanket and sense his loneliness. Prisoners were forced to work in the **chalk pit** until 1974. Conditions were so terrible, especially in the early years, that prisoners staged an indefinite hunger strike in 1967: for long trousers, more blankets, better food and permission to play football and rugby in the prison courtyard. The strike was successful. Mandela came up with the slogan »each one teach one« and organized mutual education between prisoners. In this way illiterates learned to read and write during their incarceration, and even guards were included later. Today, **visits are guided by former prisoners** such as Thulani Mabaso, Hugh Jean and Elias Mzamo, who tell moving tales of their former daily lives in prison.

Robben Island served as a **prison** from the very first years of the Dutch Cape Colony settlements in the 16th century. During the early 19th century, **whaling ships** also anchored in the island's small Murray's Bay. After the prison closed in 1843, **sufferers from leprosy and mental illness** were banished to the island. The last lepers were moved to Pretoria as late as 1931. The South African military built a post on the island shortly before the beginning of the Second World War. **Heavy artillery batteries** in the island interior still recall that era. In 1961 under apartheid Robben Island became a notorious **high-security prison** for dangerous criminals and political prisoners. Almost all **ANC leaders** were incarcerated here, and eleven of them were called to serve in Mandela's cabinet in 1994. Former prisoners have been guiding visitors around the island since 1997.

**Notorious place of banishment**

**?** **DID YOU KNOW ...?**

■ ... that one of the first prisoners was a Khoikhoi chieftain? Autshumato – named Harry den Strandloper (beachwalker) by the Dutch – worked as a translator for the Cape Town founder Jan van Riebeeck. When war broke out between the white settlers and the indigenous population in 1658, however, he fell out of favour and was deported to Robben Island. He escaped from the island in 1659, believed to be the only person ever to have done so. Today, one of the ferries that now takes tourists to Robben Island is named after him.

Bonteboks, ibex and springboks share the island's 574ha/1418 acres with thousands of **African penguins**. There are also numerous protected bird species, such as Hartlaub seagulls, black oystercatchers and great crested terns. **Shipwrecks** are visible off the rugged coast and at least seven more lie just below the water surface. There are no bathing beaches: the cold Atlantic current means temperatures never rise above 14°C/57°F, and even during high summer, there is often a stiff south-westerly wind. The almost 120 inhabitants of the island village all work for the prison museum.

**Mayibuye Archive**

🕐 The Mayibuye Archive in the library of the **University of the Western Cape**, in north Cape Town, maintains a multimedia exhibition about the Robben Island prisoners. Letters, photos and films can be seen by appointment (Mon–Fri 8am–4pm; tel. Richard Whitening 021 / 959 2935).

# Rondebosch

J–L 7

**Location:** 5km/3mi south-east of city centre

**Internet:** www.rondebosch.net

**The heart of this tranquil university district is the Rondebosch Fountain at the corner of Main Road and Belmont Road, where flower stands, small shops and cafés create a relaxed atmosphere.**

**University of Cape Town (UCT)**

✴ **Baxter Theatre ▶**

The Upper Campus of this renowned university, built on a former Cecil Rhodes property in 1928, contains neo-classical buildings and is open to the public for strolls around the grounds. The Baxter Theatre on Main Road is an important cultural institution. It was built in 1977, thanks to Dr. W. Duncan Baxter. There was furore here in 2007, when the venue staged *Impepe Yomlingo*, Mozart's *Magic Flute* in Xhosa (▶ p.128). Next door, **Rustenberg House** recalls the beginnings of Rondebosch, when the first seven settlers came to live behind the Doorn Bosje (thorn bush), on the banks of the River Amsel, in 1657. Later, it was the home of Governor Simon van de Stel.

✴ **Irma Stern Museum**

The artist **Irma Stern** (1894–1966), who was controversial in South Africa throughout her life, lived in Berlin from 1909 and met the Expressionist painters Ernst Ludwig Kirchner and Max Pechstein there.

After completing her studies in Weimar, she returned to Cape Town in 1920, where the first of her more than 100 solo exhibitions was immediately dubbed »ugliness as cult« by the critics. Today, her elegant house The Firs, on Cecil Road and north of Woolsack Drive, exhibits over 200 paintings and sculptures. Her art collection with objects from Senegal, Zanzibar and the Belgian Congo is unusual. The first floor also has changing exhibitions by young Cape Town artists. At the end of Rhodes Avenue, the Dutch windmill **Mostert's Mill** has been in operation since 1796, and its milling systems are still intact. (Opening times: daily 9am–5pm).

Opening hours:
Tue–Sat
10am–5pm; www.
irmastern.co.za.

**Rhodes Memorial**

The memorial built ten years after the death of **Cecil John Rhodes** (1853–1902) can be found via Princess Anne Avenue. The tycoon's monument was built on the model of the Greek temple of Segesta in Sicily and designed by Sir Herbert Baker. 49 steps, one for every year of his life, lead up to the bust of Rhodes designed by John Macallen. Macallen also designed the eight bronze lions flanking the bust. The equestrian statue entitled *Energy* was added by George Frederic Watts. Footpaths behind the memorial lead to the **King's Blockhouse** on Tafelberg Road. A memorial inscription taken from Rudyard Kipling's poem *Burial*, can be found there. Kipling spent some time on Rhodes' estate, living at **Woolsack House**. (Opening times daily 8am–6pm).

**Groote Schuur (Genadendal)**

Cecil Rhodes bought Groote Schuur after a fire in 1891, and also purchased all sections of the estate that had previously been sold off, for a sum of £9000. Another 600ha/1483 acres were added later, and

*The Rhodes Memorial in the style of a Greek temple*

Rhodes augmented the estate's original 1657 name of »De Schuur« (The Barn) to **Groote Schuur Estate**. Restoration work was managed by Sir Herbert Baker. South Africa's presidents ruled from the main building from 1910 to 1984. The neighbouring **Westbrooke House** was the governor general's residence until 1961, and then became the presidential residence. The historic meeting between P. W. Botha and Nelson Mandela took place here in 1990. It ended with the signing of the **Groote Schuur Protocol**, which envisaged the release of all political prisoners and the return of the ANC leadership in exile. Since 1994 Westbrooke House has been the **presidential seat** once again, but Nelson Mandela renamed it **Genadendal** in 1995.

# ✴ Route 62

D–F 3

**Location:** 170km–430km/105mi–270mi east of Cape Town

»See the Karoo on Route 62«, so says the publicity slogan for the African version of the American Route 66. The road winds through the valleys of the Klein Karoo and over spectacular passes, as well as through sleepy Wineland villages and all the way to the ostrich-farming centre of Oudtshoorn, where it joins the ▶Garden Route.

✴
**Montagu**

www.tourism
montagu.co.za ▶

Before the N 2 highway was built, Route 62 was the main road connection between Cape Town and Port Elizabeth. It starts at the charming little town of Montagu, in the fertile **Breede River Valley** where vineyards and plantations of apples, pears and apricots spread as far as the eye can see. The founder in 1851 was Cape governor John Montagu, who had many of the roads and passes along Route 62 built by convicts. The nearby **thermal springs** were already being

*Route 62* Map

# ▶ VISITING ROUTE 62 AND LITTLE KAROO

## INFORMATION

### Klein Karoo Tourism
Ladismith, tel. 028 / 551 1378
Route 62: tel. 023 / 616 3563;
www.route62.co.za

## WINE, BRANDY & FESTIVALS

16 estates belong to the Klein Karoo Wine Route (www.kleinkaroowines.-co.za). The best co-operative wine cellar is Montagu Wine Cellar, which has a prize-winning red muscatel dessert wine. (Opening times: Mon–Fri 8am–12.30pm, 1.30pm–5pm, Sat 9am–noon; www.montaguwines.co.-za). This wine can also be tasted during the Montagu Wine Festival during May. On the Joubert Tradouw estate near Barrydale, you can even try the original »R62 Wine« , made from merlot and cabernet sauvignon (www.joubert-tradauw.co.za). The best brandy at the Cape in 2007 was produced by the Southern Cape Vineyard in Barrydale, and named the Barry & Nephews Muscat Pot Still Brandy. (Opening times: Mon–Fri 8am–5pm, Sat 9am–3pm; www.scv.co.za). The Southern Cape Vineyard is also a member of the Brandy Route (www.sabrandy.co.za). The three port producers in Calitz-dorp include the Calitzdorp Winery on Andreis Pretorius Street. (Opening times: Mon–Fri 8am–5pm, Sat 8am–1pm). Calitzdorp celebrates its Port Festival in July.

## ON THE ROAD AGAIN ...

Get that endless Easy Rider feeling with the Cape Town branch of Harley Davidson on five-day escorted discovery tours along Route 62 (9 Somerset Road, Green Point, Cape Town, tel. 021 / 446 2999; www.harley-davidson-capetown.com).

## SPA

### Avalon Springs
Non-residential day guests are permitted to relax in the elegant spa of the Avalon Springs Luxury Resort Hotel and enjoy a massage or its 43°C/109°F spring water. A hit with children is the 60m/200ft water slide (Uitvlucht Street, 6720 Montagu, tel. 023 / 614 1150, fax 023 / 614 1906; www.avalonsprings.co.za).

## WHERE TO EAT

### ▶ Expensive
### Clarke of the Karoo
Main Road, Barrydale
tel. 028 / 572 1017
Connoisseurs rank Mike Clarke's restaurant among the top ten between Cape Town and Port Elizabeth. Specialties include Karoo oysters and Moroccan lamb tagine.

▶ **Moderate**

*Tractor Trips*

Popular tractor trailer tours up the 1500m/4921ft Arangieskop set off from Niel Burger's Protea Farm, 30km/19mi south of Montagu along the R 318. The panoramic round trip to the highest summit of the Langeberg Mountains takes three hours and is completed by wine-tasting and a potjiekos meal back at Protea Farm. (Departures Wed and Sat 2pm; Reservations: tel. 023 / 614 2471, e-mail: manager@montagu-ashton.info).

**WHERE TO STAY**

▶ **Luxury**

*Kingna Lodge*

11 Bath Street, Montagu 6720
Tel. 023 / 614 1066, fax 023 / 614 2405

www.kingnalodge.co.za

The hospitality at this elegant Victorian lodge was appreciated by Nelson Mandela and F. W. de Klerk in 1995, when they came here for undisturbed discussions. The best view is from the Mountain View Room with its open fire.

▶ **Mid-range**

*Rose of the Karoo*

21 Voortrekker Street
Calitzdorp 6660
Tel. 044 / 213 3133, fax 044 / 213 3133
www.roseofthekaroo.co.za

The pink guest house has three pretty B&B rooms and five self-catering apartments. During summer, there is a shaded terrace where delicious South African meals are served. The »Whatnot Shop« sells original souvenirs and craftwork from the Karoo.

*Ronnie at his well-stocked bar*

Hot springs ▶ used 200 years ago. The historic town centre now connects to the Avalon Springs Spa Hotel (▶p.241) via **Lovers Walk** along the Keisie River. No less than 14 of the 24 protected Cape Dutch and Georgian houses here lie on **Long Street**. Local history and pictures by the landscape painter **François Krige** can be seen at the **Montagu Museum**, housed in the mission church built in 1907. (Opening times:

Mon–Fri 9am–5pm, Sat & Sun 10.30am–12.30pm). Delicate porcelain dolls are exhibited at **Joubert House**, dating from 1853. (Opening times as Montagu Museum). The British fort is also open to the public (Opening times: Mon–Fri 8am–1pm, 2pm–5pm, Sat & Sun 9am–3pm). A market is held opposite the tourist office every Saturday, on Bath Street. The **Langeberg Mountains** to the south of Montagu are **a paradise for hikers and climbers**.

An unpaved road leads 7km/4.5mi to the private 54,000ha/133,434-acre Sanbona Wildlife Reserve. The turn-off is about 40km/25mi east of Montague, near Die Vlakte. The distance from the reserve gate to the lodges of Tilney Manor and Khanni Lodge is another 26km/16mi. The name of the reserve recalls the **San** people, who left rock paintings up to 3500 years old at seven different places here. Before reckless trophy hunting wiped these blue-eyed animals out 30 years ago, **white lions** were considered divine beasts in Africa. In 2003, two white lions, Jabulani and Queen, were reintroduced to the extensive bush at Sanbona. Their offspring arrived seven months later. Safaris for the »Big Five« are an opportunity to spot cheetahs, hippos, ostriches, kudus and hyenas.

**★ ★**
**Sanbona Wildlife Reserve**

◄ www.sanbona.com

From the mountain village of Barrydale, where an excellent **brandy** is produced (► p.241) and where **Anna Roux' Wildflower Garden** presents the Karoo vegetation, it is another 15km/9mi to Lemonshoek. Here, in 2001, Peter and Nola Frazer set up the **Joshua Baboon Rehabilitation Project** at their 350ha/865-acre farm, The Manger. Injured baboons, eagles, blue cranes and guenons are nursed back to health at the farm (www.baboons.co.za.). Burmese monks have built a Buddhist pagoda there.

**Barrydale**

◄ www.barrydale.co.za

According to legend, an infuriated witch is said to have split the 2189m/7182ft-high **Towerkop** mountain north of Ladismith into two peaks. Ladismith is at the heart of South Africa's largest **apricot-growing region**. Halfway to Calitzdorp lies the mission station of

**Ladismith**

◄ www.ladismith.org.za

## *Highlights* Route 62

*According to legend, an infuriated witch is said to have split the huge mountains above Ladismith*

**Amalienstein**, named after Baroness Amalie von Stein, who financed the construction of the yellow-painted Lutheran church in 1853. An unmade road branches off beyond Zoar, leading to the breathtaking Seven Week Gorge. The name is a reference to the seven-week period said to have once been needed to get through the **Swartberg Mountains** (▶p.247) by ox-cart.

Seweweekspoort ▶

**Calitzdorp** Founded in 1821, Calitzdorp is South Africa's capital of **port wine** (▶p.241). There is wonderful hiking north of town, through the untouched nature of the **Groenfontein Conservancy**. Spa and beauty treatments are available at the thermal springs of the **Calitzdorp Spa** (www.calitzdorpspa.co.za), halfway to Oudtshoorn.

**Oudtshoorn**

www.oudtshoorn info.com ▶

The **world capital of ostrich farming** is called Oudtshoorn. An oversized ostrich egg in the town centre indicates the source of local wealth. Once a source of highly desirable feathers, ostriches are now in renewed demand for their meat and leather. The **C. P. Nel Museum** on the main road tells the story of the great age of the »Feather Barons« around 1900, when ostrich feathers were fashionable in Europe and up to 750,000 ostriches were kept in Oudtshoorn. The most beautiful of the »ostrich palaces« is the adjacent **Le Roux Townhouse** built in 1909, complete with its original Art Nouveau furniture. (Opening times: Mon–Sat 10am–5pm).

A visit to an ostrich farm should not be missed! During a tour of 1–2 hours it is possible to visit breeding facilities, discover just how hard ostrich egg shells are, feed the birds, and even observe hatchlings. The oldest ostrich farm is the **Highgate Ostrich Farm,** 10km/6mi south-west of Oudtshoorn. It offers a one-hour tour, stages ostrich races, and also has a curio shop (www.highgate. co.za). **Chandelier Farm** is famous for its show and its ostrich races with professional jockeys. Furthermore, it is also possible to stay in comfortable chalets here (www.chandelier.co.za). Fascinating tours and ostrich rides are

★ ★
Ostrich farms

 VISITING OUDTSHOORN

## INFORMATION
*Tourism Office*
Baron van Rheede Street
Oudtshoorn 6625
Tel. 044 / 279 2532
www.oudtshoorn.com

## WHERE TO EAT
► **Moderate**
*Jemima's*
94 Baron van Reede Street
Tel. 044 272 0808; www.jemimas.com.
Pierre and Debbie spoil their guests
with the best of South African cuisine.
Try the Karoo lamb or grilled ostrich,
and round it off with a Demoiselles
Leroux tarte.

## WHERE TO STAY
► **Mid-range**
*Queen's Hotel*
5 Baron van Reede Street
Oudtshoorn 6625
Tel. 044 / 272 2101
Fax 044 / 272 2104
www.queenshotel.co.za
This colonial-style hotel built in 1880
is tastefully decorated with antiques.
It has over 40 elegant rooms, a
gourmet restaurant, a wood-panelled
bar, and a swimming pool.

*Hlangana Lodge*
51 North Street
Oudtshoorn 6625

*An elegant plateful: varnished ostrich eggs*

Tel. 044 / 272 2299, fax 044 / 279 1271
www.hlangana.co.za
All 18 rooms have a veranda with
views onto the tropical garden. Wonderful breakfast with ostrich paté and
smoked snoek.

## *Baedeker recommendation*

► **Luxury**
*Buffelsdrift Game Lodge*
R 328, in the direction of Cango Caves
Tel. 044 / 272 0106
Fax 044 / 272 0108
www.buffelsdrift.com
Extensive safari farm 7km/4.5mi outside
Oudtshoorn, at the foot of the Swartberg
Mountains. Exciting safaris into the un-
touched Karoo landscape lead to rhinos,
giraffes and kudus. Each of its 25 luxury
tents has a veranda looking out towards a
large watering hole frequented by hippos.
At sunset buffaloes, elephants and zebras
also congregate there.

*Take time to visit an ostrich farm in Oudtshoorn*

also run by the **Safari Ostrich Farm** (www.safariostrich.co.za), 10km/6mi south-west of town, and by the **Cango Ostrich Farm** between Oudtshoorn and the Cango Caves (www.cangoostrich.co.za).

★ ★
**Cango Caves**

The extensive **dripstone caves** 30km/19mi north of Oudtshoorn, at the foot of the Swartberg Mountains, are a miracle of nature. **Standard tours** begin on the hour, daily between 9am and 4pm, and during holiday periods it is a good idea to get there in the mornings, as there is great demand. On the half hour, between 9.30am and 3.30pm, there are also 90-minute **adventure tours**. However, these are only suitable for those with a good level of fitness and no claustrophobia problems, because the route is occasionally very steep and also leads through passages just 45cm/18in wide. The caves, whose temperature is a constant 18°C/64°F, once served as a refuge for the San people. Their drawings, however, also indicate the arrival of others: **Van Zyl's Hall**, 70m/230ft long, 35m/115ft wide and 18m/58ft high, is named after the first European to enter the darkness, in 1780. More caves, a total of 2.5km/1.5mi long, were discovered in 1972 (Cango II-IV). To protect their ecosystem, they are only open to scientists (www.cangocaves.co.za).

! **Baedeker** TIP

**Cheetahland**

Two dozen fully grown animals and six cheetah cubs belong to the successful cheetah project being run at the Cango Wildlife Ranch, 3km/2mi east of Oudtshoorn. In addition, two white lions also live here, as well as four white Bengal tigers that are presented daily during a spectacular show. Pink flamingos can be seen at the Valley of the Ancients, fragile birds of paradise, crocodiles and hippos too. (Opening times: daily 8am–5pm; www.cango.co.za).

The R 328 runs up to the Swartberg Pass (1568m/5145ft) behind the Cango Caves. The Swartberg Mountains, which make up the border between the Klein Karoo and the Groot Karoo, have been listed as a **Unesco World Heritage site** since 2004, as a region for Cape flora. The mountain chain stretches over 200km/125mi and rises to 2326m/7632ft. The most spectacular of the three passes that cross the range, the Swartberg Pass built in 1881–88, is the most spectacular. The road is not paved throughout, but is easily crossed with any car during the dry season. It does have some very steep sections, however, and poor visibility at sharp corners. **Superb views** are guaranteed, and the **fynbos vegetation** with many proteas is no less fascinating.

★★
Swartberg Pass

# ★ Rust-en-Vreugd

E 4

**Location:** 78 Buitenkant Street, Gardens    **Internet:** www.iziko.org.za/rustvreugd

**The former townhouse belonging to the Dutch East India Company lawyer Willem Cornelis Boers is considered the best example of an 18th-century Cape Dutch building.**

*The giant Cango Caves once provided shelter for the San*

⏲ Opening hours:
Tue–Thu
8.30am–4.30pm

Boers had the elegant three-storey house built in 1777–78. The Rococo lunette above the main entrance is ascribed to Anton Anreith. The estate has been a protected building since 1940, and the gardens were restored according to their original designs in 1986. Since 1965, visitors have also been able to admire part of the **William Fehr Collection**, most of which is held at the ▶Castle of Good Hope. The 17th- to 19th-century prints, paintings and drawings show the beginnings of the Cape Colony, historic events and scenes from maritime life. There are also regular special exhibitions of work by contemporary South African artists.

**St. Mary's Cathedral**

The neo-Gothic church on Roeland Street is **the seat of the Catholic archbishop** of the Cape diocese, Lawrence Henry. The cathedral was built from 1840 to designs by the Dresden architect **Carl Otto Hager** and his associate Carl Sparmann, who had both emigrated to the Cape in 1838.

# ★ St George's Cathedral

E 3

**Location:** 1 Wale Street, City Bowl      **Internet:** www. stgeorgescathedral.com

**South Africa's oldest Anglican congregation committed itself to the battle against apartheid early on. As the seat of Archbishop Desmond Tutu, St George's Cathedral gained world-wide attention and support.**

⏲ Opening hours:
Mon–Fri 9am–4pm

The church authorities reacted to the hardening of apartheid after 1948 with banners on the church façade as early as the mid-1950s. The cathedral always remained open to people of all skin colours and was regularly filled by opposition protesters. When South African television insisted on prior vetting of sermons and prayers for political content, church leaders resisted, with the result that the national broadcasting of church services was suspended. **Archbishop Desmond Tutu** (▶ Famous People) repeatedly mediated between demonstrators and the police between 1986 and 1996, and the church was regularly surrounded by water cannons. The Nobel Peace Prize holder Tutu made public speeches and granted sanctuary to asylum seekers for weeks at a time, without ever discontinuing services in the church. Today the cathedral carries the honorary title of **»The People's Church«** church services:

## ! *Baedeker* TIP

### Jam sessions in the crypt

On hot summer days, go to the Crypt Jazz Bar underneath the cathedral for a pleasantly cool lunch with delicious African dishes. The arched vaults also guarantee excellent acoustics for live evening concerts. (Tel. 021 / 424 9426; opening times: Mon, Tue 7am–7pm; Wed-Fri 7am–midnight, Sat 7pm–midnight).

*Cape Town's cathedral: Desmond Tutu's church was tolerant and open to all people, even during apartheid*

Mon–Fri 7.15am, 1.15pm, Wed also at 10am, Sat 8am, Sun 7am, ⊙ 8am, 9.15am, 6pm/7pm).

In 1827 the Bishop of Calcutta blessed the first church, which carried the title of cathedral from 1847 onwards. The foundation stone for the present neo-Gothic sandstone building was laid by the Duke of Cornwall, later King George V, in 1901. The architect was Herbert Baker. Eight years later, the crypt, choir and St David's Chapel were completed in memory of the fallen during the 1899–1902 Boer War, and St John's Chapel was completed in honour of Bishop William W. Jones. The northern transept was added in 1936. Work on the Lady Chapel and the southern transept was completed in 1969. Noteworthy features are the choir stalls of stinkwood, and the wonderful lead and glass work of the church windows and the rosette, made in 1982 and 2001. The famous **Hill organ** has been at the Cape since 1909. It is a copy of the organ at St Margaret's in Westminster, which was first played in 1675. Organist and conductor **Barry Smith** has ensured the cathedral's reputation for excellent organ concerts for the past forty years, bringing many internationally acclaimed players here. Choirs perform every Sunday evening. Concert tickets: tel. 021 / 424 7360.

**Architectural history**

✳ ✳
◄ Organ concerts

Daily between 7am and 5pm visitors can explore the **Siyahamba Labyrinth**, a replica of the maze created for Chartres Cathedral in 1220. (Tours: Richard Majewski, tel. 021 / 462 2499).

**Maze**

Cape Town's **most popular shopping strip** is St George's Mall. Take a leisurely stroll through the almost mile-long pedestrian zone with its many colourful stalls, boutiques, cafés, large department stores, fountains and lively street music. Since 2000, visitors have also admired a bronze sculpture on the corner of Waterkant Street entitled *Africa*. It is the work of the Capetonian artist Brett Murray (born 1961), and displays seven bright yellow Bart Simpson heads.

*Shopping paradise at St George's Mall*

# ✶ Signal Hill and Lion's Head

C 2, B 4

**Location:** between the city and Sea Point

**Internet:** www.tmnp.co.za; www.sanparks.org/parks/table_mountain

**The mountain ridges of Lion's Head and Signal Hill, their shape recalling a sleeping lion, offer superb views onto the districts of Downtown, ►Greenpoint, the ►V & A Waterfront and the ►Table Mountain.**

*Signal Hill*

The **350m/1148ft** Signal Hill is easily reached **by car** from the city centre via Kloof Nek Road. Alternatively, it is possible to walk through ►Bo-Kaap via Longmarket Street and climb the hill from there. Ships in port used to set their clocks according to the cannon signal. The present name was coined in 1902, when ox-carts brought two Royal Navy cannons cast in 1794 here, transported from the ►Castle of Good Hope. At the fortress, they had been fired at various times from 1803 onwards: initially at dawn, then at 1pm and, finally, on the dot of midday. At Signal Hill, the **Noon Gun** can be heard daily, except on Sundays and holidays, on the dot of noon. Computers from the planetarium in ► Observatory ensure absolute punctuality, and a second cannon is there in case the first fails. The artilleryman sends 1.5kg of gunpowder into the skies. 13 seconds later, the echo can be heard from the other end of Table Bay.

*Curry and cardamom tea*

Shireen Misbach and her family offer delicious Cape Malay cuisine and a wonderful view of Table Mountain at the **Noon Gun Tearoom & Restaurant**, at the upper end of Longmarket Street (no. 273, tel. 021 / 424 0529).

The geomorphology of the most northerly section of ►Table Mountain is made up of so-called Malmesbury slate, over 540 million years old. The shape of this ridge leading up to Lion's Head inspired this popular hill's original name of **Lion's Rump**. In fact, the **black-maned Cape lion** (Panthera Leo melanochaitus) was once native here. Larger than its northern brothers, and with a great mane covering its shoulders and stomach, it once inspired fear among settlers at the Cape. In 1653, Cape lions prowled along present-day ►Grand Parade near the first clay fort. Their bone-chilling roars often robbed Mrs van Riebeeck of her sleep. When sheep were taken by the predators, Jan van Riebeeck lost patience, and the animals were hunted until the last Cape lion was killed in 1858. Stuffed examples can be admired at the ►South African Museum, and Rembrandt made drawings of Cape lions for posterity.

**The lion's rump**

*The best view of the Lion's Head is from Clifton Bay*

**Lion's Head** The 668m/2129ft **Lion's Head** can easily be reached by a hike of 2–3 hours. There are **picnic sites** along the way, and the ascent is well sign-posted from the end of Kloof Nek Road. Mistakenly marked as »Sugarloaf« on some old maps, the mountain consists of Cape granite. The **Friends of Lion's Head & Signal Hill (FLASH)** work to protect the area and offer botanical walks, bird-watching and **full-moon hikes** (don't forget to bring a torch). Tel. 021 / 434 8456; www.friendsoflionshead.org.za).

### ? DID YOU KNOW ...?

■ ... that the massive musical hit *The Lion Sleeps Tonight* was first performed in 1939, under the Zulu title *Mbube* (lion), by the South African composer Solomon Linda and his band the *Evening Birds*? Pete Seeger, Miriam Makeba, Brian Eno and many others took the song around the world.

## ✶ Simon's Town

map p. 159

**Location:** Cape Peninsula, 50km/30mi south of the city; access via the M 4

**Simon's Town is the last stop on the metro line from Cape Town. Since 1957, it has also been the main home of South Africa's navy. Pretty Victorian houses line the »historic high street« and a small waterfront development has emerged around the harbour.**

**Local history** The town takes its name from Governor **Simon van der Stel**, who discovered the wind-protected bay in 1687 and recommended it to the Dutch East Indian Company as a winter anchorage. Thus it became **Cape Town's winter anchorage** in 1743, and from 1806 also provided a safe haven for the Royal Navy, which stood guard over Napoleon on St Helena from here. It received a town charter in 1840. The old railway station recalls the year 1890, when the railway line to Cape Town was built. In 2010 the **Marine Docks** celebrate their centenary. The **Victorian townhouses** on St George's Street, the British Hotel, the Dutch Reformed Church of St Simon and the school house all originated in the second half of the 19th century. **Tours of Simon's Town** are organized by the Simon's Town Historical Society (▶ Information, Simon's Town Tourism Bureau).

**Simon's Town Museum** The local museum also offers a tourist information service and is housed in the governor of the Dutch East India Company's former winter residence, built in 1777, on Court Road. This is where the story of Simon's Bay is told. A separate room tells the story of the legendary naval dog »Just Nuisance«. This Great Dane with the rank of able seaman got its name because it was always in the way and causing trouble. It rode trains without a ticket and drank great amounts of beer, yet was always deeply loyal to those in uniform.

Opening hours: Mon–Fri 9am–4pm, Sat 10am–1pm, Sun 11am–3pm; www.simonstown. com/museum

# ▶ VISITING SIMON'S TOWN

## INFORMATION

**Simon's Town Tourism Bureau**
111 St. George's Street, Simon's Town
Tel. 021 / 786 8440
www.simonstown.com

## BOAT CHARTERS, CYCLING, DIVING

The Boat Company at the waterfront offers harbour tours on the *Spirit of Just Nuisance* and boat charters including whale watching from May to November (tel. 083 / 257 7760; www.boatcompany.co.za). Argus Cycle Tour (www.cycletour.co.za) organizes cycle tours, and Kayak Cape Town (tel. 082 / 501 8930; www.kayakcapetown. co.za) provides guided kayak tours. Information on diving at Castle Rock and to shipwrecks off the coast can be found at www.scuba-shack.co.za.

## WHERE TO STAY

### ▶ Mid-range

*Quayside*
St. George's Street, Simon's Town

Tel. 021 / 786 3838
Fax 021 / 786 2241
www.quayside.co.za
26 rooms. A modern ambience right by the harbour, with panoramic views to False Bay.

## WHERE TO EAT

### ▶ Moderate

*Bertha's*
1 Wharf Road, Quayside Centre
Tel. 021 / 786 2138
Freshly caught seafood and spicy satay dishes are served on the terrace at the yacht marina by Laurence Burgess and Rachmat Botha.

---

The dog is even honoured by a bronze memorial on the former market square, now **Jubilee Square**. The museum offers guided tours to the grave on Red Hill where the dog found its final resting place on 1 April 1944. A memorial Just Nuisance Day Parade is held every year on 1 April. Adjacent Almay House, built in 1858 on King George Way, tells the story of the local **Cape Malay community** from the Oceanview neighbourhood, especially focusing on the era from 1967, when Simon's Town was declared a »whites only« area. The curator Zainab Davidson returned in 1995 and, together with her niece Roshini Millet, she has gathered together information on wedding customs, photos, cooking utensils and other memorabilia of the 7000 coloured inhabitants who once lived here (guided tours, tel. 021 / 786 2302).

◀ Heritage Museum

🕐
Opening hours:
Tue–Fri 11am–4pm,
Sat 11am–1pm

The old boathouse at the 1815 shipyard at St George's Street houses the **Marine Museum**, which exhibits model ships, cannons, torpe-

South African Naval Museum

*The Shosholoza sails for
the Rainbow Nation
during the America's Cup*

# SCHOOL FOR LIFE

**»Many could not even swim when they came here. Now they love the water. They swim, sail, and gain in confidence, and that is just what we need for our society ...«**

This is why the manager of the marine base at Simon's Town, Admiral Louw, supports the **Izivunguvungu Sail Academy** whenever he can. This renowned school was founded in 2002 by professional sailor Ian Ainslie (born in 1965), a world champion who has won gold at the Olympic Games three times, sailing in the Finn boat class for South Africa. The Zulu word »Izivunguvungu« means »strong wind«. Ainslie developed the sailing courses, which were initially only available to high school students, to include township children from Oceanview, Red Hill and Masiphumelele. Today, around 120 young people train in the stiff breezes of Simon's Bay after school. On Fridays and Saturdays, regattas take place in boats donated by the Royal Cape Yacht Club and the navy.

## Bravely onwards

In June 2007 a dream became reality off the shores of Valencia for second helmsman Pittmann Solomon Dipeere and his team mate and foreman **Golden Mgdeza** – South Africa's Sailors of the Year in 2001. They represented the Rainbow Nation on the yacht *Shosholoza* during the **America's Cup**. Both originally from the Kwa-Thema township near Johannesburg, they gained scholarships for the Simon's Town High School, where sailing was compulsory, in 1996 aged 15. In Ian Ainslie (the chief strategist for the *Shosholoza*), they met the right trainer at the right time. The teenagers also gathered experience on the famous South African navy yacht *Vortrekker 1*. »It is not just about sailing«, according to Ainslie: »The boys also learn to set themselves goals and that you have to work at it to achieve them.«

Youths from the **Izivunguvungu Music Academy** were also present at Valencia. Their performance in front of the *Shosholoza* was a sensation throughout the world. The band started out under Commander Mike Oldham with just six instruments, but new impetus was provided by the arrival of the SAS *Drakenberg* in 2006: the ship had 120 musical instruments on board, donations from Holland, Germany and Scotland. Information and account details for donations to the **Izivunguvungu Foundation for Youth** are available at www.Izivungu.co.za.

does, mines, life-saving objects and the bridge of a submarine. (Opening times: daily 10am–4pm). The neighbouring **Warrior Toy Museum** contains model railways, toy cars and tin soldiers. (Opening times: Sat–Thu 10am–4pm).

## Around Simon's Town

3km/2mi south of town, at Boulders Beach, a colony of almost 3000 jackass penguins live by the protective giant granite blocks. Their breeding area is part of the ► Table Mountain National Park. The **jackass penguins** settled here in the mid-1980s. In the 1930s, there were still almost 1.5 million penguins living along South Africa's coast. Today, the South African Foundation for the Conservation of Coastal Birds (www.sanccob.co.za) works for the protection of this species. The birds can be observed from raised viewing platforms. Access to the **car parks** is from Seaforth Street or Bellevue Road (opening times: Feb–May, Sept–Nov daily 8am–6.30pm, June–Aug daily 8am–5pm, Dec–Jan daily 7am–7.30pm; www.tmnp.co.za). Fish dominates the menu at the Boulders Beach restaurant (tel. 021 / 786 1758).

**★★**
**Penguin colony at Boulders Beach**

The **renowned Black Marlin restaurant** has been spoiling its guests in a lovingly restored old whaling station for the past 40 years. The menu includes oysters, kingklip, Cape lobster and a choice wine list. Whales in False Bay can be spotted from the terrace. (Tel. 021 / 786 1621, www.blackmarlin.co.za).

**★**
**Great tradition at Miller's Point**

*Stepping out: jackass penguins at Boulders Beach*

*How about a sailing trip? Catamarans are rented out at the beach at Fish Hoek*

**Chacma Trail** Guided tours on the 31km/19mi-long **spectacular nature trail** along the coast from Simon's Town, via the Swartkop Mountains as far as Cape Point, including three nights in the comfortable Cheriton Guest House, can be booked by calling tel. 021 / 786 1309.

**Fish Hoek** The **wind-protected sandy beach** of Fish Hoek, 5km/3mi north of Simon's Town is very suitable for families with children. Bead jewellery, colourful textiles and cloth from Masiphumelele township is sold at the **Ubuhlanti Cultural Centre** on the corner of Kommetje and Chasmay Road (tel. 021 / 785 7667; www.ubuhlanti.co.za).

# South African Air Force Museum

L 2

**Location:** Air Force Base, Piet Grobler Street, Ysterplaat (Cape Town)

**Internet:** www.saafmuseum.co.za

**This museum tells the story of the history of the South African Air Force (SAAF) which, by its own account, is the second-oldest air force in the world. The museum was opened by the »Father of the South African Air Force«, General Sir Pierre van Ryneveld, in 1973.**

Bus 587 as far as the stop at the corner of Koeberberg Road and Piet Grobler Street ▶

The **daredevil pilots** McCompton Patterson and Driver marked the beginnings of the SAAF about one hundred years ago, flying in Bleriot one-seaters and Patterson biplanes. During the First World War, just a single pilot protected South Africa's coasts in his Curtiss sea-plane: a certain **DH Cutler**. Transferred to East Africa, he spotted the German destroyer *Königsberg*, which was then sunk. SAAF pilots also did civilian work, for example carrying post between Durban and Cape Town, transporting diamonds between Oranjemund and Cape Town, and also providing irrigation of the eucalyptus plantations in KwaZulu Natal from the air. The trees were later used for building mine shafts. Rather less glorious military exploits included attacks on striking white miners in March 1922 and also the defeat of tribal re-bellions in Bondezwart, Rehoboth and Ovambo (in present-day Na-mibia) in the 1920s and 1930s. During the Second World War, SAAF pilots fought against Mussolini's troops in Ethiopia and in the North African campaign. By the end of the war, 2349 pilots were serving the South African Air Force. From 1960 onwards, some of them made a significant contribution towards the development of tourism in the country as bush pilots. There were also tours of duty in Korea and Angola, and in the 23-year border conflict with SWAPO, before the SAAF was substantially restructured and reduced after 1994. A good deal of air and ground equipment is on display, for example Mirage, Mustang and Spitfire fighter planes. Before the invention of radar and GPS systems, the **Spitz A 1-Projector**, built in 1923, was used for astronavigation. Exactly how it worked is explained in the museum **planetarium**.

🕐
Opening hours:
Mon–Fri
8am–3.30pm, Sat
8am–12.30pm

# ✳ South African Jewish Museum

E 4

**Location:** 88 Hatfield Street, Gardens      **Internet:** www.sajewishmuseum.co.za

**The new cultural centre for Jews at the Cape was opened for the millennium by Nelson Mandela in South Africa's oldest synagogue. Complete with its Holocaust Centre, it is among the most modern exhibitions in the country.**

The honey-coloured façade by Michael Hackner, made of Jerusalem sandstone, catches the eye. James Hogg integrated the **old synagogue** of 1863 – the oldest Jewish place of worship in South Africa – into the new museum, which also includes the **Great Syna-gogue** or Gardens Synagogue, dating from 1905. About 4000 pre-dominantly British and German Jews lived in South Africa until 1880. Among them, the diamond magnate Barney Barnato (1852–97) was the shining legend and counterpart to Cecil Rhodes. Thousands of East European Jews emigrated to South Africa prior to 1930. It is to them that the replica **shtetl** is dedicated, designed true to the original Lithuanian village of Riteve. A thora scroll and a ram's horn shofar are displayed, as well as an exhibition on the beginnings of small shops. A documentary on **Nelson Mandela** entitled *A Right-*

◄ Bus stop for the hop on-hop off City Sightseeing buses at the entrance; car park; Sun–Fri

🕐
Opening hours:
Sun–Thu
10am–5pm,
Fri 10am–2pm; clo-sed on Jewish holi-days; tours and audioguides

**! Baedeker TIP**

**Totally kosher**
Kosher meals and snacks are served at the Riteve garden café, Sun–Thu 9am–5pm. The museum shop sells Jewish cookery books and jewellery by the designer Lorraine Goodman, as well as other material on Jewish history and culture.

eous Man is also shown. South Africa's Chief Rabbi Cyril Harris described Mandela as »an example of what a person can be«. Next to Mandela and the patron Mendel Kaplan, the guests of honour at the museum inauguration included **Helen Suzman** (1917–2009), who fought for civil rights in the South African parliament and against apartheid for 36 years. A fellow campaigner, the Capetonian engineer and government advisor **Denis Goldberg** (born 1933), only returned to the Cape in 2002. He was given a life sentence alongside Mandela during the Rivonia Trial, and spent 22 years in Pretoria prison. The committed social reformer represented the ANC in London and at the United Nations. Since 1995, Goldberg's charity **Community H.E.A.R.T.** (www.community-heart.org.uk) has been dedicated to the education and health of South Africa's youth.

✳ **Cape Town Holocaust Centre**

⊙ Opening hours: Sun–Thu 10am–5pm, Fri 10am–1pm, closed on Jewish holidays; entrance free; www.ctholocaust.co.za

Complete with disabled access, the first floor houses the Albow Centre with its exhibition on the suffering of the Shoah, to which 6 million Jews fell victim. The Holocaust Centre is the only one of its kind in Africa. A multi-media presentation of the history of anti-Semitism and the Third Reich, of the deportations to the death camps, but also of resistance, release and survival, is shown. In the films, contemporary witnesses tell of their experiences. 20-minute **documentary films** about the Holocaust are shown in English, Afrikaans and Xhosa at 10.30am and 2.30pm. Although the immigration of East European Jews was severely restricted after 1930, over 1000 German Jews succeeded in fleeing to South Africa before 1935. One of them was **Harry Heinz Schwarz**, who arrived as a ten-year-old in 1934, having travelled from Cologne and then on the Giulio Cesare from Genoa to Cape Town. He studied law with Nelson Mandela and was one of his defence attorneys during the Rivonia Trial in 1964. He was a parliamentary representative for the United Party from 1974 and later for the Democratic Progressive Reform Party. A leading light in the battle against apartheid, he became the first opposition party member ever to become ambassador, representing South Africa in the USA. Today, Schwarz lives in Johannesburg with his wife Annette.

# South African Museum

**Location:** 25 Queen Victoria Street

**Internet:** www.iziko.org.za/sam;
www.iziko.org.za/planetarium

**South Africa's oldest museum has remained open throughout the restoration works that are due to be completed in 2009. The flagship of the Iziko Museums exhibits over half a million objects on the continent's nature and cultural history.**

Governor Somerset decreed the establishment of a museum as early as 1825. The earliest collection was made up of minerals and meteorite fragments, mussels, fish, reptiles, birds and mammals. The present museum building was inaugurated by Sir Gordon Sprigg in 1897. Not to be missed is the World of Sharks, where visitors can see the giant jaws of a **megalodon**: at 20m/65ft long, this was the largest shark that ever lived (around 3 million years ago). The model kelp forest includes a 5m/16ft **great white shark** and a giant squid. This 18m/60ft monster was once dubbed the »sea monk«. Even larger than that of a tyrannosaurus rex is the mighty head of a carcharodontosaurus, from the Cretaceous period, in the **Dinosaur Exhibition**

★ ★
Sharks, dinosaurs and San rock paintings

🕑
Opening hours:
Daily 10am–5pm

*The blue whale whose skeleton now hangs in the SA Museum was over 30m/98ft long*

*South Africa's cultures: traditional Sotho costume*

which was opened in 2008. Listen to whale song and marvel at the 20m/65ft-long **skeleton of a blue whale** that once weighed around 180 tons. The Karoo fossil finds are over 250 million years old. The exhibition on the various **South African cultures** of the early Iron Age is unique and includes hunters of the Kalahari, a 19th-century Nama camp, and showcases on the life of the Xhosa, Zulu, Sotho and Tswana. There is a vivid exhibition on **San rock painting**, as well as on the beliefs and traditional healing methods of the San. **South Africa's new emblem** since the year 2000 includes two figures from a San **rock painting** found on **Linton Farm** (Eastern Cape) in 1917. The nation's motto »Unity in Diversity« is also taken from a San language (►image p.39).

(►image p.39)

The **planetarium**, built in 1958, is an audio-visual theatre of the skies with its Minolta star projector, complete with spectacular shows on the stars above Table Mountain. The journey to the wonders of the universe or to »Life in the Cosmic Egg« can accommodate 140 galactic travellers seated in comfortable armchairs. The afternoon shows at weekends are especially tailored to children. (Opening hours: Mon–Fri 2pm, Tue also at 8pm, Sat & Sun noon, 1pm and 2.30pm).

**! Baedeker TIP**

**Magical San myths**

J. David Lewis-Williams examines the religion and society of the San represented in the rock art in *A Cosmos in Stone* (Altamira Press, 2002). Lewis-Williams, professor at the Rock Art Research Institute at the Johannesburg University of Witwatersrand, is a renowned expert in the field.

# South African National Gallery

**Location:** Government Avenue, Company's Garden

**Internet:** www.iziko.org.za/sang

**Those interested in contemporary art at the Cape must visit the National Gallery. The country's most important temple to the arts shows not only European masters of the colonial era, but also outstanding modern South African artists.**

The foundation of the collection of roughly 6500 items was laid by Thomas Butterworth Bayley's 1871 donation of 45 paintings. The main building, designed by Clelland & Mullins and F. K. Kendall, was not completed until 1930, however. Art from recycled materials from the townships is sold in front of the main entrance, by the **statue of Jan Smuts** designed by Sydney Harpley in 1964. The niches next to the museum entrance were designed in colourful Ndebele style by **Isa Kabini**. The permanent collection includes representatives of the New English Art Club, as well as work by the Bloomsbury Group from the early 20th century. Paintings by John Walker, Michael Porter, Gary Wragg, Alan Davie and Ronald Kitaj were purchased from 1980 onwards.

The donation from **Sir Abe Bailey** (1865–1940) has been housed at the National Gallery since 1947. Bailey was a South African mining magnate and financial tycoon who loved the lifestyle of the English landed gentry and was a passionate hunter, as portrayed in the painting *Shooting Grouse* by D. Wolstenholme, or *The Grey Hunter* by G. Towne. Bailey's enthusiasm for horse riding and cricket is also illustrated by the 400 paintings, drawings and prints that, thanks for the patron's will, came back to the Cape. The Abe Bailey Trust is dedicated to conservation and restoration of the works held at the National Gallery.

⊙ Opening hours: Tue–Sun 10am–5pm, free on Sat

**Butcher Boys**, a figural sculpture made in 1985–86 by Jane Alexander (born 1959), conveys with stirring intensity the horrific deformation of humanity during the apartheid era. Alexander also painted the 1995 portrait of Steve Biko, the founder of the Black Consciousness Movement. The conflicts and contradictions faced by the developing country are portrayed in a 9 x 15m/30 x 50ft painting entitled **Challenges Facing the New South Africa** by Willie Bester, born in Montagu/Western Cape in 1956.

★ ★ Contemporary collection

In addition, Wayne Barker is represented by his 1995 work *Blue Colonies*, and the autodidact Trevor Makhoba by *Things Will Happen* and *Azibuye Emassweni* (both 1991). In 2005 the Friends of the National Gallery purchased Claudette Schreuder's wooden bust of the president's wife Tibbie Steyn (2001).

**Township art and naïve art** A contrast is provided by the exhibited township art of bead figures by Zulu women, as well as by textiles, photos and new media installations. The **gallery café** serves tea with views of naïve art by the painter Andrew Murray (1917–98).

# ★★ Stellenbosch

**B 3**

**Location:** 50km/30mi north-east of Cape Town

**Population:** 103,000

**Unique Cape Dutch architecture, first-class museums, wonderful vineyards and superb restaurants make this renowned university town a top destination.**

**Local history** The oldest European settlement at the Cape after Cape Town was founded by Governor Simon van de Stel in 1679. The first settlers planted wheat in the fertile valley, but it was soon recognized that the climate and earth is ideally suited for wine growing. Today, the region is one of the country's **most important wine growing areas**. Stellenbosch has been a **university town** since 1918. Students who

*A picture of beauty: the former vicarage of the Rhenish Mission, which today exhibits Victorian dolls and model railway sets*

## Stellenbosch *Map*

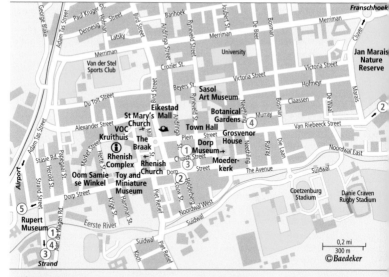

**Where to eat**
1. De Volkskombuis
2. Cognito
3. Terroir/ Kleine Zalze
4. De Oewer
5. Moyo at Spier

**Where to stay**
1. D'Ouwe Werf
2. Lanzerac Manor Hotel & Spa
3. Stellenbosch Hotel
4. Roosenwijn Guest House

went on to become prime ministers and state presidents studied at South Africa's oldest university, including Hans Strijdom, Daniel Malan and Jan Smuts. In 2007, Russel Botman became the first non-white director of this elite institution and, of the 23,000 students, almost 30% are non-whites these days. One of the university's recent success stories is also the creation of South Africa's »Silicon Valley«: the Stellenbosch **Technopark**.

Tropical orchids, bonsai trees and welwitshias (fossil plants) from Namibia's desert flourish in the university's Botanical Garden on Neethling Street. (Opening times: daily 8am–5pm).

**Botanical Garden** ⏱

On today's »braak« (village green) in the town centre, military parades were once held. The church of **St Mary-on-the-Braak** was inaugurated in 1854. In 1884 a bell tower was added. The arsenal built for the VOC in 1777, known as the **VOC Kruithuis**, is now the Military Museum (opening times: Sept–May Mon–Fri 9am–2pm). Delft porcelain, tobacco tins and VOC trophies can be admired at the **Burgerhuis** on Market Street, built in 1797. (Opening times: Mon–Fri 8am–4.30pm, Sat 10am–1pm, 2pm–5pm).

**De Braak** ⏱ ⏱

# ▶ VISITING STELLENBOSCH

## INFORMATION

### Tourism Information Centre
36 Market Street, Stellenbosch
Tel. 021 / 883 3584
Fax 021 / 882 9550
www.stellenboschtourism.co.za

## WHERE TO EAT

### ▶ Expensive

#### ① De Volkskombuis
Aan de Wagen Road
Tel. 021 / 887 2121
www.volkskombuis.co.za
This farmhouse designed by Sir Herbert Baker has been a culinary institution for over 30 years. Dawid and Christelle Kriel spoil their guests with Cape Dutch delicacies. Try the Karoo lamb with a fine shiraz.

#### ② Cognito
137 Dorp Street
Purdon Gilmore Building
Tel. 021 / 882 8696, closed Sun;
www.cognitorestaurant.co.za
Elegant surroundings and a successful synthesis of South African and Moroccan cuisine. Michelle Kromhout's specialty is b'stilla chicken and lamb with sweet potatoes and apricot sauce.

*Baedeker recommendation*

#### ③ Terroir / Kleine Zalze
Strand Road / R 44
Tel. 021 / 880 8167
www.kleinezalze.com
The 100ha/247-acre vineyard above the De Zalze Golf Club was founded by Nicholas Cleef in 1683. Today, the family firm not only offers cellar tours and wine-tasting, but also runs an elegant country house hotel with a gourmet restaurant inspired by Mediterranean cuisine. Terroir is among the Cape's top ten restaurants. Our tip: Michael Broughton's crayfish risotto with white truffle oil, along with a Kleine Zalze chenin blanc 2007.

### ▶ Moderate

#### ④ De Oewer
Aan de Wagen Road
Tel. 021 / 886 5431
www.volkskombuis.co.za/oewer
The vineyard on the Eerste River offers relaxation in the shade of mighty oak trees. The cooking is Mediterranean-inspired. The snoekopita, West Coast pike rolls, are delicious.

#### ⑤ Moyo at Spier
6km/4mi south-west of Stellenbosch on the R 310
Tel. 021 / 809 11 00
www.spier.co.za
A new generation of African wine-makers is being trained by the Zulu wine expert Jabulani Ntshangase on the 150-year-old Spier wine estate. Wine-tasting daily 10am–4.30pm.

*For high standards: Kleine Zalze country hotel with pool*

Imaginative oriental décor is part of the banquet offered at the open-air Moyo restaurant, with Bedouin tents, African music and a live show. Traditional Cape cuisine is served in the Jonkerhuis. There are also 155 smart rooms for overnight stays. Take a look at the studios of young artists and the craftwork on sale. Furthermore, the Cheetah Project has hand-reared cheetahs, and the bird of prey enclosure run by Tracy and Hank Chalmers takes care of eagles and falcons.

*Old glory: the omnibus carriage at Blaauwklippen vineyard dates from 1868*

## WINE ROUTE & FESTIVAL

South Africa's oldest wine route was been established around Stellenbosch in 1971. Today it is divided into five sectional routes (www.wineroute.co.za; ► p.269). Highlight of the year is the Wine Festival in August.

## WHERE TO STAY

### ► Luxury
① **D'Ouwe Werf**
30 Church Street, Stellenbosch 7600
Tel. 021 / 887 4608, fax 021 / 887 4626
www.ouwewerf.com
South Africa's oldest historic hotel goes back to the year 1802, and the present Georgian-style building dates from the 1890s. All 32 rooms are furnished with antique furniture. The prize-winning garden restaurant serves tender ostrich and kudu steaks cooked by Liza Engelbrecht. The »chocolate cake for millionaires« with rose-water ice-cream is irresistible!

## *Baedeker recommendation*

② ***Lanzerac Manor Hotel & Spa***
Lanzerac Road, Stellenbosch 7599
Tel. 021 / 887 1132
www.lanzerac.co.za
4km/2.5mi south-east of Stellenbosch, ancient oaks line the drive to one of South Africa's most beautiful spa hotels, with spectacular views of the rugged mountains and the green vineyards. The winery with its mansion dating from 1692 is renowned for top-class service, fine wines and exquisite cuisine (►photo p.42). All 48 rooms have balconies or a terrace. Relaxation is promised by the new spa with pool, Jacuzzi and saunas.

### ► Mid-range
③ ***Stellenbosch Hotel***
Corner of Dorp Street/Andringa Street, Stellenbosch 7559
Tel. 021 / 887 3644
Fax 021 / 887-3673
www.stellenboschhotel.co.za
Charming boutique hotel in the centre, with 27 rooms and 6 self-catering apartments. Try the restaurant where Jan Cats serves fresh oysters and game.

### ► Budget
④ ***Roosenwijn Guest House***
14 van Riebeeck St, Stellenbosch 7500
Tel. 021 / 883 3338
www.stellenguest.co.za
Enchanting mansion built in 1904, complete with pool and romantic wedding suite.

# STELLENBOSCH VILLAGE MUSEUM

**✳✳ In order to illustrate the development of architecture, domestic interiors, gardens and fashion, four 18th- and 19th-century houses in the oldest quarter of Stellenbosch have been lovingly restored.**

⏱ Opening times:
Mon–Sat 9.30am–5pm, Sun 2pm–5pm
Entrance: 18 Ryneveld Street, tel. 021/887 2902

### ① Schreuderhuis (c1709)

The German mill manager Sebastiaan Schröder lived in this thatched house with earth floors, whitewashed walls and lead windows from 1709 onwards. Half a year after its completion, in February 1710, it was recorded on the first drawing made of Stellenbosch, and today is the oldest surviving town house in southern Africa. The furniture and domestic goods date from the era between 1690 and 1720.

### ② Blettermanhuis (c1789)

In 1789, shortly before his retirement, Hendrik Lodewyk Blettermann, a wealthy justice of the peace and the last VOC official, built himself a house in typical Cape Dutch style. The house has an H-shape plan and six gables. The furniture dates from the second half of the 18th century.

*Exquisite items to admire: the stink-wood cupboard in the bedroom at the Blettermanhuis*

### ③ Grosvenor House (c1803)

The lower floors of this classical mansion were begun in 1782 for the landowner and farmer Christian Ludolph Neethling, but only completed by his successor J.W. Herold in 1803. The house was finished with a tiled flat roof. The neoclassical entrance is embellished with a pediment containing a Biblical palm for psalm 92, verse 13: »The just will flourish like a palm tree«.

### ④ O.M. Bergh House (c1850)

Originally, before it received its present form in the late 19th century, the house belonging to the deputy law enforcer Olof Martinus Bergh also had a thatched roof and gables similar to the Blettermanhuis. The wallpaper, furniture and domestic items are typical for the Victorian era between 1840 and 1870.

### ⑤ Gardens

Even the gardens of the four houses are planted in the original style, with flowers, fruit trees, vegetable patches, and medicinal and culinary herbs.

*ssical furniture
ative wood adorns
nd floor at Grosve-
use*

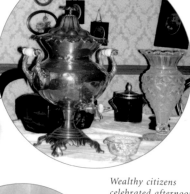

*Olof M. Bergh's Victorian desk*

ostdy

*Wealthy citizens
celebrated afternoon
tea: Empire samovar
from 1850*

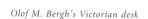

*Bedroom in the
Schreuderhuis*

Ne[...]
fro[...]
the [...]
nor[...]

*There is even a grand piano in the elegant salon of Grosvenor House*

**Van Riebeeck Street**

© Baedeker

**Entrance (Ryneveld Street)**

*The shiny fire engine of 1732 in the foyer*

**Rhenish Corner**

From 1823 slaves were once instructed from the Baroque pulpit of the Rhenish Church. The collection of buildings that make up **Rhenish Corner** is now partly used by an art school. The **Toy Museum** in the former parish house of the Rhenish Mission has an exhibition of historic dolls, cars and miniature railways. (Opening times: Mon–Sat 9.30am–5pm, Sept–April including Sun 2pm–5pm, ▶photo p.262).

**Dorp Museum (Village Museum)**

▶3D image p.266

The **Village Museum** on Ryneveld Street is dedicated to preserving and exhibiting **the rich heritage of Stellenbosch** with its carefully restored homes complete with original interiors and furniture. It is worth taking plenty of time for a tour: the museum attendants dressed in historical costumes are happy to answer questions.

**Moederkerk**

The neo-Gothic Dutch Reformed »mother church« with its thick lead windows is a masterpiece by Carl Otto Hager. The oldest of its three previous incarnations had a thatched roof until 1722.

**Sasol Art Museum**

Sponsored by South Africa's oil multinational Sasol, the university's Sasol Art Museum is housed in the neo-classical Bloemhof, built in 1907, and shows the work of South African artists from the 19th and 20th centuries. It also hosts **excellent changing exhibitions** (52 Ryneveld Street; opening times: Tue, Thu, Fri 9am–4.30pm, Wed 9am–8pm, Sat 9am–5pm, Sun 2pm–5pm). The **Erfurt Huis** built in 1876, opposite at no. 37, is the seat of the Stellenbosch Museums.

**Dorp Street**

The main boulevard of Stellenbosch is lined by whitewashed houses with fine gables and pretty front gardens. The Lutheran parish church built by Carl Otto Hager in 1851 now houses the **US Art Gallery**, which hosts art previews. (Opening times: Mon–Fri 9am–5pm, Sat 9am–1pm). **Oom Samie se Winkel** at 84 Dorp Street is a very popular general store that has been trading since 1791.

**Rupert Museum**

The immensely wealthy tobacco magnate **Anton Rupert** (1916–2006) sponsored the snow-white building complex (by Hans Meiring, 2005) for his private art collection. Three exhibition halls show **South African art**, including work by Maggie Laubser, Alexis Preller, Jean Weiz, Lippy Lipshitz and Irma Stern's early piece of 1916, *The Eternal Child*. Europe is represented by, among others, Käthe Kollwitz, Corbusier and Rodin. (Opening times: Mon–Fri 9.30am–1pm, 2pm–4pm, Sat 10am–1pm).

**Marvol Museum**

South Africa's only museum for **Russian art** is located at **Hazendal** winery, founded by Christoffel Hazen in 1699. On show are Russian Impressionist works, icons, majolica, and Fabergé eggs by Victor Meyer. The »Mandela Easter Egg« of 1997 is made of 18-carat gold, as well as diamonds, sapphires and rubies. The Hermitage

*Doing good business for the past 200 years: Oom Samie se Winkel*

Russian restaurant offers Russian specialties. (Bottelary Road, opening times: Tue–Fri 10am–4pm, Sat & Sun 10am–3pm; tours: Tue–Fri 10.30am, 2.30pm, Sat & Sun 12.30pm, 2.30pm; www.hazendal.co.za.).

## Around Stellenbosch

Almost all of some 130 vineyards around Stellenbosch offer daily cellar tours and wine-tasting. Many also have restaurants and picnic facilities. The **Kleine Zalze**, **Lanzerac** and **Spier** (►p.265) estates are especially recommended, while the **Bergkelder** winery has a wine museum and extensive cellars set into the Papegaaiberg Mountain. (Opening times: Mon–Fri 8am–5pm, Sat 9am–2pm; tours: Mon–Fri 10am, 11am, 3pm, Sat 10am, 11am, 12.30pm; www.bergkelder.co.za). Famous for its beautiful Cape Dutch mansion, the **Blaawklippen** estate, which celebrated its 325th anniversary in 2007, also has a coach museum (►photo p.265) and the excellent Barouche restaurant. Why not try the full-bodied Cabriolet? (Opening times: daily 9am–5pm, Sun till 4pm; tours by appointment tel. 021 / 880 0133; south along the R 44; www. blaauwklippen.co.za).

**Meerlust** also has beautiful Cape Dutch buildings and its wines, such as the dark red Rubicon, are exclusively aged in oak. (Opening times: Mon–Fri 9am–5pm, Sat 10am–2pm; tours by appointment, tel. 021 / 843 3587; south along the R 44; www.meerlust.co. za). The **Morgenhof** estate has a wonderful park and wine cellar with 1600 barrels: try the cuvée »première sélection« from their Bordeaux-type wines. (Opening times: Mon–Fri 9am–5pm, Sat & Sun 10am–2pm; tours by appointment, tel. 021 / 889 5510; by the Simonsberg Mountain; www.morgenhof.com).

★ ★
Stellenbosch
Wine Route

◄ www.
wineroute.co.za

! **Baedeker** TIP

### Lord Neethling

The approach through the mile-long pine-lined alley is impressive already. Neethlingshof Estate was founded in 1692 by Willem Barend Lubbe, a German immigrant. Today the magnificent property with a manor house from 1814 offers not only wine tasting – an absolute must: the pinotage – but also real gourmet experiences. Reserve a table on the palm terrace of Lord Neethling Restaurant with a view of the vineyards and try the biltong with port wine or springbok on wild mushrooms (make a reservation for a tour, Polkadraai Road, Vlottenburg, 6 km west of Stellenbosch, tel. 021 / 883 8966, ww.lordneethling.co.za, www.neethlimgshof.co.za).

The award-winning red wines from the **Rust en Vrede** estate are dry, earthy and a deep tannin red. The estate was taken over by the former rugby international Jannie Engelbrecht in 1978, and at Nelson Mandela's request Rust en Vrede supplied the wines for the banquet held in his honour when he was presented with the Nobel Peace Prize in Oslo in 2004. (Opening times: Mon–Fri 9am–5pm, Sat 9am–3pm; south along the R 44; www.rustenvrede.com). A 2km/1mi circular footpath, which also includes a very attractive wildflower garden, introduces the 200ha/500-acre **Assegaaibosch Nature Reserve**, south-east of Stellenbosch, in the Jonkershoek Valley. (Opening times: daily 7.30am–5pm).

**Hottentots Holland Nature Reserve**

Continue on the **Boland Hiking Trail** to reach the 25,000ha/62,000 acre reserve of the Hottentots Holland area, where dwarf antelopes, springboks and leopards roam.

**Somerset West**

A popular place to live 16km/10mi south of Stellenbosch is the tranquil little town of Somerset West at the foot of the Helderberg mountain chain. During summer, many artisans sell their work at the craft market on Main Road, while the best bobotie is made by Carmen Truter and can be savoured in the Victorian **Die Ou Pastorie Country House & Restaurant** at Lourens Street 41 (tel. 021 / 852 2120). Meanwhile, Andre William's cooking, for example his exquisite desserts, is true to his establishment's name: simply **D'Vine**, at Morgenstern Avenue (tel. 021 / 851 3759; www.dvinerestaurant.co.za). Monkey Town, 3km/2mi along the N 2 in the direction of Caledon, is great fun for all the family. More than 230 monkeys, including **chimpanzees**, baboons and lemurs live in a giant park here. (Opening times: daily 9am–5pm;www.monkeys.co.za).

✱ For gourmets ▶

✱ Monkey Town ▶

⊙

✱✱ **Vergelegen**

www.vergelegen.co.za ▶

⊙

Cellar tour: Daily 10.30am, 11.30am, 3pm

The 3000ha/7500-acre Vergelegen Estate 4km/3mi north-east of Somerset West is without doubt one of the most impressive vineyards in South Africa. Queen Elizabeth II, Bill Clinton and Nelson Mandela have all been guests here. The land was granted to Governor Willem Adriaan van der Stel, on 1 February 1700. It was he who built the beautiful Cape Dutch mansion and planted the first vines. During the course of its chequered history, in 1917 the holding passed to Sir Lionel and Lady »Ferrie« Phillips, who restored the winery and added a library, which is open to the public (daily

9.30am–5pm). On no account pass up the chance to take a tour around the **state-of-the-art cellars** designed by star architect Patrick Dillon in 1992, rounded off with a wine-tasting. There are four production levels here, of which three are underground. The **Cuvée Vergelegen** made from cabernet sauvignon, merlot and cabernet franc is one of the country's top wines. Take a picnic basket and settle under the 300-year-old camphor trees in the park or book a table on the terrace at the **Lady Phillips Restaurant** by the rose garden. (Lourensford Road, tel. 021 / 847 1346).

★
**Helderberg Nature Reserve**

This reserve, on the south-eastern slopes of the 1138m/3734ft-high **Helderberg Dome** is renowned for its proteas and many species of birds. (Opening times: Nov–April daily 7.30am–7pm, May–Oct daily 7.30am–5.30pm). Information on the local mountain fynbos and bird species can be found at the entrance, at the Maskew Miller Herbarium. (Opening times: daily 10am–4.30pm). A map with hiking trails leading to the summit is also available here. The **trails** leading off from the Helderberg Farm with its good restaurant are between 2km/1mi and 20km/13mi long. (Opening times: daily 8am–6pm; www.helderbergplaas.co.za).

◄ www.helderberg naturereserve.co.za

☉

★
**Nice sandy beaches**

The high-rise skyline along the fine sand of Goustrow Beach at **Strand** illustrates the great popularity of this seaside resort on **False Bay** among Capetonians. Europeans tend to prefer the fishing village of **Gordon's Bay**, 8km/5mi further along, by a rocky coast that is ideal for fishing. The panoramic coastal **R 44 route**, from Betty's Bay to Kleinmond (►p.217), is also very good for whale spotting.

*The grape harvest begins in late January in Stellenbosch*

# Strand Street

D 2 –F 3

**Location:** Connects City Bowl with the Waterkant district

**Transport:** Taxis and buses to the railway station or to V & A Waterfront

**Prior to land reclamation works, this broad traffic artery between the city centre and ▶Green Point really did follow the sea. Today, Strand Street has long-standing as well as brand new visitor attractions, such as the fascinating Gold of Africa Museum.**

**Idyllic times**

In 1790, when Cape Town's streets were given official names, Strand Street too received its first street signs. Until 1702 it was known as **Sea Street**, then as Breede Strand Straat. The road followed the historic coastline until the »strand« was moved 2km/1mi north by dumping 40 million tons of sand and earth to create around 145ha/360 acres of land for the **Foreshore**. The first house on the road was built in 1664 by the VOC baker Thomas Christian Mulder. From 1700 onwards, Strand Street became a desirable address. At the time, Cape Town's population numbered 640 adults, 605 children and 891 slaves. By the 19th century, **wealthy ship-owners and merchants** based at the nearby ▶Heerengracht lived here with their families.

✳
**Koopmans-de-Wet-House**

🕐
**Opening hours:**
Tue–Thu
9am–4pm;
www.iziko.org.za/
koopmans

South Africa's first private townhouse at no. 35 was opened to the public in 1914, and was completely renovated in 2003. The last owners were **Marie Koopmans-de Wet** (1834–1906) and her sister Margaretha (1836–1911), whose salon here was once a highlight in Cape Town's cultural life. Marie was a respected member of society because of her sponsorship of the arts and services during the Boer War, but when she organized food packets for the women in the English concentration camps, she was arrested. **Late 18th-century and early 19th-century Cape furniture**, decorative frescoes, Chinese and Delft porcelain all add to the experience of a visit here. In 1806 the house and grounds were purchased by Margaretha Jacoba Smuts, widow of the secretary of the civic council Hendrick Justinus de Wet. By then, the property had already had 14 previous owners, the first of whom had been the Frisian Reijnier Smedinga, in 1701. It was extended over two floors in 1771 by Pieter Malet from Amsterdam to accommodate his 16 children. The elegant neo-classical façade is believed to have been designed by Louis Thibault and Anton Anreith around 1790. 17 layers of paint were discovered on it during restoration work in 1994. It is said that two of widow Smuts' seven domestic slaves, the cooper Jonas van de Caab and the cook Kito van Mosambique, still haunt the place.

**Lutheran Church**

The astute merchant Martin Melck had **South Africa's oldest Lutheran church** built at the junction with Buitengracht in 1774. As a schuilkerk (school church), it could not be banned, though the 130 parishioners at the time did still pray in secret in those days. Freedom of religious worship was only granted by the VOC after 1780. The pulpit is by Anton Anreith. (Opening times: Mon–Fri 10am–2pm).

Next door is the **Martin Melck House**, which was only built after Melck's death, in 1783. The façade dates from 1820. Since 2001, it has housed the world's only museum that focuses exclusively on **African gold art**. The core of the collection is the Jean Paul Barbier/Josef Mueller Collection from Geneva (www.barbier-mueller.ch), purchased by the gold-mining multinational Anglo Gold Ashanti. It focuses primarily on the art of the West African kingdom of Akan in modern-day Ghana and the Ivory Coast. On view are gold jewellery and an Ashanti tribal throne from Ghana, gold-leaf fetishes and colourful Kente weavings, and also filigree gold work from Zimbabwe, Egypt and the Sahel region. The museum also sells 22-carat gold jewellery. (Opening times: Mon–Sat 9.30am–5pm; tours: 6pm–8pm; www.goldofafrica.com).

★ ★
Gold of Africa
Museum (GOA)

! **Baedeker** TIP

**All gold**
Those who enjoy designing their own jewellery can book a course in the museum's gold workshop. Cape Malay delicacies are served in the green courtyard of the Gold Restaurant. Dinner can be enjoyed to the sounds of drumming, and includes a museum tour and a Malayan puppet theatre show. (Opening times: daily 10.30am–11pm, tel. 021/421 4653; www.gold restaurant.co.za).

The Waterkant is squeezed between the city centre and the ► V & A Waterfront, where the Strand becomes High Level Road. Restored rows of houses, small bars and cafés, restaurants, art galleries, boutiques and the **Cape Quarter** shopping centre at 72 Waterkant Street have enlivened the area considerably. Juicy steaks, line fish and 40 top-class wines are served at the **Nose Restaurant and Wine Bar** in the Cape Quarter, with the entrance on Dixon Street (tel. 021 / 425 2200; www. thenose.co.za). The Waterkant is also known as The Village and is a popular gay haunt. Same-sex marriage has been legal in South Africa since 2008. During February's **Cape Town Pride Festival**, a gay and lesbian procession takes place in Waterkant (www.capetownpride.co.za).

Waterkant

## ★★ Table Mountain (Hoeri 'kwaggo)

**Location:** 1086m/3563ft above Table Bay

**Internet:** www.tablemountain.net; www.sanparks.org/parks/table_mountain

**Whether climbed on foot or by cable car, a visit to Table Mountain is among the highlights of a Cape Town holiday – assuming the mighty prehistoric rock is not just shrouded in dense clouds. The view down of the city centre is fabulous on sunny days and can include the entire Cape Peninsula.**

▶ 3D image p.276 By **car** the base station of the cable car on Tafelberg Road is reached via Buitengracht Street and Kloof Nek Road from the city centre. The red double-decker buses of **Cape Town Explorer** and **City Sightseeing** (▶ p.120) depart for the cable-car station from the ▶ V & A Waterfront.

Mountain in the Sea The first white man on Table Mountain was the Portuguese Antonio de Saldanha in 1503. He christened **Cape Town's emblem** »Taboa da

Caba« (Table at the Cape), which is the name that stuck. Traces of human settlement, however, prove the far earlier presence of the San on what they called **»Hoeri 'kwaggo«**, the »Mountain in the Sea«. 1085m/3560ft, 1086m/3563ft or 1087m/3566ft? The altitude of the highest plateau point at **Maclear's Beacon** is still in dispute.

*In good weather, the view from Table Mountain reaches all the way down to the Cape*

# ★ ★ Table Mountain National Park

Map p.159

**Location:** Between Signal Hill and Cape Point, Atlantic and False Bay

**Internet:** www.tmnp.co.za; www.sanparks.org/parks/table_mountain/

**Almost three quarters of the Cape Peninsula belong to the Table Mountain National Park, founded in 1998, into which the Cape Peninsula National Park was incorporated in 2004. More than 2280 plant species are native to the park, which forms the core of the Unesco World Heritage site for Cape flora.**

# TABLE MOUNTAIN

**✳ ✳** Table Mountain (1986m/6516ft) is Cape Town's emblem. Due to the south-easterly summer winds – locally known as the »Cape Doctor« – clouds often hang over the summit like a tablecloth. Hikes and ascents should start as soon as the mountain is free of clouds, because the weather can change fast. From the summit there is a breathtaking view over the city.

⏱ Cable car times:
May–mid Sept daily 8.30am–6pm, mid Sept–Oct daily 8am–7pm, Nov daily 8am–8pm, Dec, Jan 8am–9.30pm/10pm, Feb 8am–8.30pm, March 8am–7.30pm, April 8am–6.30pm. No service during strong winds. Discounts for holders of the Wildcard.
Information: tel 021/424 8181
www.tablemountain.net (includes a webcam)

### Stone witnesses to the earth's history
Table Mountain, made up of huge layers of sandstone covering an older base of granite and quartz, forms the northern end of the Cape Peninsula. The mighty coastal mountains are over 650 million years old and were once five times as high as they are today. The erosion by wind and weather that has given the colossal mountain its present form began 180 million years ago, following earlier periods when tectonic movement and changing sea levels caused it to rise and fall repeatedly. Cracks, ravines and splits around the summit area show that the evolutionary process is by no means over. To the east, the Table Mountain massif also includes the 1002m/3288ft ① **Devil's Peak;** the west, between the city and the Atlantic, rises the 669m/2195ft ② **Lion's Head** and the end of the long »lion's body« is made up by the 350m/1148ft ③ **Signal Hill**. To the south-west, the ④ **Twelve Apostles** rise above the resorts on the Atlantic at heights ranging between 780m/2559ft and 800m/2625ft. To the south, Table Mountain continues as a broad plateau that eventually descends to the Orange Kloof and the famous ►Kirstenbosch Botanical Gardens.

### Table Mountain's »tablecloth«
The »tablecloth« frequently shrouds Table Mountain due to the south-easterly summer winds. Rising air, which gathers a great deal of moisture over the Agulhas Current and along False Bay, condenses into thick cloud at a level of around 900m/3000ft. This cloud mass rolls over the mountain and falls towards the city. As it descends, the air warms and the clouds disperse, forming the distinctive »tablecloth«.

### ⑤ Table Mountain Aerial Cable Way
The cable car requires five to ten minutes for the journey of 700m/2300ft to the summit. On Friday, 13 July 2007, the cable car welcomed its 18-millionth customer since opening in 1929. The cabins of the new Swiss cable car system installed in 1997 turn a full 360° during their journey up the mountain. There is a self-service restaurant at the upper cable car station, where maps and hiking guides can be purchased.

### Plateau paths through paradise
With more than 1500 different plant species, the mountain is a **botanical paradise** that can be explored on three marked footpaths. The **Dassie Walk**, with spectacular views to the Twelve Apostles, is a route populated by **rock dassies**, which are up to 50cm/20in long and related to elephants. The popular **Agama Walk** offers all-round panorama views across Cape Town and the Cape Peninsula. The **Klipspringer Walk** leads to the plateau edge and the **Plattekip Gorge**. Many tracks lead onto the »Hoeri 'kwaggo«, but only the marked footpath through the Plattekip Gorge is recommended: a path that Antonio da Saldanha also took in 1503. Those who wish to take this route need a good level of fitness, all-weather clothes and firm walking shoes, as the ascent is extremely steep in parts and can last up to four hours. Information on the new Hoeri-ikwaggo Trails through the Table Mountain National Park can be found at the two park offices at the foot of the gorge and along the ►Table Mountain road.

### Best views
At weekends Table Mountain is illuminated during the evening. The best views for photos can then be found along the road to Signal Hill.

### Pure adrenalin ...
... is guaranteed by abseiling down Table Mountain at the 112m/367ft-long drop. Strictly for those without vertigo!

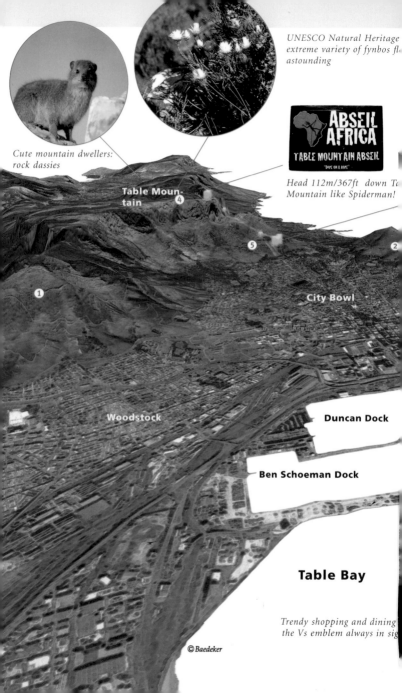

UNESCO Natural Heritage
extreme variety of fynbos fl...
astounding

Cute mountain dwellers:
rock dassies

ABSEIL AFRICA
TABLE MOUNTAIN ABSEIL
"DOPE ON A ROPE"

Head 112m/367ft down T...
Mountain like Spiderman!

Table Moun-
tain ④

⑤

②

①

City Bowl

Woodstock

Duncan Dock

Ben Schoeman Dock

Table Bay

Trendy shopping and dining
the Vs emblem always in sig...

© Baedeker

► Map p.159 After the Cape of Hope Nature Reserve was founded in 1939, nature lovers and environmental activists took it upon themselves to protect the flora and flora at the Cape in 14 individual nature reserves until 1998. Now united into one 25,000ha/62,000-acre national park, the area stretches from ► **Signal Hill**, **Lion's Head** and **Devil's Peak** to the north, to the ► **Cape of Good Hope** in the south, and from the Atlantic coast to **Boulders Beach** on ► **False Bay**.

**Species-rich flora in a small area** The main attraction is the macchia-type vegetation known as **fynbos** (»beautiful bush«) with its countless proteas, orchids and ericas. 13 of them are endemic, meaning they only exist in this park. The hardy evergreen **Disa uniflora** orchid, which can stand temperatures as low as -3ºC/27ºF and flowers red in June and July, is the much-admired emblem of the Table Mountain flora. Along with gladioli and freesias, it has long been cultivated in European gardens. The king protea, with a blossom that can reach 30cm/1ft in height, has been declared South Africa's national flower. The survival of this unique plant world is being ensured by extensive conservation measures, including the banning of flora not native to the Cape and the protection of threatened species. Mountain zebras, Eland antelopes, bonteboks, ostriches and turtles inhabit the southern section of the park. Beware of the baboons on the Cape Point hiking route: feeding and touching is dangerous and strictly forbidden. **TMNP Head Office**: Shop A1, Ground Floor, Constantia & Steenberg Road, Westlake, 7945 Constantia (tel. 021 / 701 8692; www.sanparks.org/parks/table_mountain/about/contact.php).

**✳ ✳ Hoerikwaggo Trails** There are over 300 footpaths on and around ► Table Mountain. The latest additions are the guided Hoerikwaggo Trails named after the »Mountain in the Sea«. A three-day **Table Mountain Trail** established in 2006 starts at the ► V & A Waterfront and heads up Table Mountain. Baggage transport and meals are included, as is a harbour tour, ► Robben Island and ► Kirstenbosch National Botanical Garden. While on Table Mountain, the **Waterworks Museum** and Woodhead Reservoir are also visited. Independent walkers can get the museum key from the guardian at the Overseer's Cottage. The six-day **Hoerikwaggo Tented Classic Trail** leads ambitious self-supported hikers up Table Mountain from the south. Remember to bring plenty of water! The 27km/17mi **Orangekloof Trail** is a two-day walking tour. Guides, porters, cabins complete with beds, and cook-

**! Baedeker TIP**

**What are the absolute highlights ...**

the most beautiful hiking trails in the national park? What is the best place to watch birds, see penguins or eat a meal? TMNP recommends the guide book *Mountains in the Sea: Table Mountain to Cape Point* by John Yeld and Martine Barker, STE Publishers, South Africa, 2004, for orientation and recognizing flora.

*The cabins of the cable car turn 360° during their journey*

③

Waterfront    Greenpoint

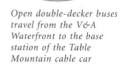

*Open double-decker buses travel from the V&A Waterfront to the base station of the Table Mountain cable car*

*More than 300 footpaths lead up the »Mountain in the Sea«*

ing utensils are available. The **Silvermine Trail** begins at Slangkop, with overnight stays in Silvermine and Orange Kloof. The spectacular six-day **Top to Tip Trail** connects Table Mountain with Cape Point, offering comfortable cabins, complete provisioning and baggage transport.

◄ Booking office: tel. 021 / 465 8515; www.sanparks.org/ parks/table_ mountain/ht/

These days, a 50-plus team of park rangers can quickly be on the scene during an emergency. Hikers should always travel in groups **of at least four** and carry mobile phones; park emergency services: tel. 086 / 110 6417; additional emergency numbers ►p.77. Obviously all-weather clothing is required, as well as stout footwear and sufficient food and drink. The **Mountain Club of South Africa** organizes mountain tours and provides a search and rescue service. Ideally, trekking tours should be registered and signed out at the MCSA (97 Hatfield Street, tel. 021 / 465 3412; www.mcsa.org.za).

**Safety first**

On the foothills of Constantia Mountain, in the heart of the Tokai pine plantations, the lovingly restored Wood Owl Cottage has three large double rooms for self-caterers, complete with kitchen, and a sitting-room with open fire. Breakfast available on request (TMNP Tokai, tel. 021 / 712 7471, e-mail: joek@sanparks.org).

**Do it yourself!**

# Townships · Cape Flats (Kaapse Vlakte)

Extra map

**Location:** 15–40km/10–25mi south-east    **Internet:** www.etownship.co.za
of Cape Town

**The flip side to Cape Town are its townships, where great poverty, high unemployment and violence are the norm. Conditions have changed only very slowly since the end of apartheid, though improvements are gradually beginning to show. The giant barracks-style neighbourhoods of the Cape Flats are home to over 2.5 million people. Formerly »no-go-areas«, they are now part of a programme organized by many travel agents. However, township tours are not without danger and should always be undertaken with a guide.**

**apartheid legacy** The townships developed as a result of apartheid. This began with the 1923 **Native Urban Areas Act**, which divided residential districts according to skin colour. Black South Africans were only allowed to reside in and own property in **specified territories**. Cape Town's oldest township is Langa, which was founded in 1927. Khayelitsha, established in 1983, is one of the most recent. With increased flight from the land, the impoverished **squatter camps** were soon hopelessly over-crowded. Social problems grew, and with them opposition to apartheid. 15 years after the end of apartheid, conditions on the Cape Flats have improved somewhat as a result of massive state intervention, but many problems remain unresolved, and the gulf between blacks and whites is still far from bridged.

**Langa** It is impossible not to notice Langa and the other townships when travelling from the airport to the city centre: the drive through the **Cape Flats** on the **N 2** takes almost fifteen minutes. **The huge and miserable neighbourhoods** on this broad plain reach right up to the motorway. Langa, meaning **»sun«** in Xhosa, is a frequent destination of the increasing number of township tours. In 1960, this oldest Cape Town township set a pattern of protest with marches against the Pass Laws. Several tour operators visit the **Eziko Cooking School** on the corner of Jungle Walk and Washington Road, where tourists can learn how to cook lamb bobotie and spicy chakalaka vegetables (tel. 021/694 0434). Langa has established itself as a cultural centre where the stars of **Afro and Cape Jazz** regularly perform. The pop singer **Brenda Fassie** (▶ Famous People) enjoyed her earliest successes at Langa High School. Since 2000, and in association with Spier Films, the theatre group **Dimpho Di Kopane** has been producing township adaptations that entertain audiences worldwide, including such works as *IKumkanikazi yeKhephu* (inspired by Andersen's tale of *The Snow Queen*, and *Carmen from Khayelitsha* (▶ Bae-

# ▶ VISITING TOWNSHIPS

## ORGANIZED TOURS

... usually last between 4 and 6 hours and are often led by locals. During the tour, there are opportunities to speak with residents and meet traditional healers (sangomas). Small groups are taken to spaza shops, schools, craft markets, aid projects and shebeens (the once illegal township taverns), where homemade beer is served. Many tours begin with a trip to the ▶District Six Museum and a walk around ▶Bo-Kaap.

### Township tour organizers
Andulela (▶ p.121)
Andy Tours (www.andytours.co.za)
Bonanitours (www.bonanitours.co.za)
Energy Tours (▶p.121)

## WHERE TO STAY

### ▶ Budget
It is possible to stay with a township family in a B & B that includes transfers, tours and meals.

### Kopanong B & B
C329 Velani Crescent
Khayelitsha
Tel. / fax 021 / 361 2084
www.kopanong-township.co.za
Thope Lekau and her daughter Mpho have three comfortable double rooms with bath. Experience genuine hospitality during a traditional dinner.

### Liziwe's Guest House
NY 111, No. 121, Gugulethu
Tel. 021 / 633 7406
Fax 021 / 633 74 06
www.liziwesguesthouse.com. Liziwe Ngcokotos opened her nice guesthouse with four double rooms in 2005. A year later, her popular restaurant serving African specialties was added.

deker Special, p.282). The people behind the **Guga S'Thebe Arts & Cultural Centre**, on the corner of Washington Street and Church Street, are rightly proud of their art exhibitions and workshops for traditional crafts, theatre and drumming. (Tel. 021 / 695 3493; opening times: Mon–Sat 9am–6pm). The award-winning **Victoria Mxenge Project** on Ottery Road is a women's aid project promoting the building of family homes. Tour guides explain the problems en-

*Khayelitsha kids have commandeered a wrecked car as their playground among the leaning corrugated iron huts*

# THE OTHER SIDE

**Well over half of all Capetonians today live in simple houses or huts built of clapboard or corrugated iron in the large townships outside the city centre. More and more deprived districts are springing up there, due to the immense increase in the population. Despite noticeable efforts by the government, living conditions are only improving very slowly.**

Originally, antelopes roamed across the 160 sq km/60 sq mi lowlands of the **Cape Flats**. Farmers avoided the terrain because of its unproductive sandy soil. The present conditions are a result of the politics of **apartheid** and **unregulated immigration** from the country's other regions and from neighbouring states wracked by economic crises after 1991. The city administrators have desperately sought to create new housing in the townships. They built massive apartment blocks, tarred the roads, provided water and electricity services, and established street lighting, garbage collection and bus transport to the city centre. Yet the **population explosion** continues dramatically, and many homes that once housed two families now have to accept up to eight families. About one quarter of all households are without electricity. In many areas there is a continued lack of water wells, piped drinking water or sewage provision. During winter, the rains cause serious epidemics. Most houses have smoothed clay floors, and every puddle is a potential source of disease. Rheumatic illnesses are the result, especially among the old and young children. It is also impossible not to notice the lack of trees and green spaces, even though a UN reforestation project is presently bringing 110,000 new plants to the townships.

## The battle against AIDS

In South Africa over 5.5 million people are infected with the HIV virus, among them more than 20% of all women of child-bearing age. The battle against AIDS has long been the main purpose of over 100 aid organizations that now work at the Cape. The non-sectarian aid organization **HOPE Cape Town** and Catholic father **Stefan Hippler** are among them. Father Hippler has been working with children suffering from AIDS in Tygerberg Hospital, in other township clinics and in Knysna, along the Garden Route, since 1987. He cares for the affected families, develops self-help groups and promotes educational programmes (www.h-o-p-e.net).

## Education and women's rights

State funds for **schools** in the townships are often just a drop in the ocean: over 10% of South Africans are considered **illiterate**. An important role is played by private initiatives such as Denis Goldberg's organization in Observatory, called **Community H.E.A.R.T.** (Health Education and Reconstruction Training). It is dedicated to fund raising for school books and computers, assists in the feeding of families with many children, and also runs the Maths & Science Bus, which brings educational materials to poorly equipped schools. Their office in Khayelitsha is especially dedicated to helping victims of sexual violence. This includes assisting abused women and girls, legal aid, education and prevention. According to statistics, 150 rapes occur in South Africa every day (www.community-heart.org.uk).

## In spite of everything

The horrors of everyday life are counter-balanced by a life-affirming music scene. **Kwaito** – a mixture of hip hop and African sounds – has made its triumphant way from South Africa's townships all the way to Europe and America. Not only pop star Brenda Fassie began her career in Langa township. Jazz greats like Dizu Plaatjes (a professor at the University of Cape Town and a specialist in traditional instruments) and Afro star Pops Mohamed perform concerts and also offer courses. The »Queen of Langa« is the singer Madosini who, for over a quarter of a century, has been performing with the star band Amampondo. Despite everything, the townships produce music that praises life: examples are the idiosyncratic version of Carmen portrayed in the film *U-Carmen e-Khayelitsha*, spoken and sung in Xhosa, and the Oscar-winning film of 2006 entitled *Tsotsi*.

## Mzoli's success story

**Mzoli's Place**, a restaurant with 250 seats in Gugulethu township, is very popular, especially with tour companies offering township tours. Here it is possible to meet South African politicians, business people, tourists, township inhabitants, TV stars, musicians and artists during a hearty BBQ of Karoo lamb, potjiekos and Umngqusho. Mzoli Ngcawuzele established a simple slaughterhouse in 2003 but, thanks to financial help from the Development Bank of South Africa, he was then able to make the transition to running a fashionable rendezvous. Mzoli's tour, Shebeen Experience, is accompanied by marabi, kwaito, deep house and Cape jazz music (tel. 021/ 638 1355).

## Baedeker TIP

**»Ubuntu – Townships in Cape Town«**
This richly illustrated book by Michael Telschow and Paul Sutton tells the story of the people of the townships, of their everyday lives, their dreams and problems. It is a book intended to inspire visitors to get to know Cape Town's other world a little better. (Clifton Publications, Cape Town, 2007).

countered during land purchases and tell of making roof tiles and construction; the adjacent Community Centre sells township art (tel. 021 / 372 4206). 200,000 new apartments are intended to be completed at the building project known as the **N 2 Gateway Project** alongside the highway; completion is planned in time for the 2010 Football World Cup. New roads and houses in Langa show that advances have been made, but the local inhabitants fear they will not be able to return to the expensive new housing development after 2010. When township residents protested by occupying the N 2 in 2007, the police banned the protest, and compulsory clearances have taken place since 2008.

**Gugulethu**  After the 1950 Group Areas Act banned black South Africans from living in the cities, the Xhosa township of Gugulethu – **»Our Pride«** – was founded 15km/9mi outside Cape Town. Migrant workers from the Homelands, such as Ciskei and Transkei, were not permitted to bring their families. Many left the purpose-built hostels and built their own **»shacks«**, which have spread across the Cape Flats ever since. The **Gugulethu Seven Memorial** at the junction of the NY 1 and NY 111 recalls March 1986, when seven young men were shot dead there during a protest march. These days, »Gugs« is considered one of the best-developed townships in South Africa. Proof of this progress is the **Sivuyile Tourism Centre** at the junction of the NY 1 and NY 4. Behind walls fortified with barbed wire, 18- to 20-year-olds are studying at the technical college of the same name, many enjoying success after completing courses predominantly devoted to commerce and technology. The centre has an internet café, and the township photo exhibition and the colourful ceramics by Uncedo Pottery are worth seeing. (Tel. 021 / 637 8449; opening times: Mon–-Fri 8am–5pm, Sat 8am–2pm). Complete with BBQ area and a stage for young musicians, **Mzoli's Place** has established itself as a favourite for sundowners (► Baedeker Special, p.282). To see just how strong the enthusiasm among **the next generation of footballers** in the townships is, join a Cape Town Football Tour run by Andulela, which also goes to Gugulethu (► www.andulela.com; p.121).

**»Our New Home«** was constructed on the barren sand flats near the Atlantic, 35km/22mi south-east of the city. An estimated 1.8 million people live in shacks made of plywood, cardboard and corrugated iron. The settlement is the **second-largest township in South Africa** – and getting bigger every day. Various government initiatives in recent years have brought many improvements, but most houses and shacks are still hopelessly over-crowded. Many have neither electricity nor piped water, and the unemployment rate is over 80%. The huge district is divided into 27 boroughs merely indicated by a letter. An overview of the muddle of houses is possible from **Look-Out Hill**, on the corner of Mey Way and Spine Road, at Ilitha Park. The feeding of small children has been a project for the **Philani Nutrition Centre** on Phaphani Road at Site C since 1987. Here 80 mothers weave mats and wall hangings that are offered for sale (www.philani.org. za). Over two dozen artisans also present their work at the **Khayelitsha Craft Market** (KCM) on Ncumo Road (tel. 021 / 361 5246; opening times: Mon–Fri 9am–5pm, Sat 9am–1pm).

*Khayelitsha*

Almost 90% of the inhabitants of **Mitchell's Plain** township are coloureds, a result of the forced clearance of ►**District Six** in the 1970s. Much of the centre is being improved as part of the 2010 Football World Cup urban restoration project. Nevertheless, many areas of this mega-township are best-known for gang crime. **Mannenberg**, founded for destitute coloureds at the end of the 1960s, became known through the unofficial Cape Town anthem of *Mannenberg* by **Abdullah Ibrahim** and Basil Coetzee (►Baedeker Special, p.46).

*Other townships*

*Despite poor living conditions, visitors encounter an amazing joy in life and optimism in the townships*

## ★ ★ Victoria & Alfred Waterfront

**Location:** Portswood Road; including the Alfred Basin and Victoria Basin

**Internet:** www.waterfront.co.za

**With over 20 million visitors per year, the V & A Waterfront is South Africa's most successful tourist attraction. Almost 500 shops, dozens of restaurants, cinemas, hotels and theatres compete for the attention of visitors in this popular entertainment district.**

*Water taxi, double-decker bus or helicopter?*

A **Waterfront Bus** departs from the V & A Hotel for the ► Adderley Street railway station every ten minutes; every quarter of an hour, one also departs from Victoria Wharf in the direction of Sea Point and the Peninsula Hotel. **Water taxis** chug up the Roggebaai Canal from the Alfred Basin heading for ► Heerengracht. There are also harbour cruises, sunset charters in Table Bay, and catamaran trips to ► Robben Island. The **red double-decker buses** run by Cape Town Explorer and City Sightseeing travel between the Waterfront and

## *Victoria & Alfred Waterfront Map*

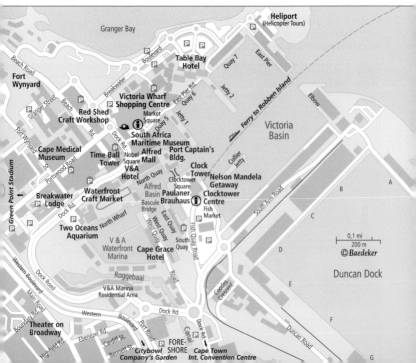

*Successful renewal: the V&A Waterfront's glass and chrome glitters at the old port*

▶ Table Mountain. **Shuttle buses** also travel to the Information Centre in the city, to the base station of the Table Mountain cable car, and to the airport. The one-hour **helicopter tour** departing from the Waterfront and flying over the entire Cape Peninsula is an unforgettable experience; helicopters take off behind the Table Bay Hotel.

The present harbour was designed by Sir John Coode in 1858. The first load of rubble from the surrounding quarries was deposited in the dock by prisoners from the Breakwater Prison on Dock Road, on 17 September 1860. The inauguration of the first **breakwater** sea defence was also witnessed by His Royal Highness Prince Alfred (1844–90). The new dock and pier were named after him and his mother, Queen Victoria. The opening up of the interior of South Africa, and the gold and diamond finds there, meant a veritable boom for the harbour. Nevertheless, completion dragged on until 1920. Its decline at the end of the 1970s was irreversible, due to the limited depth of water (just 12m/40ft) and the re-opening of the Suez Canal, and the harbour district and port facilities finally became derelict.

**Historic dock**

In 1988 the city decided on **complete restoration**, maintaining the **Victorian architecture**, and leased the land to investors. Thus, a lively shopping and entertainment quarter covering almost 90ha/220 acres was created, its backdrop the busy harbour with its shipping traffic, which also includes cruise ships. Old warehouses were turned into shopping malls, first-class hotels and smart boutiques, as well as museums, cafés and restaurants. This is not just a place for tourists. Ca-

✶ ✶
**Entertainment district**

*Shopping and gourmet dining deep into the night all around the Clock Tower*

petonians also like to come here for a stroll, not least because the Waterfront is considered very safe, not only during the day but also at night. Over the years, the vibrant port district has expanded ever more, and there is no end in sight. For example, the elegant apartment blocks of the **Marina Residential Area** are being extended in the direction of **Foreshore**, on land reclaimed in 1945. In 2006, investors based in Dubai, London and South African bought the entire V & A Waterfront from Transnet. The consortium paid 1.3 billion US dollars – the largest property deal in the history of South Africa. The new owners have plans to expand the entertainment district: in 2008, luxury boutiques selling international brands were opened and the yacht marina was enlarged.

**Ultimate in shopping** The giant **Victoria Wharf Shopping Centre** with over 240 shops, restaurants and pubs has it all: young fashion, classy outfits, expensive jewellery or original souvenirs. African craftwork and innovative design can be found at the covered **Waterfront Craft Market** at the Two Oceans Aquarium. Antiques, jewellery and souvenirs are on sale at the **Alfred Mall** next to Market Square. Glass blowers and wood carvers work in the studios at the **Red Shed Craft Workshop**, but leather shoes, bags, ceramics and art from recycled materials are also sold there.

The Waterfront's emblem, the red **Clock Tower** built in neo-Gothic style in 1887, stands beyond the harbourmaster's office and the **swing bridge** that provides a crossing over the harbour basin four times per hour. One of Munich's best beers is on tap at the **Paulaner Brewery** by the **Clock Tower Centre**, while the **Cape Town Tourism Centre** next door can provide information on South Africa's »Mother City« (daily 9am–9pm). Craft shops here welcome browsers. Right in front of the Paulaner brewery, seals often play in the shallow waters. **Chavonnes Battery**, built in 1714–25, was part of the Dutch East India Company's (VOC) fortress, but it was closed in 1861. Part of this complex

### ! *Baedeker* TIP

**Sundowner Cruises**

Brick-red sails billow in the gentle evening breeze … why not sail around Table Bay at sunset on a three-masted schooner, the *Spirit of Victoria*. Departures from Quay 5, daily at 7pm; returns at 8.30pm. Apart from sunset tours, hour-long harbour charters are also available, as well as half-day and whole-day tours (www.waterfrontboats.co.za).

was once a quarantine hospital for smallpox sufferers, and can be visited. The ferries for ▶Robben Island depart from the Nelson Mandela Gateway. The adjacent Nelson Mandela Gateway Centre with its ticket shop and museum shop is part of the **Robben Island Museum** (RIM), and its multimedia exhibition is part of the tour.

◀ Nelson Mandela Gateway

On the other side of the swing bridge, the historic **Port Captain's Building**, painted grey and white and built in 1904, is now also a shopping centre.

African Trading Port

The **Maritime Museum** in the Union Castle Building by the dock has held an exhibition on seafaring and the discovery of the world's oceans since 2006. There are model ships, historic photographs and a model of the former working harbour. There is also a description of the last voyage of *SS Mendi*, which sank in the British Channel in 1917. Outside, *S.A.S. Somerset* was once responsible for blockading the harbour with chains during the Second World War, and is now a training ship. (Opening times: daily 10am–5pm; www.izico.org.za/maritime).

★
South African Maritime Museum

⊘

On 16 December 2005 the statues of South Africa's four **Nobel Peace Prize holders** were unveiled: Nkosi Albert Luthuli (1960), Archbishop Desmond Tutu (1984), Frederik de Klerk and Nelson Mandela (jointly, in 1993). The figures of the award winners are by Claudette Schreuders, the *Peace and Democracy* sculpture by Nira Mabasa. Quotes from those honoured are inscribed on the base in the country's eleven official languages. For example, Bishop Tutu is cited: »A person is a person through other persons«. The **CD Warehouse** at the Dock Road complex has the largest selection of music CDs in Cape Town, with an excellent jazz department. Higher up, in the garden of the old harbourmaster's residence dating from 1860, stands a

Nobel Square
◀ www. nobelsquare.com

! **Baedeker** TIP

### Diving in the shark tank

Up to three divers at one time are allowed to make a 30-minute dive in the 2-million-litre Ocean Tank to observe tiger sharks and the giant hawksbill turtle Yoshi – a pounding heart is guaranteed! A diving qualification such as Open Ocean One or Discover Scuba is a pre-condition. Diving experience is also required for the two-person kelp forest dive and the descent in a historic whole-body suit diving complete with its 18kg/40lb copper helmet. (Dives: May–Aug daily 11am, 1pm; Sept–April daily 9am, 11am and 1pm; tel. 021/418 38 23; www.aquarium.co.za/diving.php).

**dragon tree** that was brought from the Canary Islands over a century ago and planted next to the **Time Ball Tower**, built in 1894. The tree's red sap is said to be good as a diarrhoea remedy.

Excitement for all the family is assured at the **Two Oceans Aquarium**, opened in 1995. Over 30 tanks containing clownfish and other exotic reef inhabitants, as well as sharks, manta rays, turtles, penguins and seals can be admired; and there are colourful corals with anemones and starfish from the **Indian and Atlantic Oceans**. (Opening times: daily 9.30am–6pm, Dec, Jan 9.30am–7pm; fish feeding: daily from 3pm; sharks only on Sun from 3pm; fish in the kelp forest only on Wed & Sat from noon; penguins daily at 11.30am and 2.30pm; seals daily at 11am and 2pm; Yoshi the hawksbill turtle is fed Mon, Wed, Fri from 3pm; www.aquarium.co.za).

★★
Two Oceans
Aquarium

*The sharks appear close enough to touch in the Two Oceans Aquarium*

Thanks to the »Canale Grande«, opened up in 2002 between the Alfred Basin and ►Heerengracht, the port and city are closely connected these days. Water taxis provide transport as far as the **Rooge-baai Canal Tourism Precinct** with its luxury Arabella Hotel and the Cape Town International Convention Centre (► p.210). The entire canal bank is being developed into a first-rate residential area with fashionable private apartments.

*Roggebaai Canal*

# ★ ★ West Coast ·
# Cederberg Mountains

A–C 2/3

**Location:** R 27, N 7, north of Cape Town

**Internet:** www.tourismcapewest coast.co.za

**During spring, the hills of the West Coast National Park and the Cederberg Mountains are covered by a wonderful carpet of flowers. Atlantic waves break on the pristine white beaches of the West Coast, sleepy mission villages are dotted about the hilly bush landscape, where bizarre rock formations and San rock art over 1000 years old can be found.**

Barely 70km/45mi north of Cape Town, an effort is being made to preserve the ancient San traditions at the **San Culture & Education Centre**. Since 2001, the 850ha/2100-acre !Khwa ttu (»watering hole«) nature reserve has belonged to the local San people, whose three-hour tours explain traditional hunting methods, tell of the amazing bird life and point out some of the medicinal plants found in the fynbos vegetation. Visitors can also have a go at using a bow and arrow. A replica of a traditional San village is also at the centre. (R 27; Opening times: Tue–Sun 9am–5pm, tours 10am and 2pm; www. khwattu.org).

★
*!Khwa ttu*

⏲

Whales can be observed from **16 Mile Beach** at Yzerfontein between May and November (www.tourismyzerfontein.co.za). **Dassen Island**, a protected bird reserve off the coast, is home to cormorants, pelicans and penguins. The **lime kilns** along the R 315 were used for burning shell limestone until 1976. Seafood fans should make sure to book a spot at the popular **Strandkombuis** (tel. 082 / 575 9683).

*Yzerfontein*

Designed on a chequerboard plan in 1853, Darling was granted the title of »South Africa's cleanest small town« in 2006 (www.darling-tourism.co.za). Lovingly restored Victorian houses and antiques shops line Main Street. The highlight of the year is the Wildflower Show in September. The **Darling Museum** on Pastorie Street illustrates how butter and cheese were made around 1900. (Opening

★
*Darling*

⏲

★ ★
Evita Se Perròn ▶

times: daily 9am–1pm, 2pm–4pm, Sat from 10am, Sun from 11am). The cabaret and theatre restaurant belonging to the comedy star **Pieter-Dirk Uys** alias Evita Bezuidenhout (▶Famous People), on Arkadia Street, is a must – especially at weekends. Drop in on the »A-en-C« shop and **Boerassic Park**, which have all manner of kitsch and satirical items inspired by well-known personalities. How Evita planned to succeed in her candidature for the highest post in state government in 2007 is explained in her show *Evita for President* (open daily, shows on Sat, Sun & Thu & Fri; tickets tel. 022/492 2851, www.evita.co.za).

## ✴ West Coast National Park

🕐
Opening hours:
June–Sept daily
7am–6.30pm, Oct–March daily
6am–8pm

www.
sanparks.org/parks/
west_coast ▶

Unesco designated the West Coast National Park, founded in 1985, as a biosphere reserve at the turn of the millennium. The 27,500ha/68,000-acre national park includes the 18km/11mi jade green Langebaan lagoon and Saldanha Bay. The region is not only well known for its **sea of flowers** alongside the cold Benguela Current, but also as a **breeding ground for migrant birds**. Africa's largest **jackass penguin colony** lives on Marcus Island. Furthermore, the national park is home to blue wildebeest, Eland antelopes, bonteboks and kudus. The private **Postberg Flower Trail** is only open when the wild flowers bloom during August and September (daily 9am–5pm).

★ ★
Langebaan
Lagoon

**Sailors and surfers** come to the golden beach at **Langebaan**, and seafood fans should definitely book a table at **Die Strandloper** (▶p.293, www.langebaaninfo.co.za). Three-hour **boat tours** set off from

*Free-style windsurfing at the Langebaan Lagoon makes for a perfect holiday*

# ● VISITING WEST COAST AND CEDERBERG MOUNTAINS

## INFORMATION

### West Coast Tourism
58 Long Street, Moorreesburg 7310
Tel. 022 / 433 8516
www.tourismcapewestcoast.co.za

### Cederberg Wilderness Area
Clanwilliam Tourism Bureau,
Main Road, Clanwilliam
Tel. 027 / 482 2024
www.clanwilliam.info
www.cederberg.co.za

*Citrusdal is the capital of citrus fruit*

## FLOWER POWER

All along the West Coast, there are wild flower festivals during August and September. The start of spring blossoming can be discovered by phoning the flower hotlines:
Tel. 083 / 910 1028 and 021 / 418 3705.

## ROOIBOS TEA

South Africa's famous rooibos (»red bush«) tea, which only grows in the Cederberg Mountains, is processed at the Rooibos Tea Factory on Ou Kaapse Weg, in Clanwilliam. This healthy thirst-quencher is named after its colour. The Tea Museum illustrates tea planting, harvest and fermentation processes, and also tells the story of Pieter le Fras Nortier, who first cultivated the rooibos plant. (Tours: Mon–Fri 8am–4.30pm; video show: Mon–Thu 10am, 11.30am, 2pm, 3.30pm). 20km/13mi west, on the way to Lambert's Bay, it is also possible to visit the tea plantation at Elandsberg. (Tel. 027 / 482 2022; www.elands berg.co.za).

## WHERE TO EAT

### ► Moderate
*Reinhold's Restaurant*
8 Main Street, Clanwilliam

Tel. 027 / 482 1101
A popular restaurant in a lovingly restored Victorian house, closed Sun.

## *Baedeker recommendation*

### *Die Strandloper*
At Langebaan beach
Tel. 022 / 772 2490
Seated on rustic wooden benches with feet in the sand, this is a great place to enjoy freshly caught mussels, crayfish or grilled snoek. Do order the freshly baked bread too. Alcoholic drinks can be brought along or purchased at the bar. Reservations essential.

## WHERE TO STAY

### ► Luxury
*Bushmans Kloof Wilderness*
►Baedeker Tip, p.298

### ► Mid-range
*The Farmhouse*
5 Egret Street, Langebaan
Tel. 022 / 772 2062, fax 022 / 772 1980;
www.thefarmhouselangebaan.co.za
Lovingly restored farmstead dating from 1860, with panoramic views across the lagoon, open fires in the rooms, and a garden with pool. Excellent restaurant with prize-winning wine list.

*Kagga Kamma suites*

### Oystercatcher Lodge

1st Avenue, Shelley Point
St. Helena Bay, P.O. Box 247,
Stompneus Bay 7382
Tel. 022 / 742 12 02, fax 022 / 742 1201
www.oystercatcherlodge.co.za
Guests sleep in giant double beds at
Luc and Sue Christen's place. From the
terrace you can see cormorants,
whales, dolphins and seals while en-
joying outstanding fish dishes.

### Paternoster Lodge

64 St. Augustine Road, Paternoster
Tel. 022/752 2023, fax 022 / 752 2083
www.paternosterlodge.co.za
Seven elegant double rooms with sea
views and delicious fish dishes available.

### Clanwilliam Hotel

Main Street, Clanwilliam
Tel. 027 / 482 1101, fax 027 / 482 2678
www.clanwilliamhotel.co.za
Hotel with very personal service and
generously large rooms opposite the
Reinhold's Restaurant

## Baedeker recommendation

### Kagga Kamma Private Game Reserve

Tel. 021 / 872 4343, fax 021 / 872 4524
www.kaggakamma.co.za
Around 120km/75mi south-east of Citrusdal. Access via the R 303, the turn-off via the
Katbakkies Pass before Op-die-Berg is sign-
posted. Opening times: Sat–Thu
7.30am–6.30pm, Fri 7.30am–9pm. Transfers
by light plane can be arranged from Cape
Town to the reserve's own landing strip.
This private nature reserve is located in
breathtaking scenery in which antelopes,
zebras and blue wildebeest can be observed
and ancient San rock paintings admired.
Accommodation is in luxurious thatched
roundhouses or unique cave suites. Sleeping
in the open under the stars is also possible.

### ▶ Budget

### Klein Boschkloof Chalets

Kleinboschkloof Road, Clanwilliam
Tel. 027 / 482 2441
www.clanwilliam.info/kleinboschkloof
9km/5.5mi outside Clanwilliam, Mrs
Colyn's idyllic farm lies in the middle
of her citrus plantation. The 250-year-
old thatched farm buildings are at-
tractively furnished and the opulent
breakfast includes freshly pressed orange juice.

Bird paradise ▶ Langebaan into the protected area of the Langebaan Lagoon, which
is a must for ornithologists. From September to March, thousands of
migrant birds from Europe winter in the nutrient-rich marshes,
where curlew sandpipers, black oystercatchers, cormorants, Cape
gannets, flamingoes and pelicans can be spotted.

15km/9mi north of Langebaan, at the West Coast Fossil Park, the exhibition of fossils dating back **over 5 million years** includes an African bear, sabre-tooth tiger, mammoths and prehistoric horses. (Opening times: Mon–Fri 10am–4pm, Sat & Sun 9am–noon; tours every 30mins; www.iziko.org.za/partners/wcfp.html).   ⊙

**West Coast Fossil Park**

The bay named after the first European to climb Table Mountain, Admiral Antonio de Saldanha, is an important military and industrial port. In the spring, **Saldanha Nature Reserve** is a sea of flowers, and from June to November it is also possible to sight whales off the coast. Gourmets should be sure to try Saldanha oysters.

**Saldanha Bay**

Snoek and rock crayfish are on the menu at the 100-year-old **Paternoster Hotel**, 25km/16mi further north, in the fishing village of the same name. All kinds of knick-knacks can be found in the Victorian corner shop Ons Winkel, with its Three Tree Teas café. The lighthouse at **Cape Columbine** has been guiding shipping since 1936.

**Paternoster**

## ✷ ✷ Cederberg Mountains

230km/145mi north of Cape Town, the highest section of the Cederberg Mountains rises to 2027m/6650ft at the **Sneeuberg** – a region famous for its **wildly jagged sandstone cliffs** and ancient **San rock paintings**. The earliest inhabitants of the Cape were also already familiar with **rooibos tea** made from the bush aspalathus linearis, which only grows in the Cederberg Mountains. Endemic plants in

**Cederberg Wilderness Area**

*Wind and weather have created the Maltese cross at Dwarsrivier*

## *Cederberg Mountains* Map

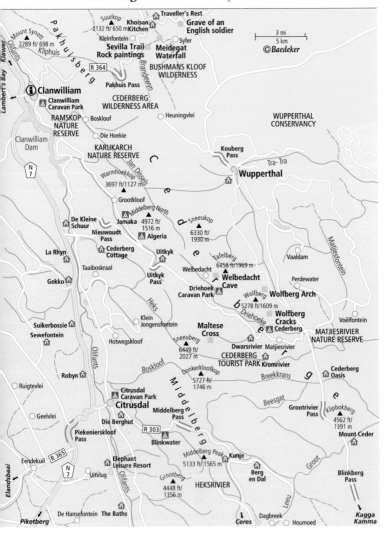

the 71,000ha/275 sq mi nature reserve, which was declared a Wilderness Area in 1973, include the rare **Clanwilliam cedar tree**, the snow protea and the medicinal herb buchu. Baboons, rock dassies, antelopes and wild boars live in the Cederberg Mountains. Very occasionally there are also encounters with mountain leopards.

The gateway to the Cederberg Mountains is Citrusdal, the **centre of citrus fruit cultivation** in the fertile valley of the »Elephant River« (Olifants River). The oldest orange tree grows to the north of town on the Hex Revier Farm. It is supposedly 250 years old and still bears fruit. Three quarters of the approximately 90,000 tons produced annually by the Goede HoopCitrus Association is for export. Spa treatments in Victorian style can be enjoyed 16km/10mi further south, at the 43°C/109°F mineral springs of **The Baths** (www.the-baths.co.za).

**Citrusdal**

◄ www.
citrusdal.info

The most spectacular sandstone formations in the southern Cederberg Mountains are in the gorges of the **Wolfberg Cracks**: the huge **Wolfberg Arch** and the 20m/65ft-high stone columns of the **Maltese Cross** near Dwarsrivier. 8km/5mi beyond Dwarsrivier, in the direction of Ceres, lie the **Stadsaal Caves** and San rock paintings that date from an era when elephants still roamed here.

★ ★
**Bizarre sand-stones and rock paintings**

The »**Flower of the Cederberg Mountains**« is among the country's oldest towns. In 1732 there were already farmsteads here, by the Olifants River, where today a **reservoir** is an excellent place for water sports. The **Rooibos Tea Factory** (►p.293) tells visitors all about how rooibos grows, is cultivated, hand-picked, and turned into tea. The **Strassberger Shoe Factory** at Ou-Kaapse-Weg, a fourth-generation family company, produces hand-made hiking boots known as »Velskoene shoes«. (Opening times: Mon–Fri 8am–12.30pm and 1.30pm–4.30pm). The Dutch Reformed Church on Main Street was built by Otto Hager in 1864. Every year, during the Wild Flower Show at the end of August, it is decorated with flowers. The **Clanwilliam Museum** in the former prison at the end of Main Street tells of the days of the pioneers, San culture, and tea planting. (Opening times: Mon–Fri 8am–noon). The region's fynbos plants can be seen during a walk in the **Ramskop Nature Reserve** above the Clanwilliam reservoir.

★
**Clanwilliam**
◄ www.
clanwilliam.info

> ! **Baedeker TIP**
>
> **Hikers & bikers**
>
> The obligatory permit for hikers and mountain bikers can be purchased in advance online from the park administration for the Cederberg Mountains at www.capenature.co.za; it is also available at the Algeria Forest Station or from the Sanddrif Winery, with its camping site and cottages in Dwarsrivier. Access from Citrusdal is via the N 7 heading north for about 30km/20mi until the Algeria turn-off, after which there is another 46km/29mi to cover on an unpaved road, as far as Dwarsrivier. Guided tours are offered all around Lot's Wife, the Maltese Cross and the Wolfberg Cracks. The panoramic views are as stunning as the sunsets in the »Valley of the Red Gods« (www.cederbergwine.com).

Barely 30km/20mi to the west of Clanwilliam, in **Graafwater**, the wealth of seafood from Lambert's Bay is processed. 25km/16mi further north, the walls of the **Heerenlogement Cave** have been marked by the graffiti of more than 130 explorers, hunters and adventurers

**Detour to Lambert's Bay**

## Baedeker TIP

**Bushmans Kloof Wilderness**

The most spectacular San rock art can be found at the luxurious Bushmans Kloof Wilderness & Wellness Centre, with its 16 stunning rooms by the R 364, at the foot of the Cederberg Mountains. More than 130 cave paintings can be viewed by torchlight during guided walks. Safari drives in open vehicles are used to spot the rare Cape zebra. Afterwards enjoy a meal in the award-winning restaurant or pamper yourself from head to toe in the new spa. Daily air transfers from Cape Town are available; tel. 021 / 685 2598; www.bushmanskloof. co.za.

who have passed this way since 1682. The beach at **Elands Bay** (Elandsbaai) is considered a surfers' paradise during summer. The harbour of **Lambert's Bay** is an excellent place to eat fresh crayfish, and not just during the Crayfish Festival in March. Among the treasures at the local Sandveld Museum is a 300-year-old bible. A pier leads across to **Bird Island** and the breathtaking odours of the colonies of cormorants, Cape gannets and jackass penguins.

**Sevilla Rock Art Trail ▶**
The R 364 winds its way over the **Pakhuis Pass** north-east of Clanwilliam. Shortly before the turn-off in the direction of Wupperthal lies **Traveller's Rest Farm**, where there is a nine-stage 4km/3mi circular footpath to the ancient **San rock paintings**; tickets are available from the farm house belonging to Koos and Haffie Strauss, who also rent out twelve nice cottages and run the **Khoisan Kitchen**: their specialty is grilled lamb and waterblommetjebredie (www.travellersrest.co.za).

**Biedouw Valley**
Drive about 20km/13mi further south to the turning into the Biedouw Valley, which is famous for its bizarre rock formations, rooibos tea and **wild flowers** in August and September.

**Wupperthal**
An unpaved road eventually leads to the first **Rhenish Mission**, founded by Baron Theobald von Wurmb and Johann Gottliev Leipoldt in 1829. Taken over by the Moravian Church in 1965, it is a collection of whitewashed thatched houses among a tranquil village of 600 people, whose **mission church** was given a new thatched roof in 2007. The former home of Baron Leipoldt now houses the local museum as well as the tourist information office, which has a pretty café with terrace. The **shoe-making cooperative** opened by Nelson Mandela is housed in a building that was once the shoe factory of German missionary Willy Strassberger. Around 1900, almost every Boer farmer wore his »Veldskoene« made of kudu leather from Wup-

perthal. The new shoe factory sells hand-made shoes at the Factory Shop at Church Square. Organic rooibos tea and rooibos soap can be purchased in the old-time **Lekkerbekkie** shop.

## From Citrusdal to Ceres

The area gets its name, »South Africa's Switzerland«, from the majestic summits, over 2000m/6600ft high, of the wonderful mountain scenery between Citrusdal and Ceres. Take route R 303 from Citrusdal heading south. Shortly before **Op-die-Berg** , a road turns off for the Katbakkies Pass and the private **Kagga Kamma** reserve, where cave paintings over 6000 years old have been preserved (► p.294). Continue on the main highway for a stunning drive through panoramic landscapes and over the 1018m/3340ft **Gydo Pass**, which is named after a species of euphorbia covering the slopes of the Skurweberg. In **Ceres** it is worth visiting the exhibition of horse-drawn carriages at the Transport Rider's Museum, as well as the Ceres Nature Reserve with its native plants and prehistoric rock art.

»South Africa's Switzerland«

18km/11mi further on there are beautiful views on the **Mitchell's Pass** route, built in 1846–48 to connect with **Wolseley**. Continue 22km/14mi north to the pretty small town of Tulbagh on the Little Berg River. Its wonderful Cape Dutch and Victorian gabled houses along Church Street were rebuilt after an earthquake in 1969. The **Oude Kerk Museum** has an exhibition on the first settlers and wine-growing. (Opening times: Mon–Fri 9am–5pm, Sat 9am–4pm, Sun 11am–4pm). The Petit Trianon at Versailles was the model for Louis Thibault's **Monbijou State House** at 36 Church Street, built in 1815. (Tours: Sat–Tue 11am, 3pm). The seat of the regional representative of the Cape government is also by Thibault, and was built in 1806. **De Oude Drostdy** (Opening times: Mon–Sat 10am–1pm & 2pm–4.30pm, Sun 2.30pm–4.50pm).
There are **renowned vineyards** in the Tulbagh Valley. Cellar tours and wine-tasting are offered by, among others, the Tulbagh Winery founded in 1906, the Drostdy Estate and the Twee Jonge Gazellen estate (www.tmv.co.za).

★ Tulbagh

◄www.tulbagh.com

◄Wine & Sherry Route

# ★ Worcester · Breede River Valley

C 3

**Location:** 110km/70mi north-east of Cape Town

**Almost a quarter of South Africa's grape harvest comes from the fertile Breede Valley, which is enclosed by 2000m/6500ft mountains on three sides. Large cooperatives in Worcester produce predominantly white wine and brandy.**

# ⏵ VISITING WORCESTER AND BREEDE VALLEY

## INFORMATION

### Worcester Tourism
23 Baring Street, Worcester 6850
Tel. 023 / 348 2795
www.tourismworcester.co.za

*Victorian coffee mill*

## LIVING HISTORY

The Kleinplasie Open Air Museum by the N 60, in the direction of Robertson, presents a Trekboer cabin and a Khoikhoi camp to show how settlers lived. Demonstrations are given of soap-making in those times, as well as methods for shearing sheep, rolling tobacco, making candles, roasting coffee beans and baking milk tarts. Visitors also discover how the 60%-proof »Witblits« was distilled. (Opening times: Mon–Sat 9am–4.30pm; www.kleinplasie.co.za).

## WITH DESSERT

A local specialty, the aromatic »Hanepoot« muscatel wine, can be found at the De Doorns Wine Cellar, as well as at the ten other cellars in the Worcester Winelands (information: www.worcesterwinelands. co.za). This fine dessert wine is 16% proof; its grapes, harvested in late March, contain a lot of natural fructose with nuances of apricot, raisons, cinnamon and honey.

## WHERE TO EAT

### ▶ Moderate

### The Pear Tree
21 Baring Street, Worcester
Tel. 023 / 342 0936
www.thepeartree.co.uk
This elegant restaurant in the Cape Dutch Beck Huis dating from 1825 serves traditional South African cuisine: ask for a table under the 150-year-old pear tree.

## WHERE TO STAY

### ▶ Mid-range

### Nuy Valley Guest Farm
P.O. Box 5298, Heatlievale
Worcester 6851
Tel. 023 / 342 7025
Fax 023 / 347 1356
www.nuyvallei.co.za
Guests are made to feel at home at the Conradie family's vineyard, 14km/9mi past Worcester in the direction of Robertson. 35 comfortable rooms, wine-tasting, a cellar tour and delicious home cooking are available.

### Arbeid Adelt
Voortrekker Road
De Doorns 6875
(Hex River Valley)
Tel. / fax 023 / 356 2204
www.arbeidadelt.co.za
This Victorian guest house shaded by century-old oak trees has six pretty rooms. Drawing courses are held, and visitors can also help during the grape harvest.

With a population of 94,000, the largest town in the Breede River Valley was founded by the governor of the Cape Colony, Lord Charles Somerset, in 1822 and named after his brother, Lord Worcester. The town's most famous son is **John M. Coetzee**, winner of the Nobel Literature Prize, who spent his childhood here (►Famous People). The fact that many Germans settled here can be seen on the local menus, which list dishes such as bacon pancakes and broad beans. The pretty gabled houses along **Church Street** were given verandas in the Victorian style in 1850. On the corner with Baring Street, visitors can admire 19th-century yellowwood and stinkwood furniture at the **Beck & Stofberg Houses**. (Opening times: Mon–Fri 9am–4.30pm).

The **KWV House of Brandy Cellar**, on the corner of Smith Street and Church Street, has 120 distilling vessels. (Tastings: Mon–Fri 10am–3pm, tours: Mon–Fri 2pm; www.kwvhouseofbrandy.com).

*Worcester*

✷
◄ Brandy distillery
🕐

The semi-desert park 2km/1mi north of Worcester has one of the world's largest collections of **succulents**, which erupt into a patchwork of flowers in August and September. It is possible to buy seeds, for example, of the kokerboom tree or Namaqualand daisies. (Opening times: daily 8am–5pm, www.sanbi.org/karoo/mainpage.htm).

✷
**Karoo Desert National Botanical Garden**
🕐

The Hex River Valley offers terrific views, especially when the leaves of the **gigantic vineyards** change to red during autumn. Many of the 18th-century Cape Dutch vineyards and farmhouses now rent out beautiful guest rooms (►p.300). At full moon the valley is said to be

**Hex River Valley**
◄ www.hexrivervalley.co.za

*Water storing plants grow in the semi-desert park at Worcester*

*Autumn morning in the Hex River Valley: an unforgettable sight!*

haunted by the ghost of **Eliza Meiring**. The pretty Eliza promised to marry her beloved in 1786, if only he would pick her a disa orchid from the 2249m/7378ft summit of the Matroosberg. He died during the attempt and Eliza lost her mind when she was told the news, throwing herself out of a window one night. With the coming of the railway, the »thornbush« farm **De Doorns** soon became a small town. 400 different roses grow in the Sonskyn Garden here. The best view over the Winelands is from the **Hex River Pass** built in 1874. The railway line was closed in 1989, after the toll tunnel was built. Only the old-time Hexpas Express still chugs up over the pass (www.worcester.org.za/hexpaseco/express.html).

Aquila Private
Game Reserve

www.
aquilasafari.com ►

A good 20km/13mi past the Hex River Pass, the R 46 turns off the N 1 in the direction of Die Venster. After around another 10km/6mi, there are signs for the 4500ha/11,000-acre Aquila **wildlife reserve**, which also has luxurious chalets set in the African bush. Just two hours' drive from Cape Town, it is possible to go on safari to spot the **»Big Five«**without risking malaria: by jeep, by quad bike or on horseback.

Matjesfontein

A little way off the N 1, almost 100km/60mi north-east of Worcester, a Union Jack announces the lonely **railway station** of Matjesfontein, which is also a stop for the luxury Blue Train and Rovos Rail. This **»Oasis in the Middle of Nowhere«** was founded by a resourceful Scotsman named James Douglas Logan during the Victorian era, alongside the new main railway line between Cape Town and Johannesburg. Around 1900 this sleepy place was a fashionable spa resort, where wealthy Capetonians and prominent individuals such as Cecil Rhodes, Randolph Churchill and Rudyard Kipling held magnificent parties. The heritage of those glamorous days of empire is preserved in the elegant **Lord Milner Hotel**. Ask at reception for a tour in the red **London double-decker bus** (www.matjiesfontein.com/LordMilner).

There are almost 50 wineries in the famous **Robertson Wine Valley** at the foot of the Langeberg Mountains, 50km/30mi south-east of Worcester. The story of the main settlement in the valley, founded in 1853, is told in the **Robertson Museum** at 50 Kruger Street. The place is also renowned for its roses and the best **race horses** in South Africa(www.tourismrobertson.co.za).

**Robertson**

Magical moments can be spent in the walled **Soekershof Walkabout** on the branch road in the direction of Ashton. This plant world, opened in 2001, has **cactus labyrinths**, a philosopher's garden, a journey through time with Albert Einstein, a Stone Age cinema and, according to the Royal British Horticultural Society, the most beautiful **botanical garden** in the southern hemisphere, complete with 2400 species of Cape flora. (Opening times: Wed–Sun 8am–4pm, closed in July; www.soekershof.com).

> ! **Baedeker TIP**
>
> ### Wacky Wine Weekend
>
> Every year, during the first week of June, Robertson celebrates its popular Wacky Wine Weekend. On offer are not only wine-tasting, but also vineyard tours, vineyard dinners, candlelight concerts, boat tours and arts and crafts from the region (www.wackywineweekend.com). Live music and wine-tasting are also part of the Wine on the River Festival in October (www.wineonriver.com).

About 10km/6mi further east, open all-terrain vehicles are used for safaris to spot Eland antelopes, wildebeest, boneboks, impalas, kudus, springboks and zebras. Two-hour **safaris**, Wed–Sat 10am, 4pm, Sun 10am; (www.patbusch.co.za/klaasvoogds.htm).

**Klaas Voogds Game Reserve**

Time seems to have stood still at this 19th-century **village idyll** of thatched cottages and historic farmer's gardens. Many artists and **artisans** have settled here. For example, the Mill Stone Pottery produces high-quality porcelain, Roy Reycraft makes sundials from brass, and the painter Jo Nowicki offers drawing classes. Meanwhile, the local wine-makers present their best efforts during the Unbelievably Festive Weekend in May.

**McGregor**
◄www.
mcgregor.co.za

The **Myrtle Rigg Memorial Church** with its Italian marble floor and lead glass windows from England was built in memory of the daughter of chief blaster Christopher Forrest Rigg (1861–1926), who died a premature death. In 1906 Rigg used 80 sticks of dynamite to blast a tunnel through the Olifants Mountains, which has been a part of the water supply system ever since. South Africa's largest **cheese factory** is located in Bonnievale and can be visited during the week. Since 2006, it has also been possible to view the antiques collected by the race-horse breeder Oom Daantje le Roux (died 2005) at the **DJ le Roux Museum** on Main Road.

**Bonnievale**

# LIST OF MAPS AND ILLUSTRATIONS

# PHOTO CREDITS

# PUBLISHER'S INFORMATION

**Illustrations etc:** 192 illustrations, 27 maps and diagrams, one large city plan
**Text:** Dr. Madeleine Reincke, Jürgen Sorges
**Editing:** Baedeker editorial team (John Sykes)
**Translation**: Natascha Scott-Stokes
**Cartography:** Christoph Gallus, Hohberg; MAIRDUMONT/Falk Verlag, Ostfildern (city plan)
**3D illustrations:** jangled nerves, Stuttgart
**Design:** independent Medien-Design, Munich; Kathrin Schemel

**Editor-in-chief:** Rainer Eisenschmid, Baedeker Ostfildern

1st edition 2009
Based on Baedeker Allianz Reiseführer »Kapstadt«, 1. Auflage 2008

# BAEDEKER GUIDE BOOKS AT A GLANCE
## Guiding the World since 1827

- Andalusia
- Austria
- Bali
- Barcelona
- Berlin
- Brazil
- Budapest
- Cape Town • Garden Route
- China
- Cologne
- Dresden
- Dubai
- Egypt

- Florence
- Florida
- France
- Gran Canaria
- Greece
- Iceland
- India
- Ireland
- Italy
- Japan
- London
- Mexico
- Morocco
- New York

- Norway
- Paris
- Portugal
- Prague
- Rome
- South Africa
- Spain
- Thailand
- Tuscany
- Venice
- Vienna
- Vietnam

# DEAR READER,

**We would like to thank you for choosing this Baedeker travel guide. It will be a reliable companion on your travels and will not disappoint you.**
**This book describes the major sights, of course, but it also recommends the cosiest pubs and bars, as well as hotels in the luxury and budget categories, and includes tips about where to eat or go shopping and much more, helping to make your trip an enjoyable experience. Our authors ensure the quality of this information by making regular journeys to Cape Town and putting all their know-how into this book.**

Nevertheless, experience shows us that it is impossible to rule out errors and changes made after the book goes to press, for which Baedeker accepts no liability. Please send us your criticisms, corrections and suggestions for improvement: we appreciate your contribution. Contact us by post or e-mail, or phone us:

► **Verlag Karl Baedeker GmbH**
Editorial department
Postfach 3162
73751 Ostfildern
Germany
Tel. 49-711-4502-262, fax -343
www.baedeker.com
www.baedeker.co.uk
E-Mail: baedeker@mairdumont.com